Race Life of the Aryan Peoples

An Ethnographic History of the Indo-Europeans - Vol. 1

By Joseph Pomeroy Widney

**PANTIANOS
CLASSICS**

Published by Pantianos Classics

ISBN-13: 978-1-78987-580-5

First published in 1907

Contents

Epos

Every masterful race of the world's history has its epic. It is the tale of the fathers told to the sons. But side by side with the spoken epic is another, unspoken, yet truer and deeper. It is the tale of the race life, not told in words, but lived in deeds done. And the epic lived is always more wonderful than the epic told. The true epic is found, not in the story of the battles or of the deeds of the rulers, but in the race life. In the perspective of time men become less, man grows greater. Race life is broader, deeper, richer than the life of any man, or of any men. The great men of a race are only an evolution of its race force; and the reserve force is greater than its product. They are indices, race marks. The great man is as the mountain peak; for the mountains that loom up above the wide-spread plain are not the land; they are only the land-*marks*, marks of the land. Kings are the accident; the people, the law. The Greek colonies, not Ilium and Atreides Agamemnon, are the true epic of Hellas, vastly more marvelous. So of the Aryan folk; not the Vedas, not the Avestas, not the Iliad, or the Nibelungen, or Beowulf, but the marvelous tale of what the Aryan man has lived how he has subdued the wild and waste lands how he has made the desert to blossom as the rose how he has built up empire with ax and plow, and has sailed the unknown paths of the seas; these are his true race epic. The others are only as the fairy tales which old wives tell to their children. We read between the lines of the written epic to find the truer and greater epic which lies beyond.

This book is an attempt to unfold somewhat of the race epic which the Aryan peoples have lived.

Los Angeles, January 1907.

Chapter One - Who Are The Aryan Peoples?

There are families of races just as there are families within races. We find in a community certain groups of individuals who bear a strong stamp of likeness; they trace their history back through some generations to a common parentage; they bear, it may be, one common surname; and we group them by these characteristics which they possess in common, and speak of the different individuals as belonging to one common family. So it is upon a broader scale with races. Among the peoples of the earth we find certain races which resemble each other more than they resemble the other races of mankind, certain likenesses of form, of features, of complexion, of speech, of mental and spiritual evolution, and it may be of traceable race history; and because of this special resemblance we infer, and are sometimes able to trace, the common ancestry back of them, and we speak of them as a distinct family among races. We so speak of the Negroid or Black races; of the family of the Yellow peoples; of the Semitic peoples; and so we speak of the family of the Aryan peoples. Within this Aryan family we ordinarily class as the one kin, and because they possess in common many of the kin evidences just adduced, the Brahmins of India, the Medo-Persians of Iran, the Graeco-Latins, the Celts, the Slavs, and the Teutons. Within these are again subdivisions into yet smaller groups or families.

Why has the Name Aryan been Adopted as the Distinctive Appellation of this Group or Family of Races?

The name comes to us through the Sanskrit, the oldest of the written tongues of the Aryan peoples. In the Vedas the Brahmins speak of their ancestors as the Arya, and of the older homeland as Arya Avarta, that is, the homeland of the Arya. In the Zend, the Iranic branch of that older Aryan speech, the word is Airya. Yet the word in both the Sanskrit and the Zend is only a derivative. The root form goes back to an older speech even than that of the Brahminic Vedas or the Iranic Avestas, and in root form is found in other Aryan speech than the two just instanced. In Latin it is found in arare; in Greek, aroun; in Slavonic, orati; Gothic, arjan; Welsh, arad; Old English, erien. In all, the meaning is to plow or till. Yet back of the verbal form can be traced a substantive form meaning earth. It is to be found in our modern English word earth; in German, erde; Danish, aarde; Latin, arvum; Greek, era. In all these tongues the root *ar* enters into many secondary forms and combinations; but back of all, sometimes difficult to trace, yet there, is that older idea of the earth. It all points back to one common speech which was mother alike to Sanskrit, Zend, Greek, Latin, and the Slavic, Celtic, and Teutonic tongues. To that primitive mother tongue the name Proto-Aryan has been given, a tongue long since unspoken, known only through its children. When the Aryans who spoke Sanskrit called themselves Arya, the thought back of it was probably the same which we find among so many of the primitive peoples of the world; that they were autochthonous (αυτοςχθων, children of the soil), the primitive, earth-born folk.

The fact that the Sanskrit and the Zend, the oldest of the written Aryan tongues, made use of this name as designative of the people and their ancestry, coupled with that other fact that the root of the name is so wide-spread among the Aryan peoples, and joined with this the additional fact that nowhere else among the primitive kin do we find even two branches of the family uniting upon a common race designation, makes this the fittest of all names to represent the whole kin. And it has the additional recommendation of being free from all entanglements with conflicting theories as to race origin and race migrations, while it is so general in character as to embrace all possible branches of the family. The term Indo-Germanic, as used by the German ethnologists, is inadmissible in that not only is it precommitted to a theory and a bias, but is also too narrow at each end. The Brahmin of India was only one of the eastern Aryans; while the German upon the west is only one of the subdivisions of one branch of the western Aryans. The term Indo-European is somewhat broader, yet this also is defective, as already shown, upon the eastern end, while the world spread of the Aryan westward makes the term European no longer appropriate. The term Aryan as the family name is justly supplanting all others.

What Reasons Do We Find for Classing the Races Just Enumerated as of Kin?

1. *The Kinship of Language*

It is to be remembered, however, in all tracings of race relationship that kinship of speech is only presumptive evidence of kinship of blood. Presumptive, but not conclusive. It needs to be confirmed by other and different lines of proof. The Negro of Haiti speaks French, yet he is not French. The Frenchman speaks a Latinized form of speech, yet he is not Latin, but Celtic and Teutonic. Only in the Mediterranean lands of Provence is the Latin even an important ingredient of one of the most mixed bloods of Western Europe. Yet the exceptions do not render worthless the rule. The rule remains as before stated, that kinship of speech is upon its face presumptive evidence of kinship of blood. And while the kinship of tongues is shown by words, subject to Grimm's law of phonetic change, it is often yet more strongly shown in the grammatical structure. Words are often borrowed, as is shown in the Latinized English of the Elizabethan writers, but grammatical structure is among the unborrowable things of speech. It must be grown, not borrowed; and it, even more than words, is characteristic of races. Neither is written speech always the truest test. Stronger, more conclusive than the written, is the unwritten speech. The Lingua Rustica of the Roman people, as seen in its successor, the modern Italian, is a safer guide than the rounded sentences of Cicero or the quips and jests of the courtly speech of Horace; ἡ κοινη γλωσσα of Hellas, as living in the Romaic, than the neatly turned sentences of Sophokles; just as one finds the true English, the kin English, in the speech of what Lincoln termed the common people, rather than in the elaborate rhetoric of Webster or the polished turns of Milton. It is the vernacular, not the school speech, which keeps best the family likeness. So the simple tale of folk-lore gives a safer clue than the more ambitious drama; Mother Goose jingles, than "Paradise Lost" or Gibbon's "Decline and Fall." It is because they are artless, because they are natural. Therein lies their especial value in tracing relationships of kin.

2. Myths, Traditions, and Folk-lore Held in Common

These may often be traced in their variant types among widely separated and often apparently slightly related races of men; and their ethnic import can never be wisely neglected. The so-called Arthurian legends of the Celt, and the various versions of the Teutonic Nibelungen Lied are cases to the point. And it is never to be forgotten that the apparently nonsensical jingle of a nursery rhyme, passed on from mother to child, will survive the centuries after the granite obelisk is crumbling to dust. The genesis of Mother Goose can be traced in the old Aryan days out on the highlands of Asia four thousand years ago. When the fond English-speaking father tosses his child up into the air and catches it as it comes down, crying to it, "Upadā'!" he little thinks that the word is literally the Sanskrit Upadā, to catch; and that so the old Proto-Aryan forefathers four thousand years ago must have tossed and caught their little ones to the same cry. The nursery has bridged over the chasm, and kept the record of race kin for forty centuries.

3. Likeness in Mental and Spiritual Types

I have in my library a book written by a Chinaman, a man of education and ability, and thoroughly conversant with the ways and the thoughts of the world outside of his own land. He is writing upon a topic which is international in interest and touch. The English of the translation is faultless. And yet to read it is to enter within a mental and spiritual world so unlike that of the Aryan mind that one almost rubs his eyes to see whether he be not asleep. It betrays the radical difference in type between the Mongol and the Aryan minds. The whole vision is from a different mental and spiritual standpoint. The same unlikeness, but to a far less degree, may be noticed even between the different branches of the Aryan kin. A French book is not an English book. No skill of translation can conceal the fact. There is a mental race stamp which can neither be counterfeited nor disguised. And so the English book is to the Frenchman. Yet there is a likeness also, clear, strongly marked, within each family of races, with all the minor differences. A Japanese book is not a Chinese book; yet it is a Mongol book. Homer is not Milton; yet both are Aryan. These instances are given as illustrations of the fact that in tracing race kinships or race divergences mental and spiritual characteristics afford a valuable clue.

4. Trend to Similar Political Institutions

It has been said by some one that all Asia has never known one republic. Likewise may it be said that all Asia is Mongol and Semitic. If the primitive Proto-Aryan home land lay, as has been claimed, in Asia, the great mass of the Aryan peoples early left it, and the few who remained behind were swallowed up in the teeming millions of the Mongol and the Semite, and so failed to develop an Aryan political life. Despotism is the one type of government which seems to be normal to the mind of the Negroid, the Mongol, and the Semite; and to-day is to them as three thousand years ago. Two of them, the Negroid and the Semite, have dwelt about the shores of the Mediterranean also, but migration and new climatic surroundings worked no change in the type of government. Carthage was no less a despotism because an oligarchy.

Trace, on the other hand, the Aryan races in the European home. Slowly but surely, often with long backsets, yet always turning again to the effort, the Aryan peoples have been emerging from the despotisms of the past. In the process of political evolution the despot becomes the constitutional monarch; then a mere figurehead; then quietly disappears; and "government of the people, for the people, and by the people" becomes the ultimate law of the land. It is one of the birthmarks of the Aryan peoples, and by it we help to trace kin.

5. Race History so far as Traceable

While much of the history of the past seems to be hopelessly lost, there is yet much which may be traced, for two thousand years with reasonable certainty, for a thousand years before that more vaguely but still with enough degree of probability to give it weight upon questions of race relationship. During all that time the Mongol has been sharply and distinctively Mongol; the Semite, Semitic; the races which we call Aryan neither Mongol nor Semite, but peoples having a race life and a race history apart from both and resembling neither. On the contrary, their race life, the type of race evolution, and their race affiliations have been along lines distinctively unlike and apart from all others, and as distinctively in a class by themselves. There have unquestionably been in many of the subdivisions of the Aryan family, as with Celt, Graeco-Latin, and Slav, admixtures and incorporations of extraneous and alien bloods, less so apparently with the Teuton; and these admixtures have left their trace in well-marked variations from what would seem to be the normal Aryan race type; yet in it all the general trend of race evolution, as shown by ascertainable race history and by the other characteristics which have been mentioned under the several headings, has been sufficiently alike to justify their classification as one in kin. The admixture of alien blood to which allusion has been made will be traced more fully under the different race headings.

Chapter Two - Original Homeland of the Aryan Peoples

Are the Lands now Occupied by the Aryan Peoples the Original Homeland of the Race Stock?

Certainly not in South Africa, New Zealand, Australia, America, for their incoming to these lands is a matter of only recent history. Presumably not upon the shores of the Mediterranean, for the Greek has well-kept tradition of the immigration from the north in the Dorian influx. Inferentially not with the Latin, for while he has no such tradition of his own, his close kinship with the Dorik Greek renders probable a like origin. Questionably with Celt and Teuton, as will appear in the discussion of the next question, and as there appears to be fairly reasonable evidence of the occupation of the land before them by the Iberian, whoever he was, in the south, and dimly traceable, yet traceable hintings of a Mongoloid before him upon the north. Of Slav land less can be even probably said; yet this we know, that within historic times even it has been swept by successive waves of different peoples. In fact, there seems to be in man some deep-seated, instinctive impulse to change, so that it may be fairly questioned whether any of the world's great races now occupies the land of its origin. Periodic change of race home, within certain climatic bounds, seems to be an essential to the perpetuity and vigor of a race, as does the admixture of fresh blood within certain limits of kin. It may even be questioned whether Europe does not show signs of wearing out upon the Aryan blood. Its greatest vigor is no longer found there, but in still newer lands.

Where Was the Common Race Home of the Aryan Peoples before the Separation into the Different Sub-Families Took Place?

From a common Proto-Aryan speech we infer also a common Proto-Aryan homeland. It is the same line of reasoning which leads us back in the individual family through the common ancestry to a common home. The one implies and requires the other. Where was this primitive home from which the Aryan blood went out in so many different streams over the earth? This much would seem to be fairly settled, that it was somewhere in the climatic belt of the mid-temperate zone. The word temperate as applied to a climatic belt upon the map is broad. It embraces upon the one hand a sub-arctic margin, as Siberia, the north Russian plains in Europe, the regions north of the Great

Lakes in America. Upon the other hand it takes in a sub-tropic region, as the shores of the Mediterranean littoral and the shores about the Gulf of Mexico. Between these two lies the mid-temperate belt which partakes of neither extreme, and which in America includes the greater portion of the United States, in Europe the British Islands and what might be termed the Mid-European plain, a region which is drained by the Seine, the Rhine, the Danube, the Don, the Dnieper, and the lower Volga, besides some rivers of lesser note. In Asia elevation largely neutralizes latitude, the vast uplifted Mid-Asian plain of the Pamir and Tibet bringing the sub-arctic climate southward until from the high passes of the Himalayas it looks directly down upon the tropical plains of hither and farther India. Only in the Trans-Caspian plain drained by the Amuand the Syr-Daria, and bounded eastward by the snowy crest of the Thian Shan Mountains, does the mid-temperate plain of Europe find an eastward expansion. Upon the Pacific coast, beyond the great uplift of Central Asia, is an imperfect attempt of nature to resume the mid-temperate climatic belt, but the southern exposure, and the warm winds from the Japan current, in part neutralize this and then that is Mongol Land.

The reasons which lead to the assumption that the primitive homeland of the Aryan peoples lay, not in the sub-tropic, not in the sub-arctic, but in the middle belt of the temperate zone, are fairly and reasonably conclusive We have a hinting of the homeland in the Vedas. They tell of the land where the Brahminic Aryan dwelt before he removed southward to the Indian plain. It was a land of "winter snows" and "stabled cattle," a land of "sheep, and clothing of wool," but it was a land also of "pastures and meadow grasses," of "butter and milk," of the "red apple," and of "autumn harvests" and the "grass piles" of the haying.

A similar picture is given by the Irano-Aryan in the Gathas. The Airyana Vaejanh is a land of winter snows and summer rains, of woodlands and pastures, and cattle, of grain-fields and harvests. It is a picture of a land free alike from the enervating heat of the sub-tropic and from the depressing chill of the sub-arctic clime; a picture of a climatic belt such as we find to-day in Mid-Europe or the northern and middle portions of the United States. And it is in this climatic belt that the Aryan has developed the highest and most enduring types of his race life and has proven himself to be able to keep up the race standard without the necessity of periodical rejuvenation by an incoming of fresh blood.

That the primitive homeland of the Aryans is thus to be looked for northward of the sub-tropic belt of the temperate zone is further shown by the earlier traditions and myths of the Greek peoples. It is from the north that the Dorian wave of Greek blood pours down over the Thessalian plain and across Attika to the Peloponnesos; and upon the Asiatic shore it is past the Phrygian upland, northward in the river valley of the Sangarios as it faces out toward the Euxine that the Phrygian Greek blood locates the scene of its earliest myths, of King Gordios, him of the famous knot which Alexander cut, and of King Midas of fabled wealth. The Latin is singularly lacking in race traditions, yet the fact that we first find him a man well advanced in the knowledge and use of the metals, and with no trace of a stone age, in his home by the Tiber, would indicate that his earlier home had been elsewhere; and the seagirt peninsula would leave to an incoming primitive race, as yet without maritime skill or ability, only one pathway possible, that by land from the north.

That the primitive homeland of the Aryan could have been in the sub-arctic belt of the temperate zone could hardly be possible as the contest with nature is there too unequal for primitive man to wage successful battle in the struggle for existence. It is only as man can take with him into the rigors of the northern climate, the skill and the accumulated appliances of a somewhat advanced civilization, that he begins to carry any form of a higher civil life into the sub-arctic lands. Then, too, the race history of the Slavs, the great northern branch of the Aryan folk, points southward toward the lower Volga and the shores of the Black Sea as the initial point whence they have spread. Of the Celts it may only be said that as their race life has become absorbed in that of the stronger incoming bloods, all reliable race traditions have disappeared. When they first appear in history their home is in the mid-temperate belt of Western Europe, upon the British Isles, in Gaul, in the valley of the Po, and in the mountain valleys of Switzerland. The Teuton, the one remaining member of the Aryan peoples, has no tradition of any other climatic home than the one he now occupies, the mid-temperate belt of the eastern continent. All his traditions, all his myths, all his race habits and customs point to this as his one and abiding race home.

The conclusion would then seem to be not only reasonable, but unescapable, that somewhere within the mid-temperate belt of the eastern continent we are to look for the 'primitive race home of the Aryan peoples, the region where the 'old Proto-Aryan blood first, began to evolve that autogenetic type of civilization which has so strongly stamped itself upon all his descendants, and whence the widely scattered Aryan peoples went out upon their diverging pathways over the world.

But where? In east - or in west? In Europe - or in Asia? Have we any means of determining, or even reasonably surmising, where within the mid-temperate belt that original primitive homeland lay?

Two theories have been advanced. One that the original homeland of the Aryan blood was somewhere amid the highlands of Central Asia; the other, and a more recent theory, claims the Scandinavian lands by the shores of the Baltic as the primitive race home. Both theories can not be correct. The most that could be claimed would be that one might be a second home of a part of the Aryan peoples, from which again this division branched out. The whole question probably does not admit of a final answer in the present state of historic research. We can only take the weight of preponderating evidence, and draw a tentative conclusion. This whole question of the primitive race

12

home of the Aryan peoples has, however, been discussed possibly too exclusively by the student in his library, and from the standpoint of the antiquarian and the philologist. It should be discussed as well, and even more fittingly, from the practical standpoint of the frontiersman. Of far more weight than philological research, or the question of metal or stone implements, are the matters which pertain to climate, possible food supply, practicable lines of migration, and the many questions which the frontiersman has to face in all lands and all ages, and which are the determining factors in settling the line of his migrations and the location of his new home. As antiquarians and philologists stand divided between the two locations, the shores of the Baltic, and the highlands of Mid-Asia as the original Aryan homeland, these more practical points may well help to settle the question, so far as a final conclusion may be reached. Among such points to be weighed are the following:

1. Scandinavia lies upon the extreme northern edge of the temperate zone. Even with the warm southwest winds from the Atlantic it is still sub-arctic in climate, and wet and chill with excessive rains and snows. The struggle of an infant civilization starting in its first efforts from savagery would in such a climate be so severe that of its own unaided powers the chances would be largely against success. The historic rule is, that civilization is imported into such lands rather than that it originates there.

2. Scandinavia, even within historic times, was a densely wooded country, and the history of the rise of primitive civilizations is that of location in more open lands. The reason lying back of this fact is, the unpreparedness of man in the infancy of mechanic arts to battle successfully with the forest. The stone ax is but an inefficient tool with which to fell a tree and clear the land for agriculture. It was the lack of the metals possibly, even more than aught else, which held back the infant civilizations of the Algonkins and the Cherokees, and which kept the American Indian for ages a savage. The battle with the forest was to his stone ax an unequal one. Any one who has helped, even with the steel implements of an advanced civilization, to hew out a home amid the beech woods of Ohio will realize the almost hopeless struggle which would lie before a savage race making its first start with stone ax and sharpened stick toward subduing a densely wooded land such as Scandinavia was. That they could succeed, and succeed with that measure of success in the building up of the mother civilization which the Aryan problem requires, would be one of the utterly improbable things in the history of race development. Then, too, a forest land is not a land of game to supply food while man is yet in the hunter stage, for with the dense forest growth grass is not found, and no grass no game is the law; and the first requisite of an incipient civilization in an unsubdued land is a sufficient supply of wild game to furnish food until the forests have been cleared and the land made ready for cultivation; and this in the slow evolution of man is a process, not of years, but of ages. It is for this reason that civilization first attacks the great wooded regions of the world upon their outer edge and advances always with its rear

resting upon the cleared lands whence it may at the first draw its supplies of food. And this is even more necessarily the case with man in the infancy of civilization when as yet the means of transportation are limited and inefficient. It was the existence of the open grass reaches of the Tennessee and the Cumberland with the game they fed which rendered possible the rapid advance of that wave of settlement which crossed the southern Appalachians, coming even as it did with the superior implements of a fully developed civilization; while farther north in the dense forests of the Ohio valley the waterway of that river, running for a thousand miles directly westward, practically extended by its easy transportation of food the base-line of civilization into the heart of the continent.

The fish of the Scandinavian waters would not take the place of game upon the land as an efficient food supply to men in a savage state, for even in the comparatively sheltered waters of the fiords and island channels the sea boat, so indispensable, implies in its construction a mechanical skill already well advanced beyond the stage of savagery.

Yet the Scandinavian theory would maintain that under all these disadvantages the whole fabric of Aryan civilization had its inception here, and under these unfavorable surroundings; and, tho thus weighted, had in prehistoric times already gained numbers and strength sufficient to pour out and overrun the lands from the British Isles to the Mediterranean and on to the plains of Persia and India. But in view of the facts just given, and knowing the history of man's settlement of such lands elsewhere, it is hard to see how the verdict could be other than not proven - even more, improbable.

The history of the rise of primitive civilizations shows them to have had their origin rather in the more temperate, semi-arid, and more open lands of the world. It was so that the primitive seats of population and of power for the Negroid and the Semite clustered about the warm, semi-arid, comparatively treeless valleys of the Nile and the Euphrates; and it was so that the earlier historic civilizations of the Aryan of the west were upon the warm, open shores of the Aegean and the Adriatic. And the reasons for this also are plain. With the lighter rainfall forest growth is restricted rather to the line of the streams in the river bottoms, while the open grassy upland plains afford an abundant supply of wild game for man when as yet in the hunter stage, and an already prepared field for the pasturage of his herds and flocks as he passes on to the next stage of upward evolution, the pastoral life. It might indeed be truthfully said that all civilization is in the beginning based upon grass. It is such a life as this that the Vedas hint of before the Aryan man descended to the Indian plains from the highlands of Central Asia. Then, too, in life under such conditions the lighter rainfall, the sunnier skies, and the semi-arid lands tax less severely the vitality of a crude people and thus conduce to the more rapid increase in numbers and the consequent ability to make their way against opposing races. It was the discerning complaint of the American Indian that under the exposure and the less certain food supply of their forest life they multiplied less rapidly than the white man with his superior comforts of shelter and his assured means of subsistence, and so the battle for race supremacy must go against them in the end. They simply discerned a general law which holds good in all ages and among all races.

To locate the beginning of a primitive, autochthonous civilization in the cold, humid north is to reverse the whole teaching of history. Other infant civilizations sprang up, not in the cold, wet forest lands of sub-arctic regions where the forces of nature were arrayed against them in an unequal contest, but in the warm, sunny, drier, more open regions which lay farther south where nature was a friend and not a foe. The civilizations which had their birth in the valley of the Nile, amid the semi-arid plains of the Tigris and the Euphrates, about the mild shores of the Mediterranean, and in the upland valleys of Mexico and Peru are instances. All these facts would logically point away from the inhospitable west shores of Europe and toward the drier, warmer, more open lands farther east and nearer the Heart of the continent as the more probable primitive homeland of the Aryan peoples, and from which, with a knowledge of the use of the metals already gained, and with a measure of mechanical skill already developed, they could go out at least reasonably equipped for the battle with the forests, the cold, and the inclemency of the West European peninsula.

Again, the natural roadway from Central Asia into Europe is a constantly dividing and diverging one, as will be shown further on. This fact would readily account for the wide-spread character of the Aryan settlements toward the west, if the original stream of migration was from the east. But assume a Scandinavian origin, and we have to face the difficulty that the lands of the west are by nature more inaccessible to each other by direct lines than if approached by a diverging stream of population from the east. Witness the high Pyrenees as against the low Mediterranean littoral, and the lofty passes of the western and central Alps as against the low, easy passes of the Julian Alps to the Italian plains. The assumption of a Scandinavian origin for the primitive Aryan stock would almost necessitate the explanation of a secondary return current from the east to account for the wide-spread Aryan settlements of the southwest. Then, too, we naturally look for the earliest evidences of civilization of a race in, or at some point near to, their primitive race home, for migrations retard the development of civilization, which comes only as the population grows fixed and stable. But we find the Aryan civilizations of the Far East antedating those of the west by many centuries; and the evolution is a successive one from east to west - Brahmin, Persian, Greek, Roman, Teuton.

The theory of an eastern origin of the Aryan peoples is confirmed by the evidences of history so far as traceable. Historically the problem is similar to the problem which lay before the geologist in trying to trace backward the trend of the great ice-sheet which pressed down over the American continent in the glacial period. Upon the smooth faces of the rocks throughout

New England he found scored lines and grooves made evidently by the cutting edge of stones held as graving tools in the frozen under-surface of the advancing ice-sheet. While many of these lines were often deflected by local causes, yet the greater number of them pointed always in the one general direction toward the northeast. From these the scientist reasoned back to the Labrador ice-fields as the starting-point; and the reasoning is accepted as legitimate and sound. Race traditions are way-marks, the grooved furrows in the ages back of written history, which often give clue to race migrations.

Not all the Aryan peoples have such traditions of their past. The Slav seems to have none. Yet when we consider how mixed is the blood which we now call Slavic - Aryan probably, Ugro-Finnic and Tartar assuredly, Gothic and Germanic historically - and then overrun by successive waves of conquest and oppressed for centuries, we could scarcely expect the preservation among them of the folk-tales of the earlier race migrations. The Celt, like the Slav, has apparently no traditions of his race migrations in the past; but here also we find a mixed blood, for there are several well-marked and distinct race bloods all classed as Celtic; and the Celt, more unfortunate even than the Slav, has not even retained his race identity but has become merged into other branches of his Aryan kin until all distinctive folk tradition of possible race migration seems to be lost. The Teuton also has no well-marked tradition, unless we take the epic of the Nibelungen as a vague hinting; and if the epic of the Iliad could after three thousand years prove to be a reliable topical guide to Schliemann in his excavations we may hesitate before discarding any hint that any epic may give, and especially as the scene of an epic is most apt to point backward along the trail of migration of the older race life, and this because of the fact that the land that way is familiar to them and is as yet allied with the earlier deeds of the kin. In the Nibelungen it is eastward to Atli's land that the heroes of the Nibelungs go in quest of adventure, and find - death. The Latin likewise, as separate from the Greek, has no known folk tradition of other land than that of the Tiber. Of course Vergil's pretty epic romance of a Troad myth is only poetry, hardly disguised enough to tickle even the willing ear of Augustus. Yet with the marked similarity between the Latin type and that of the Dorian Greek it may be well questioned whether they are not entitled to a common history. In the Greek tradition of the Dorian incoming we find a clear-cut narrative of the migration of an important division of their race blood from the north; while the numerous and more ancient Ionik branch of the Greek km along the whole coast line of Asia Minor with their ancient civilization, and eastward of them in the highlands of the interior that archaic Phrygian Greek tarrying as one left behind, and with his myths and traditions reaching back yet again northeastward down the river valley of the Sangarios to the Euxine: all these point toward a Greek migration down from the Asiatic interior at a time when Dorian and Ionian and Trojan and Phrygian were probably one, or else successive waves of one common stock following a common pathway westward toward the Mediterranean shore. If, as claimed by opponents of this view, the Phrygian had been only an outpost of the checking eastward wave of Greek life, we should have to face the anomalous fact of the lone frontier outpost developing its civilization before that of the more populous and powerful homeland behind it; for the myths of Midas and of Gordios point back to a settled and wealthy civilization which long antedated that of Attika, and the Peloponnesos, and the Ionian shore.

When we come to the Indo-Iranic branches of the Aryan peoples, however, the trail becomes warmer and footprints clearer. It is down out of the north by the mountain passes of the Hindu Rush that the older Brahmin of the Hymns to the Maruts descends to the Indian plain of the Five Rivers. And it is down from the northeast through the passes of the same range that the older Iranian of the A vestas descends, and as the years go by gains strength to pour westward and overthrow the Semitic power upon the Tigris and the Euphrates. And the land which both the Vedas and the Avestas describe as the older homeland is not a land by the sea, but such a land [as may even yet be found, but steadily, with the ages, becoming more arid through some vast telluric change, on the inland plains which stretch from the westerly slopes of the Thian Shan Mountains and on to, and about, the shores of the Caspian. In fact, once that the borders of the Black Sea are passed, this is the first region in the mid-temperate belt of Asia where a fertile area sufficiently extensive for the homeland of a people as numerous as the Proto-Aryan folk seem to have been is to be found; for south are the rugged mountains of the Hindu Kush, and then the tropic plains of India; eastward are the forbidding crests of the Thian Shan and the upland deserts of the Gobi, the Chinese Sha-mo, "Sand-sea," while upon the north are the bleak Siberian steppes. And that the Proto-Aryan folk must have been already too numerous a people for a narrower homeland, even before they started upon their migrations, would seem to be fairly inferable from the number of branches into which they divided. Mere numbers of descendants prove little, for time will bring this about from small beginnings. But a folk few and feeble are not apt to divide up into so many branches. Rather are they apt to keep together for the sake of mutual protection among strange and hostile peoples, and to migrate together as one body. For it is to be remembered that among primitive peoples the words stranger and foeman are practically synonymous terms.

Neither climatic law nor race traditions taken alone may be accepted as conclusive in deciding the question of the original home of the Aryan peoples; yet when we take both together, and add to them the thought that if we are to accept the theory of a common origin for all races of men, and couple with it the fact that geologically Asia is old and Europe new, and that Asia would thus be first fitted to become the home of man and the birthplace of civilization, and the further fact of the widespread belief in ancient times that Asia was the birthplace of man, and the yet further fact that within historic times the great waves of migration and of conquest of the eastern continent have been almost universally from Asia westward:- when we consider all these facts we can hardly escape the conclusion that the burden of proof, and the more reasonable presumption, would point away from the sea to the mid-continental lands as the primitive home of the Aryan peoples, from which they scattered and spread over the world; and that the later homes by the western seas were only secondary homes of separate branches of the common stock, won from the dank, chill forests and the inhospitable climate after this portion of the earth's surface had become geologically fitted for the abode of man, and after the race had developed mechanical skill, and devised implements and appliances with which to wage successful battle against the less favoring forces of nature in these newer lands. That this solution is the simplest, and answers more nearly to all the requirements of the problem than any other which has been offered, would seem to be hardly a matter of dispute even.

It is to the heart of the continent then, away from the sea rather than to the ocean rim or the sea-girt peninsulas, that we look for the Proto-Aryan home. It is a land continental, not insular or peninsular. Here seems to have been, so far as we can trace, the primitive race home. But what manner of land was it? What was it topographically, climatically, as well as geographically? If these points be known, we may better reason as to the type of man who was a dweller therein; for man is a resultant not simply of race alone, but is the product of race modified by physical surroundings. If we know the land we shall better know the type of man to which it would give birth.

This is the land as it is to-day:- a land of elevated plateaus rather than of low plains; with a background of lofty mountains; arid rather than humid, yet watered by streams fed from the perpetual snows of the peaks beyond; winds wrung of their moisture in crossing the high crests of the mountain chains upon the south; a winter cold, dry, with light snowfall except upon the mountains; a spring quick coming, short; then the long dry summer, with a day heated up by a fervent sun which pours its rays down through a sky almost devoid of atmospheric moisture; a night cooled, even chilled by the rapid radiation of heat which occurs in such climes with the coming on of evening; a latitude of 40°; an isothermal line of 50° annual mean; home of the barley, the wheat, the rye, the oat, the apple, the blackberry, the onion, the lentil, the pease. Upon the plains bloom the rose, the campanula, the honeysuckle. In the forests of the foothills are to be found the maple, the birch, the hawthorn, the pine, the tamarisk, the ash, the oak. In its fauna are to be found the ox, the sheep, the dog, the horse, the swine.

Yet while the climate is now semi-arid, the evidence is that the land was once less arid than now, the rainfall greater, the margin of fertile plains broader. Even within historic times the change has been marked. Under the slow working of some wide-spread telluric cause, possibly upheaval, the rainfall is diminishing, the rivers shrinking, the inland seas drying up, and what was once a fertile land is becoming desert.

18

Chapter Three - The Type of Man to Which the Homeland Gave Birth

And the man himself , this older Aryan? What of him? Is it possible after so many ages to form a race picture of that Proto-Aryan, the manner of man he was physically, mentally, spiritually? A composite portrait might after a fashion be made by combining the salient features of his various race descendants. He certainly had within him the germs at least of a masterful man, for each of his descendants has been somewhere, at some time in the world's history, one of its masters, and the history of the world is largely of their making. In fact, the history of the world is largely only the history of the Aryan man. It must have been a vigorous stock that could thus stamp its impress so indelibly upon the ages. Reconstructing him physically from the transmitted features which mark his children in all lands, as one produces from a group of photographs a composite picture, and especially reproducing the picture from the race types of those of his children who are living their race life amid climatic environments similar to those of the original Proto-Aryan race home, and making due allowance for the variations which are incident to migration and civilization, we may judge him to have been in stature of medium height, yet varying from this toward tallness rather than toward undersize; full-chested; long-limbed, yet symmetrical of build; a free stepper; a clear striker whether with the hand or the sword; in build rather spare; of active habit; a lover of outdoor life, of the field, of the chase; a man already feeling that he was the superior of the races about him, feeling already the stir of the masterful spirit within him; features well-marked and clean-cut; nose finely chiseled but rather prominent; chin well developed; mouth large yet not gross; teeth regular, showing ample jaw space; eyes blue or gray, rather than dark, and set well under brows that project in a strongly developed supra-orbital ridge; a forehead high rather than broad, yet swelling out above and behind the temples; dome of the head well arched; head long rather than thick through, the dolichocephalous rather than the brachicephalous type, broad above rather than at the base; hair fine, light in color, reddish or brown rather than black, straight or slightly wavy; complexion tanned by the winds of his life afield, yet back of the tan the ruddy skin of the blond: in all things the opposite of the Mongol upon the east or the Negroid upon the south; more akin in form and feature to the Semite. This tall, fair, dolichocephalous type we find everywhere among the Aryan peoples; and where another type is mixed with it, the first type as here given dominates as leader. It is inferentially, and indeed may be assumed to be logically, the true Aryan type, as, while it remains constant in all the family ramifications, the other types vary and change.

Mentally, Spiritually, what was this Proto-Aryan Man? How did he live his Daily Life? What was his Home Life? What were his Thoughts?

Here again we might reason back from the children to the ancestors, from the races which have sprung from him to that older Aryan man himself. But we have here the advantage of other lights, side lights it is true, yet lights which reveal to us much of the working of both mind and soul. It is such a light as the "Iliad" and the "Odyssey" throw upon that old Greek life about the shores of the Aegean three thousand years ago; and by means of it we look down, as from an upper window, and see the primitive Aryan man living his old-time daily life. It was a life which we, after all the years, are too apt to look back upon as to the vagueness and unreality of a dream, not feeling that it was just such a real life as we are living to-day, with its planning and scheming, its work, its hopes, its ambitions, its loves, its hates. It is such a view as Vergil pictures Aeneas to have had out of the invisible cloud from the hill-top down upon the busy scenes of that newer Tyrian city, himself all un-seen.

The oldest view we gain of that primitive Aryan is through the channel, the race stream, of one of his descendants, the high-caste Brahmin of India. A second record comes down to us through another branch of the family, the ancient Iranian, the ancestor of the present Persian. Both early developed the writing habit, a habit which was only developed in other branches of the family centuries later. The record which comes to us from Brahminic sources is through the Sanskrit, that of the Iranian by means of an old dialect of the Zend, both languages which long since ceased to be spoken, but each re-tained, and so insured continued existence, as the sacred tongue of the reli-gion of a race, yet neither being the primitive Proto-Aryan speech. Both were simply the oldest written daughters of a common Proto-Aryan mother tongue, spoken by the common ancestor of both strains of blood, the primi-tive Proto-Aryan, as his home speech, but both yet near enough evidently to still bear the strongly marked linguistic stamp of the mother tongue. In spirit and in the race life which they portray both records are older than the type of speech in which they are told, "just as the scenes of the "Iliad" and the "Ae-neid" belong to a more ancient era than the form of speech in which they are preserved. They all belong to the epic age of a race literature; and the epic of each people goes back of choice into the fading, yet still remembered, years of a folk youth for the subject-matter of its song. It is so with Beowulf, with the Nibelungen, and with the Arthurian cycle.

The picture of that older Proto-Aryan man as coming to us through the Sanskrit and the Zend will be given in the next two chapters under the head-ings "The Indo-Aryan" and the "Irano-Aryan."

Chapter Four - The Indo-Aryan

When the Sanskrit and its treasures of early Brahminic literature became known to western scholarship it was as the discovery of old, long-forgotten family portraits where none had been before supposed to exist. It at once carried the family history, and the family gallery, back three thousand years. Not that these were in the direct line of ancestry of the western races, but that the collateral branch of the family thus brought to light was so much nearer in time to the common ancestral home as to yet retain the original family stamp, with the reasonable presumption that little departure from that type had as yet begun to show itself. In this fact lies, to the ethnological historian, the especial value of the Vedas as being possibly the earliest of the known race literatures of the Aryan peoples. An especial value attaches to the Sanskrit as an authority in that it had ceased to be a spoken language some three thousand years ago, and hence for that length of time has remained practically unchanged. It is thus the oldest form of the Aryan tongues now known; as the others, with the exception of the Zend, remained for ages after spoken but unwritten, and have consequently, in the unceasing changes which are ever going on within unwritten speech, constantly grown farther and farther away from the forms of the primitive Proto-Aryan tongue. What that primitive Proto-Aryan speech, common mother to all Aryan tongues, may have been in structure can not now be told with any great degree of certainty. Probably itself far removed from the yet more primitive monosyllabic speech of man's infancy, with the agglutinative stage of word formation already passed by, it was still, if we are to judge from the simpler form of some of its derivatives, less elaborately framed than the Sanskrit with its ten cases for the noun and its elaborate verb.

Out of the mass of the Vedas the Hymns to the Maruts, or storm gods, stand as probably the most ancient, certainly the nearest in freshness and spirit to the original race home. They are the folk-songs of the childhood of a race. As you read you feel that you are back in the days when the world was yet fresh before men, and full of hope. It is that race childhood when as yet the close sympathetic touch with the physical world around has not been dulled. It is the glad abandon of youth - or is it that the centuries have hid the shadows? Yet it could not be entirely this, for the thrill of early pastorals, as of a May morning, is in it, with the raindrops glistening on the spring leaves, and all nature astir with the awakening. This can never be entirely simulated. The old can not sing the songs of youth; the weight of the years is too heavy. There will creep in the somber undertone of the contralto of life. Horace may laugh, but the laugh is not the laugh of Plautus. It has in it the covert bitterness of a sneer, the sneer of a heart no longer sweet with youth; for Rome grew old at heart quickly. But these songs - they float to us across three thousand years with the freshness, the crispness, the cheer, of the morning breeze from the mountains. They have in them the sough of the wind in the upland pines, the early call of the birds, and the varied, homely sounds of a primitive folk life as it wakes from the sleep of the night to go afield for the labors of the day. They are full of the lowing of the kine, the herdsman's cries, the whistle of the plowman, and the floating of the great cloud-shadows across the sloping grassy hillsides. We should forget the three thousand years and remember only that it is a song of the living, as much so as the morning song of the plowman to-day as he drives his team afield in the early dawn by the banks of the Ohio or the Isis.

Where was the homeland of the folk that sang these songs to the STORM GODS? for it is not the tropic life of the Brahmin of the Indian plains that is to be felt in them. They go back of the life in the dank, steaming plains of the land of the "Five Rivers" to a fresher, freer race home. The journeying may be traced as one reads between the lines. The songs have in them the sweep of the winds in mountain passes, the roaring of winter gales down from the snow peaks, the sharp rattle of the thunder amid rocky crags. It is not the lurid storms of tropic India; not the sweep of the monsoon in from the sea; these came to the later Brahminic literature; but it is the clearer air of the uplands which breathes everywhere throughout these Hymns to the Maruts. There is a striking similarity in spirit and style between these earlier Indo-Aryan hymns and the rugged songs of the Norse skalds; the same rude strength in each, the same sense of oneness with nature. The Graeco-Latin seemed to have in a measure lost this - more as a city man describing nature; not quite at home with her, especially in her wilder moods.

These primitive folk-songs go back to a time when the Brahminic Aryan of the Indian plains was still in the mountain passes and the uplands of the Hindu Kush, not yet having emerged into the lowlands of the plain country. But they have in them hintings of a time and a life anterior even to this, a time when he was as yet a dweller out upon the Mid-Asian upland. It is of this yet older race life that they give hintings; and it is in this fact that their great ethnographic value to us lies. It is a hinting of a time when the folk was not yet Brahminic, the speech not yet Sanskrit; a time read in the backward un-folding of the fragmentary skeleton of a still more ancient grammatical struc-ture, as the naturalist rebuilds the Elephas primigenius or the Cave Bear from stray bones found scattered over the earth; a time seen also in the root meanings of words coming up through the superimposed forms of later cen-turies and telling of that older speech, as the basaltic dike which through all the superimposed stratification of the ages tells of the yet more ancient world of igneous rock below. That older Pre-Brahminic man was the Proto-Aryan; his home, as has been shown, probably somewhere in the uplands of Mid-Asia; his speech presumably the common mother tongue of the Aryan peoples.

Let us take the picture which this old-time kinsman of ours paints of him-self and of that primitive homeland of Aryan peoples, as he sings his spiritual songs in the Vedas. The song is of the upland plain with its, "ice and winter snows" and its "stables rich in cattle," showing the need of winter shelter for domestic animals; "sheep, and clothing of wool," thus telling of the rigor of the cold; a life "of a hundred winters," a time measure not born of tropic lands; then the quick coming of spring-time with bursting blossoms, and pas-tures rilled with "lowing kine," and "wild deer in the meadow grass"; a land

22

of "butter and milk"; a land of "grass piles" and of "autumn harvests," and of the "red apple"; a land of farm life and of hamlets, not cities; a people who prepare their grain for food with "grinding stones of the mill" (the quern stones of the Norse man?); they speak of the "spokes of the chariot wheel," not the rude solid wheel of the Mexican; of "wife and child and home," of "kith and kin," showing the family ties; of "kings and chiefs," and "anointed priests," thus showing a settled order of society; of "physicians and healing medicines," indicating some advancement in science; of men going forth to conflict armed with "spear and bow and sword and ax"; and the "singer" to soften stern lives with the strains of music, as the Norse skald, or "long-haired Iopas with his golden lyre."

It is a picture of a people settled, yet still largely pastoral in type, as are most primitive peoples; already well advanced in the arts of war, of government, and withal of a gentler living; a people of the upland home in the open lands, yet, as the commingling of pictures of the rocks and storms of mountain passes shows, having already, when these songs were sung, left the older life in the plain country, and become entangled in the hills and the mountain passes which led to the fertile lowlands of India.

And as this Aryan man comes out to the plains of India, and to the Negroid who dwelt in the land before him, he comes as the superior race. Even the very name by which he called himself came to indicate this. The word Aryas, root AR, to stir or plow, Latin arare, in the newer relationship to subject races took upon itself a secondary meaning, noble. The plowman of the upland Asian plain thus became the nobleman of the Indian lowland, overlord of the less capable Negroid whom he found already dwelling in the land. When he contrasts himself with them, he is the "well-born" man. The distinction has in it already the germ of caste.

What has become of this older brother of the Aryan family in his Indian home? Ten degrees south of his normal home, but owing to the great change in elevation having in that short distance passed from the mean annual isothermal line of 50° to that of 70°, from mid-temperate to sub-tropic, and with no winter to counteract the debilitating heat of the summer, this man of the north who conquered the Negroid of the tropic Indian plain was himself conquered by the climate of the Negroid. Not all at once, however; not before he had placed an indelible stamp upon land and people. Caste, and his religion, are the two abiding marks which tell of the old Aryan supremacy in the land. Enervated by climate, overwhelmed by subsequent waves of invasion, Greek, Scythian, Mongol, Moslem, he yet remained the one masterful spirit. No longer the conqueror, he remained the priest; and still remains. And in it all he does not forget that he is the "well-born." And he has placed his mental stamp upon yet other lands; for the Buddhism of Tibet, of China, of Japan, of Ceylon, is of Aryan birthright through the blood of Brahminic India; a religion dying out ultimately in the land of its birth to take firmer, more lasting root in the Mongol bloods of farther Asia.

Yet it is not to Brahminism as we know it now after all the centuries of change and contamination in India, the land of gods innumerable and unnamable, that we are to look for the intellectual and spiritual picture of the Aryan of three thousand years ago. And in speaking of this picture it is to be borne in mind that in primitive races the intellectual and spiritual are divided by no such sharp lines of demarcation as in the modern man. With their narrower horizon, intellectual and spiritual were as yet largely one. It is away from Brahminic India, to the earlier hymns of the race, the hymns of the race infancy, that we turn to learn of the man. Nor need it be wondered at that to man, even to the Aryan man, in his infancy the incomprehensible forces of nature about him became as gods. In our artificial life of a complex civilization we can scarcely enter into the feelings of primitive races as they dwell face to face with nature. It is only as we go back to their simpler life, and as we also face nature away from the hurrying crowd and alone, that a conception comes to us of what it all meant to them. I can never forget my own life upon the desert for months that ran on into the years, in danger and hardship, and the revelation which the physical world about held for me:- the dawn coming to me almost as a sentient being as the long perilous night watches passed away; the desert wind breathing across the waste as with the voice of an unseen form; the torrid hush of the noonday heat resting down upon the land with the weird spell of some strange enchantment; the constellations in the loneness of the midnight seeming in their solemn march across the sky as an unceasing procession of the great silent gods of nature; and the unspeakable mystery of the waste brooding over it all. Earth, air, sky, all seemed to be filled with myriads of forms unseen yet felt, and life seemed to reach out and touch yet other life that quivered and palpitated and glowed all around.

It was not spiritual darkness, it was spiritual light that came to that older Aryan man as he dwelt upon the upland plains, and afterward passed on through the rocky passes of the mountains; light which with only the revelations of nature made him see the divine in all about him. And if with the dazzled eyes of human vision he failed to perceive the unity, seeing instead only diversity, and found not God the one but gods many, we need little wonder. Rather may we wonder that he saw so much. Withal it was an honest, true-hearted, earnest soul reaching out with the light it had, and not ashamed or afraid to confess what it found. Yet he had glimpses of something more. And this, too, he told, for he was honest of heart. This Aryan man who saw the gods many caught a glimpse also of the God One. It was only a glimpse, for a moment, but with the quick impulse of a soul at heart monotheistic he at once turns to him as the One Above All. It came to him with the power of that vision of Isaiah when across the ages he caught a far-off glimpse of the Prince of Peace. That older Aryan was looking away past and beyond the storm gods of the hills and the upland plain that day when he saw the vision and sang –

"Who is the God to whom we shall offer sacrifice?"

And again and again is the question put to his soul; and as the refrain to a chant the answer comes floating across three thousand years

"He who founded the earth and the heavens."
"He who giveth health and strength."
"He through whom the heavens and the earth are made fast."
"He who alone is God above all gods."
"He it is to whom the supreme sacrifice is to be offered."

It was the glimpse which came once, may be, even to the fickle, laughter-loving Athenians when they built that altar "To the Unknown God." It was the glimpse which came once and again to nobler souls in that old Norse theogony when after Ragnarök, and the overthrow of the gods many, the God One, the All-Father, comes to judge gods and men alike, and to make all things anew and free from mar or stain. That old Aryan song from the highlands of Asia is worthy to stand beside the dying speech of Sokrates before his judges, or the groping prayer of that lone Icelander ages after, who, looking out past the winter skies and the ice-floes, by faith also caught glimpse of Him "who alone is God above all gods."

These points are to be especially noted in the Indo-Aryan when he first comes into historic view as he emerges from the Asiatic highlands to enter upon the low-lying Indian plain:

That he is already well started upon the pathway of civilization;

That he already has a settled form of government, and a well-ordered social and civic framework;

That he is mentally intensely active and alert;

That he is spiritually alive and healthy, not morbid, nor moribund;

That he is a masterful man; and comes as the superior race, and as conqueror, to the Negroid and the Mongol of the Indian plains; but is himself in the end overcome by climate.

Chapter Five - The Irano-Aryan

Side by side with the Indo-Aryan possibly, even probably as shown by certain word forms held in common, and starting apparently from the original home as an undivided stream, was another off-shoot of the Proto-Aryan folk which may be traced to Southern Asia. The record is to be found partly in the Avestas. Like the Hymns to the Maruts, these also are not the production of an advanced civilization, but the voicing of a primitive folk life. They are the devotional hymns of a community of herdsmen and tillers of the soil. They show the soul of a primitive folk reaching out and groping into the darkness about them. The great value of these hymns to the student of folk life lies, as was the case with the Hymns to the Maruts, in the fact that they afford a picture of the folk life and the folk mind which reveals to us, as we read between the lines, what manner of man that old Irano-Aryan was. It is not of the upper

Persian plains that they speak. They, too, like the hymns of the Indo-Aryan, reach back to an older race life and an older race home in yet another land. And they also, like the Vedic hymns of the Brahmins, are as a window through which we may look down and see that older Aryan man in his primitive home; for it is an older Aryan land of which they also speak.

The picture as given in the Gathas, the most ancient of the Irano-Aryan hymns, is of a folk, tillers of the soil yet still semi-pastoral in habit, and in much the same state of primitive civilization as the Indo-Aryan as he is pictured in the Hymns to the Maruts. Yet it is a picture of one who has pierced more deeply into the mysteries of the spiritual world than his brother Aryan of the Vedas. The simple child-faith is a thing of the past. He too, like that old Hebrew Adam, has learned "to know good and evil." The mystery and the agony of sin are upon him. To this Irano-Aryan the conception of a great spiritual battle between good and evil has come. Back of and above a world of spirits, apparently at times inferior deities, is the one "Great Creator," "Living Lord," who is the embodiment of all good; and opposed to him a Spirit of Evil and of Darkness; and between these two is waged a war which never ceases: and man's soul is a storm center. And in his own relationship to the Spirit of Good he recognizes the duty of right doing, of "holy deeds to be done with faith toward God" and a "desire for the coming of righteousness within the soul." He looks beyond the present state and sees the promise of "immortality." A dividing line runs for him in this life between the "righteous" and the "wicked." This Irano-Aryan man is out upon a distinctively higher spiritual plane than his Indo-Aryan brother of the Vedas. Yet as he grasps the monotheistic idea of One Supreme Lord, Creator of all things, he is confronted with the problem of the existence of a Principle of Evil which is apparently independent and equally powerful. How shall he reconcile these startling facts? His soul is torn and distracted in the conflict. Yet with a faith in the ultimate overthrow of evil he clings to the good. It is the first skirmish of a spiritual battle which broke in all its fury upon the soul of his far-off kinsman, the Puritan of Britain, thirty centuries later.

The race life pictured in the Gathas, like that of the Indo-Aryan as given in the Hymns to the Maruts, is the life of the uplands. There is not, however, the same marked contrast between the older and the newer life as pictured for the Indo-Aryan, for the newer home of the Irano-Aryan on the eastern slopes of the watershed of the Tigris and the broad plain which lay beyond was also temperate-zone upland, only it bordered upon the tropic margin; while the Indo-Aryan had upon the contrary emerged from the mountain passes of the Hindu Rush to descend at once to the tropic lowlands of the Indian plain. The older homeland of the race from which this Irano-Aryan came is spoken of in the Avestas as "Airyana Vaejanh," Older Aryana. Sometimes the word used is "Vaego." The Spanish *viejo,* "old," is the same word almost unchanged.

The picture of that older Irano-Aryan homeland is much the same as the picture given in the Vedas of the older Indo-Aryan home before they had come in their race migration to the headwaters of the Indus. It is a region of woodlands and pastures, of winter snows and summer rains; a land rich in cattle and domesticated animals; a land of grain-fields and harvests. It is a picture also of an organized social order. They have the "house chief," the "village chief," the "tribe chief." They knew the sea but what sea? It could only be that great inland sea of Central Asia, now shrunken and broken into three.

The after-history of the Irano-Aryan is found in the masterful race history of the Medo-Persian. Darius assumed as one of his titles, Darius "The Aryan." From his new home about the headwaters of the Tigris the Irano-Aryan overran the lands until from the Oxus to the Nile, and from the Indus to the Bosporus, the ancient world knew him as conqueror. Babylonia, Egypt, Syria, Lydia, went down before him. His career of conquest was only stayed when he finally crossed arms with his brother Aryan of the west. Yet, like the Indo-Aryan, in the end he failed.

Why have these two of the Aryan peoples, after a comparatively brief career of conquest and dominion, now for ages practically disappeared from the world as race powers among men? Each drove southward as a wedge into the bulk of a strange population, the one into the Negroid mass of the Indian plain, the other into the Semitic peoples of the Tigro-Euphratean plain. Each came as conqueror, and the native races went down before him. Yet each after a while lost his initial momentum; failed to permanently hold his power; and each ultimately succumbed to the reassertion of the older race power about him. Why is this? Why has their fate been so different from that of the Aryan peoples elsewhere? Does the explanation lie in the fact that they both had wandered away from the normal race habitat; had abandoned the climatic belt which is the Aryan's normal race home; and leaving behind them no reserve of race population in the old home from which to renew the race vitality by fresh immigrations, failed to maintain the race vigor, and in a measure the race fecundity, under the new and alien climatic environments? What the Punjab did for the one, the Mesopotamian plain did for the other. Alexander at Arbela only toppled over the structure which long before had been undermined by the, to the Aryan, unnatural heat of a sub-tropic climate. Salamis and Plataea had shown the incipient crumbling of the foundations.

Yet the Irano-Aryan, as the modern Persian, has retained his race characteristics, and his race vitality, better than his Indo-Aryan brother. Does the explanation of this lie in the fact that his change of climatic surroundings has been less radical? for while the Indo-Aryan came to the low, steaming tropic valleys south of the Himalayas, the Irano-Aryan came to the less humid, only semi-tropic upland plains of the Tigris and the Euphrates. The deterioration which came to both of these strains of Aryan blood is only the assertion among the races of mankind of a law which holds good in the vegetable world also, that the natural habitat can not be widely departed from and vitality and vigor of species retained. The law holds good with that modern Aryan, the English-speaking man who has gone to India as conqueror. Only the constant influx of fresh blood maintains the political ascendency, for Englishmen can not be bred and reared in the tropical Indian climate. There is no power of self-perpetuation. The Englishman has conquered the Hindu; but - the Hindu's climate in turn conquers the Englishman. Even the mingling of bloods does not change the law; for the Eurasian who, like the mulatto of the South, betrays the crossing of bloods, is only the Asian over again, the force, the vitality of the superior race lost in the inferior stock.

Another cause was probably at work with both Indo-Aryan and Irano-Aryan to change the race constitution and deteriorate the race character. It is the same cause which has for ages been at work upon the mixed Aryan races of Eastern Europe to their detriment, namely, the constant influx of new and alien bloods in overwhelming waves of invasion, often to remain as the dominant race. Mongol, Scythian, Mogul, Arab, have in turn overrun the lands, as Scythian, Hun, Turk, have overrun Eastern Europe, until the older blood has been overwhelmed, and in the never-ceasing struggle of contending peoples has lost much of the original race type.

The Aryan was an alien in Southern Asia. He met the fate of the alien; for about the intrusive stranger blood, thus weakened by climate and to a certain extent by inevitable miscegenation, the older indigenous Negroid blood of the Indian plains, and the Semitic peoples of the Tigro-Euphratean valleys, closed in again as the growing wood about an indriven wedge, until it in a measure has become covered from view. It is the working out of the law of the survival of the fittest; but in the case of the Indo-and the Irano-Aryan the fittest, under the working of climatic law, has not proven to be the more powerful northern blood but the indigenous races of tropic blood. And it must ever remain so until, in the slow-working telluric change which is going on over the globe, the constantly advancing cold belt of the north shall have encroached upon, and included within the temperate zone the tropic plains south of the Himalayas, and the steaming marshes of Mesopotamia; and the jungle and the tiger shall have given way to the wheat-field and the ox. Then, and not until then, may the man of the north find a climatic habitat wherein he may abide and breed Northmen, in the south Asian plains. It is the working out to its inevitable result of the same climatic law which gives to the northern man his unequal battle upon the plains of the Amazon, and which will work to a like inexorable end in the valleys of the Kongo and the Niger.

For these laws are as the Laws of the Medes and Persians, that change not. Men may come and men may go; but the law abides, fixed, inexorable, and will ever work out the same ultimate physiological results in the race, whether it be primitive man, battling for a subsistence with club and stone ax; or the wandering nomad with flock and herd, and life out under the stars; or whether it be the man of the twentieth century, with all the appliances of an advanced civilization at his command.

Chapter Six - The Going Out from the Old Home Westward to the Sea

We have already traced two branches of the Aryan peoples, the Indo-Aryan and the Irano-Aryan, southward through the passes of the Hindu Rush to their new homes. We now go back to trace the wanderings of the other branches of the family. But what was the influence at work to first force out the Aryan folk from their primitive home and scatter them abroad over the face of the earth? Races do not ordinarily go out from their old family home to find a new unless forced or led, and often both influences are at work. The mere wanderlust may be the heritage of the nomad, but the true nomads are few among the races of men. If we accept, as the burden of proof would seem to show, the theory of an Asiatic birthland for the Aryan peoples, can we discover a sufficient reason to account for their going out from it? A possible reason may be found in that slow climatic change which is still going on in Central Asia, and which, beginning back in geological eras, is yet unfinished; and under which the land is century by century becoming more arid and less capable of supporting animal life. The time was, how many ages ago no man can say, ages probably before the day of the Aryan even, yet the record of the change is there, when a broad shallow sea, similar in many respects to that other inland sea which once covered the now arid plains of the inner American plateau, occupied the great depression in which lie the Caspian, the Aral, and the Balkash. These three are only the shrunken fragments of the one ancient inland sea. The old water-marks, the beach lines, and the marine deposits are all over the land telling of its former existence and its extent.

This inland marine plain of Asia does not, as I have said, stand alone in its geological history. Similar inland seas once existed not only in the Utah plains between the Rocky Mountains and the Sierra, but also in portions of the great desert of North Africa, and in Australia. In the year 1867 I crossed and examined the basin of such an extinct sea in the depression of what is now the Colorado Desert in Southern California. The water-marks of the old beach line were still, after centuries, so plainly shown upon the mountain-sides that the water-level could be readily traced by the eye when miles away. Riding out from camp I spent a day examining it. The storms of ages had failed to dim the tracing.

With the modifying influence upon climate of so extensive a body of water in the Mid-Asian plain, and the greater atmospheric humidity and heavier rainfall which it implies, the surrounding shores would be less arid, altho the same general type of inland, continental climate evidently prevailed then as now. Under the working of some widely acting general cause not now clearly apparent, possibly continental upheaval, possibly a further upheaval of the huge ridge of the Himalayas upon the south, thus shutting off the monsoons from the interior plateau, the time came when precipitation no longer kept pace with evaporation, and this inner sea began slowly to shrink in size and to dry up. As the process of desiccation went on, the one sea became three, with broad intervening plains but little elevated above the receding waters. It is that plain which now makes the broad salty levels of the desert of Kizil-koom. Even at present the process of desiccation is still going on so rapidly that surveys made at intervals of only a few years show marked recession of the water from the former shore line of both the Aral and the Caspian. Under the diminished productiveness of the land which would come with the increasing aridity would arise the necessity of race migration. Diminishing food supply and increasing population would compel it. And then possibly rumors of lands beyond where the food supply was more abundant, and life easier, just such rumors as to-day are drawing the overworked, underfed poor of Europe by the hundreds of thousands yearly away from the old homes to new lands across the Atlantic, drew them on. A second cause leading to race migration may possibly have been extraneous race pressure from the hordes of Mongols who apparently then as now possessed the vast steppes of the North Asian plain, a race which from its pastoral and nomadic habits would be better able to subsist in the midst of the ever-increasing aridity than would a people who were, at least in part, dwellers in fixed abodes and subsisting in a measure by agriculture. Possibly also some deep-seated race instinct of migration which may have been designedly implanted in this especial people to make of it a pioneer, a hewer of ways through the wastes of a new world, possibly some such instinct, some unrest in the blood, may also have been at work urging on to the journey. For there is unrest in the Aryan blood, an unrest which is ever urging it out and on.

And so, influenced by some, possibly by all, these varied causes, the long journeying of that older Aryan began. But whither should he go? Let us examine into the general laws which govern and direct race migrations in all ages and among all men, before we seek an answer; for the same laws of migration lines must have governed the primitive Aryan upon the plains of Central Asia with his flocks and herds and his household goods as governed the frontier American upon the plains of the West along the line of the Platte, the Humboldt, and the Gila. The needs were the same in either case, namely, means of subsistence from day to day for his flocks and herds and, in the absence of all roads, lines of travel at least comparatively free from natural obstacles such as large bodies of water, mountain chains, deserts, and long stretches of broken, rugged lands. Such migrations will select, and in fact are forced to select, lines of natural food supplies and of easy grades. And for the migrations of antiquity these requisites must be not stinted but ample, the food supply abundant, the way broad and easy, as migration was then, through necessity of mutual protection among hostile races, tribal, rather than as now, under the security of better settled forms of civilization, individual, or of the family. And while it is true that short stages could be made then as now over the lower passes of mountain chains which might lie across the way, yet the rule would be that mountain regions would be avoided, and the valley lines followed. Another fact might be noted here. An examination of the migrations of antiquity shows that they were of the pastoral or semi-pastoral peoples rather than of the more fixed agricultural races. Contrast, for instance, the rapid and wide-spread migrations of the pastoral peoples of the Central Asian plain with the fixity of abode of the agricultural communities by the Nile, and about the great Chinese rivers, and upon the plains of India. The reasons which lie back of this fact are at once plainly apparent. In the absence of the efficient appliances for transportation which have been the outgrowth of the mechanical development of modern civilization, it was only the pastoral peoples that could take with them in the form of flocks and herds their accumulated property, and the means of subsistence, in long journeyings. Even the comparatively short removal of Israel from the plains of Goshen to Canaan called for the explanation of a miracle that they did not perish of starvation by the way. An apparent exception to the workings of this law which governed and restricted migration among ancient peoples is found in the case of the Phoenicians and the Greeks; but their migrations, while far-reaching in results, and, as seen from the distance of centuries, apparently extensive in character, never involved large numbers, and were not tribal but made in small groups, and were amply provided for even by the limited resources of ancient navigation; for to them the water was the traveled road. They were seafarers.

In the list of requisites for lines of tribal migration may be particularized:

1. Water, in abundance, and to be constantly found by the way, that herds and flocks, no less than their owners, may not suffer or perish of thirst. Forced marches of twenty to thirty miles might then, as now upon the great plains of the West, be made occasionally with families and herds when there was a certainty of abundant water supply beyond, but these must be only occasional or the route would be avoided then, as now by the pioneer who follows the transcontinental trails of America. With flocks even these water-less reaches would be impassable. A route might also be passable during the cooler portion of the year, and during the rainy season, which would be impassable at other times. Yet the general law remains; and it would be only along lines of well-assured water supply, where there could be no question at any season, that the line of migration would fix itself; for while the skin-bottles of the Asiatic, like the water-kegs of the emigrant of the West, might carry a limited supply for a dry camp, neither could afford sufficient for the flocks and herds which accompany the train.

2. Grass. No less essential for flocks and herds is an abundant supply of grass for forage. The migrating tribe can not carry with it, because of lack of transportation facilities, a supply of grain or hay. And grass for forage in the arid Asian plains, no less than upon the similarly arid plains of the Central American plateau which lies between the Rocky Mountains and the Sierra, would be found during the dry season only in sufficient quantity along the valleys of the permanent watercourses.

3. Wood. This again is one of the requisites for comfort in the migration of large bodies of people. It is to them the only material for fuel either for cooking their food or for warmth. I well remember in long months spent upon the plains the desire always to make camp near timber, and the care with which every small stick would be picked up and placed in the wagons when a camp without timber was expected. In slow tribal migrations such as seem to have been the type of the Aryan removals westward, wood for the various mechanical arts would also be requisite apart from the need as fuel. In the arid and semi-arid regions of the world timber growth is only found as a fringe along the banks of the watercourses. Wood, water, and grass explain the long and apparently purposeless detour of Abram northward by way of the river valley of the Euphrates and then across the short divide to the overbranching and interlacing headwaters of the Jordan, when called to go out from the old home at Ur of the Chaldees to the Promised Land. The shorter, more direct way across the deserts of the Hinter-Moab Upland was to him, encumbered with flocks and herds, practically impassable.

4. Easy grades. The wheeled cart seems, from the earliest times, to have been the common possession of the Central Asian races. Rude and weak in structure, it was yet the only means of transportation apart from the beast of burden. Laden with household goods and utensils, ill adapted for rough roads, and heavy of draft, its possessor would be forced whenever possible to select a line of easy' grades and smooth natural roads. I take it that the same laws held good with men in the olden times as now; that when that older Aryan man found it easier to go around a hill than to go over it, he would do so; just as his far-off descendant on the Oregon trail did thousands of years after. Easy grades would be found along the lines of the river valleys. They would also be found upon the open upland plains; but here would be lacking wood and water.

5. In race migrations a well-established rule is that the same blood will, so far as possible, keep within the same climatic belt. This is seen in the migrations of European races to the New World. The Latin naturally seeks the lands bordering upon the Gulf of Mexico. The English and the German man, the central and the southern portions of the United States. The Norse man, the tier of Lake States. The French Canadian is an apparent exception, yet only apparent, for he is the descendant of the Breton and Norman fishermen who in the early days of America sought the cod banks of Newfoundland and the shores of the St. Lawrence, and they, altho of Latin speech, were not of Latin blood, but were the direct descendants of the Celt and the Norseman. Yet this law of climatic line, while general, is not invariable. Many circumstances and so-called accidents come in to modify and interrupt its workings.

6. Yet another law comes into play in deciding the immediate route of primitive migrations, subjective rather than objective in character, yet none the less active. There is in man an instinctive dread of losing himself. It was strong in primitive man as well as now. When men upon the plain of Shinar

looked abroad over the face of the lonely land and then said to each other, "Go to, let us build us a city and a tower whose top may reach unto heaven, and let us make us a name, lest we be scattered abroad upon the face of the whole earth," they only gave expression to this instinct of all men in all ages. Men cling to landmarks. If wandering upon the great plains, they will find themselves insensibly bending their course toward any mountain peak that may lift itself to break the loneliness of the vast level. If traveling along a watercourse they will defer the departure from it to the last possible moment. In primitive man, without compass or guide save the rising and setting of the sun, this dread of becoming lost in the trackless waste of the unknown land must have been even stronger than in man now with his superior knowledge to direct his course. To him the mountain and the river were as the friendly faces of sure guides. With them he would feel that he was *somewhere*. It was this same lost feeling which to the primitive navigator lent an added horror to the trackless wastes of the sea. The mind of man craves something definite, even to the fixing of a little space of time in eternity. Can we imagine the bewilderment of those older chronographers who could only date by such a year of such a king; to whom all before was blank, all to come unmeasurable? It is as one lost out upon the desert.

The first three of the requisites in primitive migrations which have been enumerated, water, wood, grass, may be disregarded for short distances, and probably will be under strong inducements from in front, as the attraction of a fertile country immediately beyond, or under the spur of race pressure from behind with no choice of other line of outlet. The fourth and fifth, easy grades and normal climatic belt, may be disregarded, and will be under the same race pressure, or if the direct way of advance be blocked up by natural obstacles as desert, sea, mountains, or by strong and hostile races, and the line of migration be deflected from its normal race course; and conversely, deflection from such normal course will almost certainly be found to have back of it as a cause some one or more of the obstacles enumerated. There is no such thing as chance in this. A race is too broad, the interests too varied, for the play of so-called chance. It may therefore, in accordance with the foregoing facts, be accepted as a well-settled principle that lines of migration will be decided largely under the working of the natural laws as just given.

If we accept then the theory of the Mid-Asian origin of the Aryan peoples, we come again to the question, Whither would this Aryan man go when thus forced out from his old home? And with it comes another question, Can we by any natural laws account for the rapid divergence of the pathways of the various branches of the kin, and the marked variations which have come about in race characteristics? The answer to these questions will appear as we trace the lines of migration and the race life in the new homes. Eastward the Aryan could not go; for there lifted the forbidding peaks and the almost impassable gorges of the Thian Shan, crossed even now only with difficulty and peril for a few weeks in midsummer by occasional bands of wandering

Chinese traders clad in sheepskins. And beyond lay the long stretches of cold, desert upland of the East Turkestan plateau. Upon the north, reaching on to the arctic seas, spread the forbidding, wind-swept steppes of the Northern Asian plain, roamed over by the Mongols who centuries later precipitated themselves upon Europe, and at one time threatened to blot out the whole fabric of western civilization. Only two ways lay open, south and west. The two branches of the Aryan kin which passed southward we have already traced. The one which afterward became the Brahmin of India making its way through those low northwest passes of the Hindu Rush which have always been the gateway to India, and entering the plain which is traversed by the headwaters of the Indus. This branch of the primitive Aryan family, as before told, subjugated or drove before it the lower races of the Negroid which were then in possession of the land, and founded the great Brahminic empire of India, that empire which after ages of the enervation of a tropic climate upon northern blood, and under the varying vicissitudes of successive waves of invasion and subjugation, yet proves the old race vitality by its persistence in the form of a religious domination. For wave after wave of conquest rolled into that Aryan Hindu mass, Greek, Scythian, Mongol, only to be dissipated and spiritually absorbed by it, leaving little trace. Brahminic it was, and despite Greek, and Scythian, and Mongol, Brahminic it remains. It is the stubborn race persistence which comes of a strong primitive race type.

The other southward stream of migration, possibly separate from the start, but more probably as indicated by certain words made use of in common, branching off from the Hindu stream while yet in the uplands before the Indian plain was reached, crossed on still southerly but farther westward to the plateaus of ancient Iran, becoming in the new home the Mede of Herodotos, but afterward incorporated together with adjoining tribes into the kingdom of Persia. This branch, also, gave birth to one of the great religions of the world, that which comes to us in the Avestas from Zoroaster. Less enduring than the faith of the Brahmin, possibly more exposed to the shock of contending races and race beliefs than the Brahminic faith behind the comparative shelter of its mountain wall, it yet for ages swayed the minds of millions. It too, like the Brahminic faith in the days before the one was known as Brahminism, or the other as Zoroastrianism, seems to have been originally a comparatively pure theism, afterward overlaid through the centuries with a growth of superstition. Altho driven from the land of its birth it still survives in a corrupt form among the Parsees of India.

Why did these two streams, apparently in violation of the law of low grades for lines of migration, and of that other law of race climatic belts, cross the high rugged mountains southward instead of passing across the plains westward? Possibly because back of them, and between them and the open plains, lay the dense mass of their own kin to bar the way, leaving only the road southward open with no choice. Possibly also rumors of the broad fertile plains beyond these mountains and of a feeble folk dwelling thereon as possessors may have reached them to draw them on. And then the first portion of the way, while still in the mountain slopes of either side of the range, would not even be a change of climate to them. Afterward, when in the course of slow migration the mountains and the after-following current of population barred the backward road, there would be only the low tropic plains open before them. Return would be impossible. But for the Aryans who remained behind another way lay open, that toward the setting sun. Take a map of Central Asia. Westward, at the foot of the well-watered upland of Bactriana is the arid plain now known as the desert of Kizilkoom, at the farther edge of which lies the shallow, rapidly disappearing Aral. Of the geological history of this and the Caspian mention has already been made. What the area of the Aral might have been at the time when the supposed westward march of the Aryan began from his assumed Central Asian home, it is impossible now to determine; yet allowing for even the most rapid change, there must still have remained, between the margin of its waters and the fertile plains of Bactriana, the supposed Proto-Aryan home along the west slopes of the Thian Shan range, a long stretch of some hundreds of miles of desert plain, as impassable in its barrenness to the herds, the flocks, the families of a migrating race as the waters of the sea.

For it must be borne in mind that migration which, as before said, under the settled order and the assured protection of modern civilization is of the individual or of the family, was then for purpose of mutual protection tribal in character. And with the tribe went not only its flocks and herds but also its stores of accumulated wealth, its household utensils, its implements of agriculture, its tools of mechanic arts, things which were to it as truly impedimenta as were the stores of Caesar's legions. It is also to be borne in mind that such race migrations, instead of a continuous forced march across long reaches of territory, are so slow as at the time scarcely to seem to be a migration. The land before them is unknown. They are as men reaching out into the dark. They have no fixed destination; and as soon as they find what they seek, fresh lands and an assured food supply, they stop and settle while others overtake and then pass on beyond them. It is only as one looks backward across the land and the years that the change of location and the continuous march onward may be detected and traced. The front edge of the wave, like a flood wave in a river, is continually overlapping new land, the farther edge abandoning the territory which lies in the rear, and so it travels on, but slowly. For the means of subsistence for man and beast must be continuously provided, and so the land is occupied and tilled it may be for generations from the time when the front edge of population spreads over it until the last receding margin has passed on, may be forced on, and left it. Then, too, these tribal migrations of antiquity were seldom accomplished peaceably. They had to fight their way forward, for there were yet other dwellers in the lands before them who would resent the intrusion and battle against dispossession. It was so that the southward-moving Aryan had to fight his way down into the plains of India, battling with and forcing back the dark-skinned Negroid, his predecessor in the land, as shown in the earlier Vedic hymns. It was so that older English man fought his way across Britain. It is so the man of the greater English land has fought his way slowly but surely from the rim of the sea across the Alleghenies, beyond the Mississippi, over the broad plains, across the Rockies, then over the inner plateau and another mountain chain to the borders of yet another sea. For this Aryan man was born with the instinct of battle in him, and there is unrest in the blood.

It is this slow yet ever progressive tide which is to be borne in mind, or one entirely misapprehends the character of the older tribal migrations and misreads their lesson. We are too apt to think only of the initial and the terminal points of a race removal, and to overlook the long centuries of the slow advance which often lie between. Slow - yet in race migrations the score of the centuries is to the race as the year-marks to the individual. This slow yet ever advancing march of the primitive races in their tribal migrations was of such a type as the frontier American has been repeating in his march across the continent ever since the landing at Jamestown and Plymouth Rock - out from the Atlantic littoral, up the Appalachian slope, over the crest of the Alleghenies, down the valleys of the Ohio and the Cumberland, fighting his way mile by mile across the Dark and Bloody Ground with the Indians who held the land, building his log cabin, planting his little patch of corn amid the blackened stumps of his clearing, and after a while coming to possess the land in peace. I remember, when a boy, watching the never-ceasing stream which crossed the Alleghenies by the Great National Road and took its course westward along the highways of the Ohio valley; the lumbering wagon with its white cover; shy-eyed women and children peering out timidly from beneath the canvas at the new scenes which met their gaze; the flocks and herds driven behind; the men with rifle in hand trudging beside the wagons footsore and weary yet with eyes set hopefully toward the promised land which lay but just beyond. It was the rear wave of population passing on and overlapping the wave which had preceded it, to be again in turn, when it should have become fixed, overlapped by the next wave from behind. My grandfather, while yet a young man, leaving the old home in Pennsylvania, moved on farther west, securing lands and building a new home upon the extreme verge of population in Western Ohio. About him were the forests of the frontier, and the Indians. Within his lifetime the advancing wave of migration had already passed on and left him far within the line of a settled and comparatively dense population. Within another generation his descendants, with the unrest of ages in the blood, were again leaving the older home in Ohio and moving on to again pass beyond the new frontier line of a Farther West and build homes where the lands were again fresh and untaken. It is a history which in America has held good for nearly three centuries, and across three thousand miles of new lands.

But before the Aryan as he would face westward from that supposed old race home in the Central Asian plain stretched the broad reaches of desert which lie east of the Aral, and which even then must have been poorly watered and at least comparatively barren. How would the race with its flocks and herds and the impossibility of transporting adequate supplies of food for man and beast, the impossibility even of laying up such supplies in advance of a season's needs, probably also the lack, in common with other rude and primitive peoples, of that provident forethought which leads to the storing up of food supplies much beyond the season's needs - how was the race in the face of such obstacles and difficulties to make its way westward?

Several ways would lie open. They might flank the desert upon the south, following the well-watered tho narrow and broken plain at the north base of the Hindu Kush and the Elburz Mountains to the south shores of the Caspian, a route which would no doubt be made use of, and which will be described more fully in the chapter upon the Graeco-Latin migration. Or a similar flanking movement might be made north of the desert by way of the grassy steppes of what is now the Kirguis land, a route more strictly pastoral in possibilities than the other. This also will be described more in detail in the chapter upon the Teutonic migrations. As auxiliary to these two just mentioned are two others which are of interest more because of the light thrown upon them by the line of flow of the modern return wave from Europe upon Asia; for after all the centuries the current is now reversed, and Europe is beginning to overflow upon Asia. Directly across the desert stretched the long lines of two great natural highways; highways whereon were water, wood, grass, the three things which to the migrating herdsmen then upon the plains of Mid-Asia, as now in Mid-America by the Humboldt or the Gila, mean food, shelter, comfort. And along these highways the race might, year by year in its slow march, plant and reap and provide for the surely coming winter. And along the line of these highways that older Aryan would find, as his American after-type ages later found by the valley ways of the Humboldt and the Gila, the line of low grades for his journeying. These highways which thus opened up before him were the lines of waterways.

The numerous mountain streams which, flowing down from the melting snows of the Thian Shan, watered the northern portion of Bactriana, gathered together to mingle in the common current of the ancient Jaxartes, known now as the Syr-Daria. Turning to a course west by north the river entered upon the arid plain which spread before it, and began its battle with the desert, its waters drunk in by the thirsty sands, sucked up by parching winds whose drought was never satisfied, yet its current constantly reinforced by the melting snows of the mountains behind. Surviving the long struggle with the sands and the drought, its shrunken stream is at last poured into the Aral near its northern border. Southward three hundred miles a parallel road also leads over the desert from the mountains to the inland sea, and this also is a waterway. The ancient Oxus, the Amou-Daria of modern geographers, has its sources in the western slopes of the Beloor and the Hindu Rush. The branching headwaters of the two streams interlock and overlap before they start on their westward way to the sea. The Amou-Daria, larger than its companion on the north because of its greater mountain drainage, has its origin partly in the elevated snow plains of the Pamir, that lofty "Roof of the World." Flowing like its comrade northwesterly, it also has to do battle with the thirst of the same desert, which it also must cross to reach the sea. Fed by more numerous tributaries it pours a greater volume of water into the Aral as it enters near its southern border. Did it always thus empty into the Aral?

A hundred miles above the point of entrance into the Aral, at the head of the delta, is found an old river channel branching off southwestward away from the Aral along the south border of the Khivan desert. It may be readily traced in this southwesterly direction for six hundred miles until it leads, not into the Aral, but into the Caspian at the Balkan Bay, and by branches even farther south. At the point where this old channel leads off from the present course of the Oxus the difference in levels is so slight that a dam thrown across the river would easily change the course and divert its waters six hundred miles southwestward to the Caspian. Did it ever flow in this channel? The writings of Strabo, Pliny, and Ptolemy, and of later geographers indicate that from about 500 B.C. to 600 A.D. it did so follow this way to the Caspian. About the year 605 A.D. it turned to the Aral, and dams built for purposes of irrigation retained it in this channel. In 1221 these dams were broken down by the Turks, and it again found its way to the Caspian. In 1643 it was again flowing into the Aral. The whole physnorthward along the branching arms of the Syr-Daria to mingle with a more northerly stream of migration following down the valley of that river. At times, however, when the Amou-Daria chanced to turn its 'course and flow on over the Khivan desert to the Caspian, thus opening a direct road six hundred miles farther to the west, the current of population instead of checking, or may be deflecting northward, would naturally follow the course of that long river valley until it reached the Caspian at the point where the river emptied into the Balkan Bay. It is so that population followed the long valleys of the Nile and the Ohio. But arrived at the shore of the Caspian, again the desert would hem them in upon the north with its eight hundred miles of rocky plateau, mountainless, and therefore in that semi-arid interior climate deficient in water supply. Upon the south, however, the way opens up to rejoin the other stream of Aryan blood which, upon this supposition of a Mid-Asian homeland, would probably be working its way westward along the more broken but well-watered foothill plain of the north base of the Hindu Rush and the long rugged line of the Elburz Mountains. South of this mountain wall lay the dense populations of the well-organized and powerful monarchies of the valleys of the Tigris and the Euphrates barring the way from the Persian Gulf almost to the tablelands of Anti-Taurus. How then could this Aryan man, with the road blocked on the north and on the south, make his way from the interior and reach the larger open sea, for we soon find him settled about the east shores of the Mediterranean? There was a way by which he might escape the desert upon the one hand and the bar of opposing races on the other.

Around the south margin of the Caspian, between the long wall of the El-burz Mountains and the shore-line, is a narrow coast plain which forms for a migrating race a natural highway four hundred miles farther westward to the river valleys of the Aras and the Kur in Georgia. Northward again the way is barred by the to them, with their crude means of transportation, impassable wall of the Caucasus stretching from the Caspian to the Black Sea, while southward still lay the civilization and the compact power of the Semite. Yet still the way opened westward on from the plains of Georgia by the shore-line of the Black Sea north of the Anti-Taurus range; and from this shore plain of the Black Sea the river valleys of the Halys and the Sangarios with their rich alluvial lands give ready access to the heart of Asia Minor; and beyond are the Meander and the Hermos, and the open plains of the Ionik coast.

Thus far in the line of advance at no point has the land been extensive enough to long detain a migrating people or to long support a rapidly growing population; yet it has been a highway with wood, water, and grass, for its numerous streams from the mountains above make it even now a comparatively well-watered land. Here, too, the migrating Aryan would still find his old-time friends, the oak, the beech, the elm, walnut, sycamore, ash, together with the shrubs, the fruits, the flowers, and the grains of the old Mid-Asian home, for he would still be within the margins of the same climatic belt. Looking at the question in the light of all the facts thus far given it would not seem unreasonable to conclude that by this route only could an Aryan man of Southern Bactriana have found his way westward to the shores of the Mediterranean, for by this way he has escaped the desert upon the north; he has found wood, water, grass; he has avoided the great mountain chains; and he has flanked the densely populated and powerful Semitic kingdoms of the river valleys of the Tigris and the Euphrates upon the south, through which his as yet more limited numbers, his weaker tribal organization, and his cruder civilization incapacitated him to force his way. And as confirmation he has left behind him along the line of march a trail of Aryan peoples and Aryan tradition.

Two great divisions of the Aryan kin presumably worked their way westward by this southern route, the Graeco-Latin, possibly as forerunner, the Celt presumably following after. Of the Celtic migration little, if any, trace remains. Their route is largely only a matter of inference drawn from the location of their after-home in Southwestern Europe, and the natural lines of approach thereto as deduced from the laws which have been stated as governing primitive migrations. This will be discussed more in detail under the heading of "The Celto-Aryan." The Greek division of the Graeco-Latin branch, however, has left behind it waymarks which time has even yet not entirely obliterated. It is possible that somewhere about the south shore of the Black Sea a division occurred in the main stream of this Graeco-Latin migration, the ancestors of the Ionians of the Asiatic seacoast and of the adjacent islands following the open valleys of the Halys and the Sangarios inland, yet leaving behind them as they passed on over the uplands that Phrygian offshoot which remained fixed in the central highlands of Asia Minor and never reached the sea; leaving behind them also as hinting of a Greek life by the way, a life which afterward became obliterated, the race myths of Midas and his hoard of gold, and of Gordios and his fabled knot, to linger about the headwaters of the Sangarios. And myths of persons will go back of their homeland along lines of race migration even when all other trace of the journeying is lost. And one other thing the Greek left behind him as a waymark which to the student of race migrations is full of import; and it was something which in all his further migrations he never forgot. He left a name. In all his after-familiarity with other and greater waters, this always remained to him, Ὁ Πόντος, The Sea. He might sometimes call it Ὁ Πόντος Εὐξεινος; but if a Greek ever spoke simply of Ὁ Πόντος, no man doubted for a moment which sea he meant. And the very land where he would linger upon its shores before taking his departure inland by the open river valleys, and to which he would in his slow race migration long look back, the fertile plains of the lower Halys and of the Sangarios, even this was ever after known to him as Πόντος, The land by the Sea.

The other portion of what was possibly a combined Dorik and Latin wave of migration would seem to have passed on more directly westward, probably by the law of grades following still the Black Sea shore to the narrower waters upon either side of the Propontis, and so to have crossed over directly into Europe. Possibly the Propontis itself became another dividing barrier, that branch which afterward became the Dardani of the Troad passing to the south and leaving their name as a waymark stamped upon the watercourse which after-ages have known as the Dardanelles. That the Dardani and the Ionian Greeks could have turned southward as a common stream is improbable, as they had no tradition of a common origin, and did not look upon themselves as kin. It remained for the philologist and the antiquarian to prove this. That the Latin and the Dorian peoples continued together for some time after the splitting off of the Ionik Greeks would seem to be clearly proven by some peculiarities of speech which they held in common, but which are lost in the Ionik tongue. As such may be instanced the broad vowel sounds of the so-called Aiolik, which seems to have been only the older, ruder Dorian tongue, sounds which the Ionian in his sunnier clime soon flattened and softened; and also may be instanced the lingering use of the Aiolik digamma, which appears in a modified form in the Latin V; and also the increasing approximation, as we trace backward, of that older, pre-classic Latin and of the primitive Aiolik Greek to each other in terminal forms.

Let us leave for a time the Graeco-Latin stream, and go back to that other current of westward migration which presumably departed from the old race homeland in Central Asia by the way of the plains north of the Aral and the Caspian, and possibly also by the river valley of the Syr-Daria. As that river enters the Aral near its northern border, any current of migration following down its course would naturally in its onward march flank the sea by its northern and more fertile margin, slowly skirting along its shore, and joining with any current advancing by a still more northerly route over the plains; and, pushed on from behind by the ever-crowding waves of population, and keeping as nearly as possible within the same general climatic belt, would cross over the plains which lie between the North Aral and the North Caspian to the margin of the latter sea. Along this line are no great desert stretches after once the Aral has been left behind, as the numerous streams which flow southward to the two seas leave only short interspaces which, even if much more arid than they now are, might be readily crossed over during the rainy portion of the year when water and grass are to be found in sufficient abundance to meet the daily needs of tribal migration, while farther back, about their interlacing headwaters, the grassy plains would at all seasons offer an open highway toward the west. Working around the head of the Caspian the current of migration, repelled by the rugged Alpine center of Mid-Europe, would naturally follow the low grades and the fertile lands of the Volga, probably here dividing and a portion passing over where that river makes its turn to the northward, to the valley of the Don and on through the low, well-watered, and grassy plains northwestwardly across Europe to the south shores of the Baltic, while another portion would probably follow up the valley of the Volga itself and on by a still more northerly route also to the shores of the Baltic but farther north.

That these conclusions as to the highway by which the northern current of that old Aryan migration must have entered Europe have sound reason back of them is shown by the fact that it is the line of the great race irruptions from Asia into Europe within historic times, and by the further fact that it is the identical route by which Northern Europe is now, after all these long ages, turning back upon Central Asia again. Trace the line of the Russian aggressive advance upon Central Asia which is in reality only a movement of regression; down the Volga to the head of the Caspian; across the Caspian (for now the returning stream of population has ships, which the older had not); across to the Aral, but now by rail; and then on by the well-watered valleys of the Amouand Syr-Daria to the heart of the continent.

But this course westward has led the migrating Aryan, in apparent violation of climatic law, ten degrees north of the old race home. Why should he not rather, the north shore of the Caspian once passed, have turned southward again to the latitude of his primitive home? In answering this question it must first of all be borne in mind that climatic belts are not things of parallels of latitude but of isothermal lines, and these vary with elevation, exposure, prevailing wind currents, and proximity to or remoteness from the sea. Owing to the lower elevation as an offset to the more northerly latitude, and also to the great inlet of the waters of the Baltic which on the one side, with the Black Sea upon the other, partially bisect Europe at this point, carrying the tempering influence of the sea and its warm southwest winds far inland, the line of milder average temperature deflects northward in crossing from sea to sea. Central Europe, the Europe of the Balkans, of the Carpathians, the Hartz, the Alps, because also of the greater average elevation, is colder, more inhospitable than the more northerly yet lower plain.

But other influences besides that of mere temperature would help to divert the line of migration northward. The course of the first great waterway, the fertile river valley which leads out from the Caspian toward Europe, is northwesterly rather than directly west; and, as the line of migration passed over by easy crossings from this to the adjacent waterways of the Azov and the Black, the same general trend would be found in the valleys of the Don and the Dnieper. From these again the natural line of migration (natural because easiest) would be over the scarcely perceptible divides to the valleys of the Duna, the Niemen, the Vistula, and on down these to the shores of the Baltic. The line of milder temperature and of easier grades across Europe from the Caspian and the Black is thus northwesterly to the Baltic and not directly westward through the Alpine center to the Atlantic.

Another point is to be borne in mind. What slight history we have shows, as before stated, the primitive Aryans to have been a semi-pastoral people, and in their migrations they would naturally and even necessarily follow along the grass belts of the world, rather than the timber belts; and these broad level plains which stretch from the Black Sea to the Baltic are the natural grass lands of Europe, seemingly an extension of the Asiatic grass plains westward to the sea; while the Alpine center was largely clad in those dense forests which even yet, after ages of human settlement, cover the mountains and give harbor to the bear and the wolf. This central mountain region, because of its rugged, inhospitable character and its dense forests, must have been settled more slowly and at a later date; possibly settled by offshoots from the main current, possibly also by some streamlets from that Aryan wave already described which, going out from the Mid-Asian homeland, passed westward by the plain south of the Caspian. This as Celto-Aryan may have followed up the course of the Danube, to be finally overtaken and lost in that mass of warring and contending tribes which later became known to the Latin under the one general name of Alamanni. The main northern current of what (for now the returning stream of population has ships, which the older had not); across to the Aral, but now by rail; and then on by the well-watered valleys of the Amouand Syr-Daria to the heart of the continent.

But this course westward has led the migrating Aryan, in apparent violation of climatic law, ten degrees north of the old race home. Why should he not rather, the north shore of the Caspian once passed, have turned southward again to the latitude of his primitive home? In answering this question it must first of all be borne in mind that climatic belts are not things of parallels of latitude but of isothermal lines, and these vary with elevation, exposure, prevailing wind currents, and proximity to or remoteness from the sea. Owing to the lower elevation as an offset to the more northerly latitude, and also to the great inlet of the waters of the Baltic which on the one side, with the Black Sea upon the other, partially bisect Europe at this point, carrying the tempering influence of the sea and its warm southwest winds far inland, the line of milder average temperature deflects northward in crossing from sea to sea. Central Europe, the Europe of the Balkans, of the Carpathians, the Hartz, the Alps, because also of the greater average elevation, is colder, more inhospitable than the more northerly yet lower plain.

But other influences besides that of mere temperature would help to divert the line of migration northward. The course of the first great waterway, the fertile river valley which leads out from the Caspian toward Europe, is northwesterly rather than directly west; and, as the line of migration passed over by easy crossings from this to the adjacent waterways of the Azov and the Black, the same general trend would be found in the valleys of the Don and the Dnieper. From these again the natural line of migration (natural because easiest) would be over the scarcely perceptible divides to the valleys of the Duna, the Niemen, the Vistula, and on down these to the shores of the Baltic. The line of milder temperature and of easier grades across Europe from the Caspian and the Black is thus northwesterly to the Baltic and not directly westward through the Alpine center to the Atlantic.

Another point is to be borne in mind. What slight history we have shows, as before stated, the primitive Aryans to have been a semi-pastoral people, and in their migrations they would naturally and even necessarily follow along the grass belts of the world, rather than the timber belts; and these broad level plains which stretch from the Black Sea to the Baltic are the natural grass lands of Europe, seemingly an extension of the Asiatic grass plains westward to the sea; while the Alpine center was largely clad in those dense forests which even yet, after ages of human settlement, cover the mountains and give harbor to the bear and the wolf. This central mountain region, because of its rugged, inhospitable character and its dense forests, must have been settled more slowly and at a later date; possibly settled by offshoots from the main current, possibly also by some streamlets from that Aryan wave already described which, going out from the Mid-Asian homeland, passed westward by the plain south of the Caspian. This as Celto-Aryan may have followed up the course of the Danube, to be finally overtaken and lost in that mass of warring and contending tribes which later became known to the Latin under the one general name of Alamanni. The main northern current of what we now distinguish as Teutonic blood, and which occupied the lands about the Baltic and the North Sea, seems to have remained almost unknown to the Latins. They only knew of it as a vast hive of rude barbarians who dwelt in little known and inhospitable lands far to the north, lands which bordered close upon the home of the Hyperboreans.

This then, under the working of the natural laws which govern and direct the migration of primitive races, would seem to have been the line of advance westward across Europe to the shores of the Atlantic followed by that Mid-Aryan wave which, as said, we distinguish by the name of Teuton:- the line of the open grassy plains of the Don, the Dnieper, and their counterparts on the Baltic, the Duna, the Niemen, and the Vistula, rather than across the rugged woodlands of Central Europe.

What Modifying Influence upon Race Type and Characteristics Would the Wandering Life' of this Long Migration Tend to have upon the Aryan Peoples?

To one who has watched the change which comes to the individual man in even the few months of a similar life spent by overland emigrants upon the western plains, the question is by no means an idle one. The mere fact of an entire breaking up of the comparatively fixed habits and manners of a settled home, however rude, and entering upon the unsettled life of migration, is not without its influence. When to this is added a continuance of this unsettled, migratory life through generations, the effect must be marked. My attention was first called to this thought when stationed for a year at Camp Bowie on the Southern Overland Road. It was the great highway of migration from the Southern States to California. My position as post surgeon often called me among the emigrants who were accustomed to camp at the spring below the post, and I studied them with great interest, for I found what was to me a comparatively new type of American. Erect, spare-bodied, alert and active, no ounce of superfluous flesh, long straight hair bleached by the winds, skin tanned by the constant outdoor life, features strongly marked, wary, watchful eyes, taciturn, shy of approach, most at home amid their wagons and their herds, habitually armed and quick in the use of arms, they were unlike myself, yet we had come of a common stock. They were the product, however, of over two centuries of frontier life, with its developed instincts and its unsettled habits. One of these men told me that in fifteen years he had lived in sixteen different States and Territories. Another told me it was his third migration back and forth across the continent with his family and herds. They were become almost nomads. They were representatives of that wave of frontier population which, landing more than two centuries before at Jamestown and in the Carolinas, had ever since kept in the front line of westward migration until it now knew no other life than that of the nomad.

And again, I, with generations of frontier blood in my own veins, altho not as an individual trained to frontier life, having been reared amid schools and books, found that I differed in aptness for frontier life from my associates at the post who had come from the Atlantic seaboard with its generations of more settled life behind them. The woodcraft, if one may apply the underly-

44

ing idea of the phrase to life upon the woodless plains, which by night or by day never loses its bearings, the keenness of sense which in scouting could take and follow the faintest trail, the cunning and wariness of Indian warfare, these things which to the frontiersman are a birthright, came to me as the arousing of a slumbering instinct. And so it was. Yet in many of my associates upon these scouts, men who for a number of generations had come of a more fixed and settled blood, even the instinct seemed to be almost gone.

In the long journey westward to the shores of the Baltic this migrating Aryan must have given up the comparatively fixed habits of his old home and taken on somewhat of the ways of the nomad. In foods the unsettled life and the newer lands into which he was continually moving with their greater abundance of game would make him more of a hunter and a meat-eater. It is just such a change as came to the pioneer Americans as they crossed the Alleghenies and moved on into the wilds of the Ohio valley. The less attention to agriculture and the greater dependence upon his flocks and herds in the unsettled semi-pastoral life, which during the long migration he must necessarily lead, would tend still more to make him depend upon meat and the milk foods of the dairy rather than upon grain and vegetables for sustenance. The central plain of Europe across which he slowly made his way was also at that time less favorable to agriculture than the Asian lands of the old home. Geologically this plain was one of the last portions of Europe to emerge from the waters of the sea. Long after the Alpine center of Europe stood as a great rocky island above the sea-level, a broad arm of the ocean extended from the waters of the Baltic across the North German and South Russian plain to the waters of the Black Sea. Rising slowly from the shoal waters it remained, as it yet is by nature, badly drained, dotted with morasses and swamps, its sluggish waters keeping the soil cold and unfruitful and as yet unsuited to the needs of agriculture. It would be better adapted to grass of which it, and not the Alpine uplands, became the natural home and consequently the well-filled habitat of the deer, the elk, the bear, the wild boar, and of the bands of wolves which preyed upon them.

The hunter life which he would thus necessarily lead, and the probable battling with opposing tribes in his passage over the land, would strengthen in this wanderer the original combative spirit which the whole blood seems to have possessed as a common heritage, and would accustom him still more to the use of arms and to a self-reliance which still marks his descendants. How much of that jealous guarding of the right of the individual to keep and bear arms which appears in the Constitution of the United States dates back in spirit to those old days of migration and self-reliance of the Teutonic forefathers is an interesting question. The same migrating life, with its need of taking care of self and of family, would also develop an individuality which in a large portion of this especial branch of the Aryan peoples and their descendants has made of the individual man the basic unit upon which the state is built up.

Yet while this long migration would bring with it a gain in rude strength, in self-reliance, in individuality, there would result certain other changes which, for the time at least, might seem as a race retrogression. Tribal lines would weaken, and as each man learned more and more to depend upon his own strength and his own arms for the protection of himself and his own immediate household, the authority of chieftain, whether hereditary or elective, would be lessened. It would apparently be a step backward toward the lawlessness of the savage. The same tendency is shown in a marked degree in the race migration of his descendants across the heart of the American continent. It still shows itself in the rough lawlessness of the Kentucky and Tennessee mountains. And even in the more law-abiding early Ohio days I remember to have heard grave discussion as to whether it was compatible with the dignity of a free man ever to submit to arrest at the hands of an officer of the law. And I myself grew up to carry the rifle, and to look upon the boundary fence-line of the farm as a line within which the one supreme law was the law of the family, while without that line was the unfenced, neutral land upon which all freemen met upon terms of equality. It was the survival of the old Danish land and law of The Mark; and that was a survival of the still older days of Teutonic migration when all the land was free, and each family was law unto itself. Yet out of this immediate evil, and from the civic standpoint it was an evil, came an ultimate and a compensating good; for this feeling of personal independence and reliance upon self is, as has just been intimated, the indispensable groundwork of that democratic form of government toward which the Teuton's descendants seem to be everywhere evoluting as their one common form of race government.

There would also naturally and inevitably come as a result of the long wandering a loss of culture and an impoverishment of mental life; for the wanderer would be leaving behind him in the march the more fixed forms of civilization of the old home, with such culture as it possessed; and the Vedic hymns show that one branch at least of the old stock was possessed of no mean degree of culture only shortly after it must have gone out from the common home. And then his westward march to the sea, unlike that of his Graeco-Latin kinsman, would bring him in contact only with races still ruder than his own. Yet in this also there would be a gain as compensation; for the civilization which he might afterward develop would be his own, not borrowed; and it is the self-evolved civilizations which alone have shown vitality and power of endurance. In it all the very hardships, the exposure to danger, the adventures of the long migration, while at the inevitable expense of culture, would bring with them a gain in strength of those rude virtues which make a more manly man and lay foundation for a broader, more enduring culture in the end. The race as it gained the shores of the Baltic would be a stronger even tho a ruder folk.

His religious faith would naturally share in the same change. It also would tend to become ruder and simpler, dropping off subtilities and creeds, going back to the primitive groundworks of religious faith, and becoming more personal in character. His gods would tend to become more like himself, great simple-hearted men, hunters, woodsmen. For it is to be borne in mind that in non-inspired religions it is man who makes his gods. Take again as an illustration his descendant upon the frontier wave of migration as we find him in the Mississippi valley half a century ago. The abstruse theology of the introspective Puritan of the New England shore, the somewhat simpler creed of the Cavalier of Jamestown, the formal tenets of the 'Huguenots of the Carolinas, seemed to have been strained out of that broad wave of population which everywhere rolled up and over the long line of the Alleghenies, and left behind as subtilities for which the frontier life and the battling with forest and savage gave no time. Religiously they became a people of one book, and that not a book of theology. And the circuit-rider with his saddle-bags and his copy of King James's Bible, and a few quaint hymns that rang out through the aisles of the great forests like the clang of a trumpet, sang and preached his way from the Lakes to the headwaters of the Tennessee in the simple faith of Methodism, a faith with only a half-formed skeleton of a creed, but with an intensity of personal feeling to which the older forms were strangers.

Thus far in tracing the history of the Aryan peoples we have been working largely in the region of conjecture. It has been chiefly the prehistoric age of race life. The qualifying words *possibly, probably, presumably* had through logical necessity to be constantly made use of to guard the statements made and the conclusions drawn therefrom. It has been an attempt to rebuild a race history, and chiefly from collateral and fragmentary material. And it has been a portion of the family history over which men may reasonably differ. Even in tracing the history of the Indo-and the Irano-Aryans the work has had to be largely a reading between the lines to inferential conclusions. Yet in it all, when we apply to the information thus derived the test of the working of the natural laws of climate and the laws which govern primitive race life and race migrations, we are apparently justified in applying to the conclusions reached the more forceful word *probably* rather than the less positive word *possibly*. And we have a logical right to thus reason and thus announce the conclusions reached in the investigation.

But we now enter upon a different field. While there will still be some points concerning which we can only infer, we are largely leaving behind the region of uncertainty, and are entering upon the region of fairly reliable historic record. The facts of history are here in the main well established. It is only in the philosophic conclusions drawn therefrom that differences of opinion might legitimately arise.

Chapter Seven - The European Home

Asia is continental. It, more than any other division of the globe, is the triumph of the land. Its distances are vast; its elevations awesome; its bulk massive. Here men might live and only know of the sea as some far-off, vague, unreal dream. It is the land that is real. To them the vision of the measureless outlying and encircling ocean of Homer had not yet come. It was the land that was measureless, and ever stretched on and on. It was the waters that were pent up and prisoner to the land, as in their inland seas, which, waging an unequal battle with the ancient earth, were everywhere shrinking before the thirst of the desert and disappearing. The fathomless depths were of the blue sky which spread above, and beyond, pierced by mountain peaks snow-clad and inaccessible, but which fell short of the abyss that reached on and on past the stars.

The new homeland was the antithesis of all this. Europe is peninsular, not continental. It is encircled and pierced and overawed by the sea. Draw a line from the Baltic to the Black Sea. East is Asia; west is Europe. For Russia is Asia. The Volga is a mid-continental river. It, too, is Asia. The Black Sea is half-way Asiatic. East of the line given the land triumphs; west of it is the triumph of the sea. The waters of the sea enwrap the land. Their long arms cut into it. The sea winds blow over it and temper it. The climate of the sea dominates it. Even within historic times the moisture of the sea clothed valley and mountain and plain with dense forest. Man in Europe, as afterward in America, has since subdued the forest. The surrounding waters, with the islands which line many of the shores, invited man to measure his cunning with the waves and go out to a new life upon the great deep.

It was to this life peninsular, and then to the life insular, that the Aryan peoples who took up the westward march went out. So radical a change from the old life continental could not but leave its impress upon the whole afterhistory of the race. It is to the Celtic and the Teutonic peoples especially that the full influence of this peninsular life came, for the Graeco-Latin never quite cut loose from the old Asiatic life and affiliations. His history can never be entirely separated from that of the Asiatic peoples. Asia left its impress upon his whole after mental development. Its imperium shaped his entire political existence. It is Lydia, Persia, Babylon, and half-Asiatic Egypt, that influence and color his civilization. This was not so with Celt and Teuton. Asia was not to them even a dream. The Asiatic life of their forefathers was as tho it had not been. A cloud of oblivion settled down between old and new, and the old was blotted out. And no Asiatic army ever threatened them. No Asiatic despot ever demanded tribute of earth and water. The shadow of no oriental imperium cast its modifying influence over the shaping of their political life only the reflected shadow from the Latin overlapped the Southern Celt of Gaul and Iberia, and left its mark upon his after-history.

Chapter Eight - The Graeco-Latin Aryan

Let us go back for a while to that other wave of Aryan blood which presumably flowed westward from Asia into Europe by the southern route. If the Mid-Asian origin of the Aryan peoples be accepted as fairly proven, it is interesting to note how the two great westward streams of migration, the northern and the southern, would in their journeying be continually forced farther and farther apart, and how by the interposition of natural barriers they would be kept from ever uniting or even drawing near to each other again. First, the diverging lines of the two rivers and the lateral plains, with the broadening wedge of the desert of Kizilkoom between; then the forbidding wastes of the Khivan desert; then the snowy wall of the Caucasus; and still beyond the black waters of the Euxine and its adjunct, the Azov; and yet beyond all these the rugged crests of the Balkans and the Carpathians; and then the great Alpine center of Mid-Europe to force them still farther apart. And so the two streams, starting from one common home, would keep ever diverging, and never again intermingle, or cross each other's paths even, in their long march westward to the waters of the greater seas which lay in the dimness beyond. This much we know, however, that it is a separate race life, a separate race history, a separate and distinct race development which we are to trace in peoples who were once of one kin. It is this fact with which we now come to deal, and to which the discussion thus far has largely been preliminary.

Whether the two peoples which we now know respectively as Greek and Latin left the primitive race home as one people and afterward separated, is not settled, possibly never can be definitely settled. Yet certain peculiarities of speech, such as words held in common, grammatical forms which resemble each other more closely than they do the grammatical structure of the other Aryan tongues, consonantal and vowel similarities, all these point toward a bond of yet closer kinship within the race lines of the broader kin. It would seem to be, as with the Indo-Iranians and with the Teutonic peoples, an instance of a minor kin growing up which ranks as a single unit within the lines of the larger family circle, a compound algebraic factor as it were in the calculation of the broader race equation. It is through the Dorik tongue and the Dorik character that the evidences of kinship between Greek and Latin are most clearly to be traced; in speech the same tendency to harsher consonants and broader vowels, with the more terse and even awkward diction; in character the same grave, taciturn, realistic, unpoetic temperament. In type of character, indeed, the Dorian was more Latin than Ionik.

The Greek peoples first appear in reliable history as settled about the shores and upon the islands of the Aegean. Back of this are vague traditions of the incoming, and of successive migrations to and fro within the Greek lands. One thing the excavations at Mykene and Tiryns, and at Knossos upon the island of Krete have taught us, and that is to lengthen out the centuries of the Greek separate race life and of the life by the Aegean far anterior to the time at first conceded. Where we had allowed centuries we must allow millenniums. It is rather the Greek in his decadence that we know in history. Only the echoes of the days of the Greek youth come to us across the unnamed ages - the days of Minos, and of Herakles, and of Theseus, and the Argo, and the Troad, the days when as Herodotos plaintively says, "All the Greeks were still free." The evil days came later, even with all the gilded after-glory. Then too the Greek language was no new thing. Even as it first comes down to us it bears in its grammatical structure the wreckage of long ages before it became a written speech. The classic Greek verb as we know it is only a patchwork of yet older and fragmentary forms. The antiquity of the Greek race life is recorded in the Greek tongue. That fragmentary verb is letters patent of a past long antedating written Greek speech; the middle voice, only a supplanted passive; the dual number throughout, a primitive and displaced plural; augment and reduplication not yet entirely settled even in Homer's time; the uneasy ghost of the digamma ever rising like a tombless and troubled shade to mar the metric peace of the poet; euphonic contraction not yet fixed and stable. It is the hither verge of linguistic chaos out of unwritten and long-forgotten ages.

And that primitive, broken conjugation in μι, predecessor of the form in ω, which, like the irregular conjugation of the verb in all tongues, goes back of those decorous and orderly after-conjugations we call regular to a time when words were few because thought was simple, and hence the necessity of a more uniform system in conjugation as a mental labor-saving device had not yet been forced upon men. And then that old-time second aorist, the displaced tenant of a once verbal past; and the parvenu first aorist, still uncertain of its social rank among grammatical forms even in classic Greek, but depending upon the ecclesiastical indorsement of the New-Testament Greek to secure to it general standing; and the second perfects, with their roots abraded by the wear of untold centuries - all are grammatical derelicts, the drift of the ages, telling of a long-gone, prehistoric past. Or they are as the smooth coins which linger in circulation side by side with their smarter successors, date, motto obliterated, effigy worn and dim, only the polished disks remaining to tell of the days that are no more. And when the grammarian stopped short, the spade of the antiquary took up the uncompleted task, and at Mykene and Tiryns and Knossos, and upon the old Dardanian plains of the Troad in that other Greek home, dug down through the buried stratification of a long-forgotten past and uncovered again to the light of day the Greece that had been. It was a Greece which had lived its life and grown old before the days of the Persian, before the days even of Lydia and of Kroisos, and of the outflowing of the Greek colonies, for all this was only the Greece of the Dorian Renaissance, not the Greece of the beginning.

Rome we know from her beginning; Greece, only in her decline and fall. It is as tho Rome's written history had begun with the Goth at her gates. Greece was already retreating from her outposts when the dawn of written history set in. We have been accustomed to look upon the age of Perikles as the summit of Greek greatness; it was only a revival. It is the glow of the afternoon, not of the morning, that comes reflected to us across the centuries. The Greek was then past the noontide of his race life. The days of expansion were over. He was already upon the defensive. It is to be remembered that Thermopylai, and Marathon, and Salamis, and Plataia were battles fought upon Greek soil to drive back the invader from the Greek homeland. The advance of the Greek wave had been checked. The Ionians no longer were free. This was not a contest for the acquisition of new lands, but a fight for life itself in the older homeland. These were such battles as Rome fought in the third and fourth centuries against Alamanni and Goth when she was already rebuilding the walls of defense of the Imperial City. Flood-tide of Greek power passed with the dimly historic days when the Greek peoples went out and built up that Magna Graecia which spread from the Euxine to the shores of the Tyrrhenian Sea.

I have said that it was the afternoon sun of the Greek day that slanted down upon the Greece of Marathon and Salamis. Noontide was back in the days of which Herodotos so sadly speaks. Greece did not then have to fight for her freedom. The evil days began when the Lydian power overshadowed the clustering Ionian cities of the rim of the Asiatic shore. The brave days of the old Greek race were the days when the Greek colonies possessed the shores of the Mediterranean out to the Pillars of Hercules, those old Πυλαι Γαδειριδες, beyond which Gades looked out over the sweep of the ever-circling River of Ocean; days when Greek ships carried Greek trade to the farther shores of the Euxine and brought back their lading of fish and grain. We have been accustomed to speak of Greek power as short-lived. May be we do not go far enough back for the beginning. If Mykene and Tiryns and Knossos could speak from their ruins they might tell somewhat of the earlier manhood of the Greek peoples. But history then was not: only song; and the song was already growing faint upon the air. Age writes history; youth sings.

Altho Greek and Latin seem to have been closely akin in blood, and linked together in race migration, yet the dividing line historically between them is the dividing line between old and new. Upon the one side lie the vague, shadowy, long-departed Asiatic days; upon the other, the stir of modern life. When we speak of the Greek somehow we think of Ilium and of the Lydian shore, and of Kroisos, and of Cyrus and Babylon, and of the March of the Ten Thousand, and of days and of lands which were before time was; for time historically seems to begin west of the Aegean. But the Latin somehow links on to the present. We are in at the birth. Even Romulus and the wolf-fostering do not seem so very far away. And then Rome still lives.

But Greece:- the Akropolis is only a tomb; beautiful in its desolation; but still only a tomb, where men linger in the ghostly moonlight dreaming, but it is the elusive fantom of a dream within a dream. One picks up Caesar, or

Livy: it is as Grant's Memoirs, or as Hume. But Herodotos: it is as the Egyptian Book of the Dead. And Homer - he might have sung the Hymns to the Maruts.

The Latin had also his prehistoric days about the slopes of the Apennines. Of these we know less, for here we lack even tradition. Yet to him also we have learned to give more time for the process of race evolution. The *ante urbem conditam* is lengthening out. The *post urbem conditam* is dwarfing. But the essential historic fact of it all is this, that here, by the shores of the Mediterranean, in some prehistoric time the Graeco-Latin Aryans *did* find a race home, driving out or absorbing other men who held the land before them, and *did* build up an Aryan civilization which has left an indelible mark upon the whole after-history of the world.

What were the Changes in Physical Surroundings and in Climate which Came to the Greco-Latin in his New Home?

He has left the interior of the continent and has come to dwell by the shores of the sea. He has ceased to be a man of the highlands; he has become a lowlander. Yet only in part, for even here are the mountains also where he may quickly climb the steeps which form the backward rim of the seacoast plain. In latitude, unlike the Teuton, he has scarcely varied from the old home line: he is still within the parallel of 40° north. But he has departed from his old isothermal line. He is now upon the annual mean of 59°. This fact has an important bearing upon the question of the comparative time of race maturity, as will be seen in the further discussion of the subject. He has also, like the Teuton, left the dry air of the interior of the continent and passed progressively on to the moister air of the sea; yet not into the fogs and the mists which enveloped the pathway and the final halting-place of the Teuton. While the air of the sea, it is yet the warmer, drier atmosphere of the Mediterranean with its comparatively cloudless skies, and over all the kindly summer sun of the Orient. And this fact stands prominently forth in his case as in that of his Teutonic brother, that he, a man born and reared in the heart of a continent, having his race constitution fixed in lands away from the sea, has left the inland and become a dweller by the shores of the sea. He has changed the physical surroundings and the skies which had helped to make him the man he was. He has found a land of softer, kindlier skies. He is still a dweller in the land of the wheat and the barley, but he has gained the olive and the vine. He has carried with him his domesticated animals, but coming to a land more favorable to the cultivation of the soil he begins to lose his pastoral habits and becomes more of an agriculturist; and with this change he changes also, and resultantly, somewhat of his food habits, eating less meat, more of grains and fruits. And with this change he becomes more fixed in his habitation, for the tiller of the soil can not roam at will as can the man who is fed by his flocks and herds.

The laws which regulate and govern race development are in many respects much like the laws which regulate and govern vegetable life. The plant, removed from a colder climate to warmer and more genial surroundings, takes on a quicker development. Under the stimulating rays of a southern sun and the favoring influences of a longer growing season, it flowers and fruits more quickly. So it is with races. And races, like plants in this respect also, with such surroundings show all the more quickly that decay and death which come after flowering. Races, not men. For while the race as a race seems to lose vitality and decay, the individuals, the units, the elements, live on to recombine after a while in new race forms. The race seems to lose capacity for united action and for forward movement; not the individual the power of reproduction. The ability to bring things to pass as a race is gone. It is a mental and moral, rather than a physical, decay which seems to result, a race inertia. The race, like the plant, has flowered and fruited; thenceforth the rule is for it, as for the plant, only decadence. And normal flowering and fruiting seem to come only once to each race even when no external force, as of war or conquest, has supervened to check the current of race life. It was so with the Brahmin, the Iranian, the Israelite, the Arab, the Chinese. No power of self-rejuvenation, no second coming of youth, no rebegotten tide of vitality in the race veins, has ever brought force to lift either up from the race torpor which has fallen upon them. Two things may, however, for a time suspend the normal working of the race law to its ultimate end, may even for a time bring back the slighter harvest of an aftermath to the race. The first is, the stimulation of new race environments; as when that older Phoenician passed oversea from Tyre and made a new race home at Carthage. The second is, the incorporation of new blood; as when to the failing civilization of Knossos and the Aegean came the fresh wave of Dorian blood which upbuilt classic Greece; or as when to dying Rome came that wave of Teutonic blood which made possible to the Latin the Renaissance of the Middle Ages.

What were the Physical Surroundings in the New Home of the Graeco-Latin Aryan which would tend to stimulate & hasten Race development?

They may be thus briefly enumerated: a somewhat higher mean of annual heat; a more equable temperature; a more genial climate; a better-watered land, with a greater degree of atmospheric moisture and hence more favorable conditions for agriculture; with these a fresh and fertile soil; and as a result of all these a more abundant and more varied food supply; and as a result of this more plentiful and more certain supply of food, in accordance [with a well-established law of population, a more rapid increase in numbers, wealth, and power. This Graeco-Latin Aryan also found here, for the first time Probably, since leaving the primitive race home, a fixed habitation and gave up the wandering habit. It was the end of the long march. The Aryan man is not by temperament a nomad. The Mongol and the Semite in some of their branches furnish the only true nomads of the world. That this Graeco-Latin branch of the Aryan family had been upon the road through necessity, and not by choice or from any rambling instinct, is fairly shown by the fact that having found this new race home, they have not departed from it in the at least thirty centuries since first taking up their abode therein. The nomadic life seems to belong only to the great plains of the world. It seems to be a part of the boundless reaches ever stretching on and on with no natural features, as mountain or lake or river to anchor the race - of this, and the pastoral life with its attendant lack of personal ownership in the soil. And then this Graeco-Latin Aryan has come to the broken lands where it is less easy to change habitation and transport his household goods. The growth of the agricultural habit also would help to fix him from month to month as the season's crop was maturing, and to a certain extent from year to year, for now he begins to have a more permanent interest in the soil which his own labor has cleared of its wild growth and fitted for the plow. This he can not carry with him if he removes, and it represents to him too great an expenditure of labor to be lightly abandoned. The change which came in the habit of life of the race was not then a mere matter of choice alone, for having passed in its migration southward from the great grass belt of the world it adopts through necessity the agricultural habit and becomes attached to the soil.

Several causes may readily be inferred as lying back of their final location about the east basin of the Mediterranean. Here, about the rim of the sea, apparently for the first time in their journeying they found a suitable and ample race home, with all the agricultural and climatic requisites fully met. Here, too, for the first time the way was in a measure blocked about and before them. Upon the north were the forbidding waters and the harsh shores of the Euxine, and the inhospitable mountains and forests of eastern Mid-Europe. Southward spread the "Great Sea," and about its shores were settled the powerful and fixed Semitic and Hamitic nations of Syria, Arabia, and Egypt. In front lay the as yet untracked waters of the Aegean. Eastward the oncoming tide of Asiatic population closed in behind them over the road they presumably had just traversed. And so here this Graeco-Latin wave of the Aryan blood rested from its journeying and began to build up a new homeland.

Let us pause for a moment and take a view of this land which was to be for all these centuries the Graeco-Latin race home and the scene of so much of the world's history.

From the upland center of Asia Minor flow down westward to the sea numerous streams of purest water making fertile the broad plains of Karia, of Lydia, and of Mysia. Notable among these streams are the Meander, giving from its devious course and winding curves a word to modern tongues; and the Hermos, which from the golden sands of its tributary, the Pactolos, gives another to the words coined to our use from the land. Here was the chosen home of the Ionik Greeks. The exact lines by which the Greek folk first entered upon these lands which lay about the shores of the Aegean may always remain, if viewed solely in the light of race tradition, a matter of question.

Whether, coming first to the narrower waters on either side of the Propontis, they gradually worked their way down both shores of the Aegean, or whether they first reached the sea at the Ionik coast and then gradually crossed oversea westward from island to island until the mainland of peninsular Hellas was reached, no man can now say, for tradition is confused and uncertain; nor in the dim hintings of successive crossings and recrossings of this island-studded sea which have come down to us are the traces of their footsteps sufficiently clear.

But it is upon the Ionik coast and the near-by island of Krete that we first discover the beginnings of their civilization. Why? Probably because here lay the more favorable lands. Here life first began to grow easier to the race. Here amid the rich barley-fields and the rank grasses of the alluvial plains, and not upon the more sterile hills of peninsular Hellas, was the struggle for daily bread first made lighter by a more genial and kindly nature, thus leaving leisure from irksome toil for the development of civilization and literature and art. It was by these shores Homer sang, and around them clustered the legends upon which was based that epic which through all these centuries has kept upon it the freshness of the world's youth. Across the waters, almost in sight of the Karian shore, with Rhodes and Karpathos as the stepping-stones, lay the wooded hills of Krete with tree-crowned Ida, and the rim of rich soil which girt it about, land of Minos, and Knossos, and the hundred towns, and seat of the earliest settled state of the Greek peoples. Then the clustering islands of the Aegean, 'οι κυκλαδοι, still tempting on over the blue waters; and then, as they learned to cross over the narrow seas, the mainland of Hellas. And yet beyond, for the Latin branch of the family, which possibly crossed over the narrower waters on either side of the Propontis, and moved thence on by land never taking to the sea but skirting about the headwaters of the Adriatic for them were the sloping plains of the west flank of the Apennines, and in later years all the broad lands of the Po and of Cis-Alpine Italy, with the slopes of Etna, and the winding coasts of Sicily, the older Trinakria of the Greek colonists, just across the slender ribbon of water which later washed the walls of the island town of Messina.

Some of these lands had to be fought for, it is true. There were the Pelasgians, whoever they were, for the Greek to displace; and the older Etruscans and Iapygians for the Latin; or if these also were Aryan, as seems possible, then other yet older dwellers, akin may be to the Iberians and the Basques of Western Europe, those truer autochthones of the soil, and then later the Semite. For the seafaring man of Tyre and his children were upon the Sicilian coast with their sea cities before him, and gave valiant battle for the rich prize. But in the end the stronger Aryan blood prevailed, and the whole north shore of the Mediterranean, from Syria to the Pillars of Hercules, was in his undisputed possession; this, and the fertile islands which dotted the north waters of that Latin Mare Internum. Altho the south shore of the sea in after-years called the Latin-speaking man master, yet it was the north shore as given which remained to him and to the Greek as home. Southward oversea he passed only as conqueror. That south shore continued always a dwelling-place of the Semite.

It was a goodly heritage, this land which in the settling of the races fell to the lot of the Graeco-Latin Aryan; fair to look upon, and full of the good things of life. It was in very truth a land of wine and corn and oil. To the rude plow of this early Aryan it was a virgin soil, not yet exhausted by the drain of an old and dying civilization. And over all were the softer skies of a more genial and kindly climate than that which belonged to the older home of the inland. The summer sun, tempered by the increased moisture of the air, shone down without the fierce, dry heat of the midland plateaus. The nights were free from the rapid radiation and the sudden chill of the uplands of the world. The winter, moderated by the same agencies, was equally free from extremes of cold. In this land the mere struggle for daily existence which must have been a part of the long rough journeying, and which continued the lot of the Teuton for ages after, became less exacting. The kindly earth ceased to be only a harsh step-mother, and became indeed, as that earlier Dorian caressingly called her, Γεά Μήτηρ, "Earth Mother," and to be repaid by her children for all her poured-out stores with a love which breathes through the whole spirit of the primitive Greek life.

Of all the homes which have fallen to the lot of man this by the east basin of the Mediterranean is probably the most favorable to a rapid race development. A region of varied landscape; of mountains and hills, interspersed with fertile plains watered by ever living streams; dotted, yet not smothered, by a broken forest growth; circling the borders of a friendly and sheltered sea which tempered to comparative equability the climate of the surrounding lands; from its borders looking out and across the blue waves to clustered islands wrapped in the soft poetic haze of a semi-tropic sky, and ever tempting on and on over the placid waters; a climate neither retarding race development by its harsh chill nor sapping its strength by enervating heat. It was in its varied groupings of mountain and plain and sea a world in itself, this belt of territory which circled about the shores of the Aegean.

Here under the stimulating influence of favoring skies and a bountiful land the Greek branch of the rude Aryan took on a quicker life. The flow of a gentler blood warmed its veins. Upon the harsh yet strong soil of the older Aryan race life sprang up the luxuriant life of the Aegean. The old wanderings ceased. Men began to build cities and towns, and to develop civic life. Now, probably for the first time in ages, possibly for the first time in his history as a people, the individual begins to merge into the citizen. Settled states begin to line the shores. The islands become strongholds of power. And in addition to all, for the first time in his whole history as a race, the Aryan man becomes a sailor and takes to the sea; at first hugging the quiet shore; then creeping timidly from headland to headland, pulling his flat-bottomed boat out upon the sand when night overtakes him; ever in dread of strange monsters of the unknown deep; believing in syrens and fell spirits haunting the waterways of the sea to bring sore harm to the wandering sons of men. Hardly is he past the age of the raft, man's first float upon the sea; for it is by a well-built raft of dry logs guided by rudder and sail that Homer pictures Ulysses to have escaped from Kalypso's isle. It was a sea raft such as the Peruvian balsa which the Spanish found in use among the natives of the west coast of South America, and which was probably the first frail water craft of many races. But as the years went by we find evidence of more venturesome voyaging. He crosses oversea by the long chain of islands to other lands beyond. And learning no doubt from the Phoenicians, he at length cut loose from the shore, and, trusting to the guidance of the favoring stars, boldly explored the mysteries which lay northward through the straits of the Pontos, and westward over the broader reaches of the Great Sea; at first as pirate and robber, then as the peaceful barterer in quest of gainful trade.

And this early maritime love never afterward left him. He ever remained a man of ships and the sea. The salt spume of the waves was to him as the breath of the pines to the man of the uplands of the world. Away from it he never was content. It was to him what it became to the Norseman centuries later. The broad plain of the great deep was his empire; and the seats of his power were by its rim. From his home upon rocky islet or jutting headland he looked down upon its restless waters. In the sheltered haven below lay his ships. Θαλαττα! θαλαττα! The sea! the sea! was the glad shout of Xenophon's army as they emerged from their long wandering in the tangled maze of the Asiatic highlands and caught sight of the blue waves of the Euxine.

It was a genial, kindly civilization, this which grew up about the borders of the Aegean, so kindly, so full of the springtime joyance of early youth that the world even yet looks back with longing to it, and lingers lovingly over its memory as over the sweetness of some long-gone day in June. It was the first glad abandon of the westward-marching race; the first time in its journeying when merely to live became a joy. For life became an easier thing here by the rim of the summer sea; no longer all taken up in hard battle for a bare subsistence; with leisure from bodily toil, for mental growth; better fed; betted clothed; better housed; with time for the comforts and the elegancies, the refinements of life; leisure, and the growing of a taste, to carve the rustic doorpost into the first rough semblance of a Korinthian column; leisure to modulate the harsh earlier speech of the Alolic highlands to the simple cadence of a song, and then, as the ages went by, to the finished measures of the stately Greek chorus. The chisel of Praxiteles, the metrical but even yet rugged strength of Alschylos, the more rhythmic verse of Sophokles, were not born at once, complete. Athena might spring full-grown, in the finished beauty of the goddess, from the cleft head of Zeus, but not so comes the finish of a cultured civilization. It is of slower growth. It took centuries of slow polishing before these things could be a possibility. Long before these, and making the pathway by which the Greek mind had slowly climbed upward, were the rustic carvings of Dionysos, the unskilled songs of Hylas, of Linos, and of Eumolpos. And it is not probable that to the untrained perception of that earlier Greek man the possibilities of the after-civilization came even as a vision of things to be. To him as yet the block of marble gave no hint of the living statue within, but was only a rude mass of stone, ungainly, unpolished. Even the new world of beauty in the streams, the hills, the waters about him, possibly was only seen by untaught eyes which, seeing, as yet saw not. To him also, no doubt, as to that other untrained man ages after by the muddy banks of the Thames,

> "The primrose by the river's brim;
>   A yellow primrose was to him;
>   And it was nothing more."

Probably to him as yet the blue depths of the skies were only the blue vault, carrying no higher poetic meaning; and the song of the sea was as yet a song sung to ears that heard not; and the voice of the night wind in the pines only the soughing of the breeze. Yet they became more as the sleeping soul awoke. As the years went by the harsh, battling, Aryan blood here took on an artistic development, a poetic type, such as nowhere else in all its wide wanderings have ever come to it. Somewhat of this may be explained by the supposition that, like the sporting of a plant in vegetable life, this especial branch of the Aryan blood had born in it an artistic and poetic possibility which was less marked in the others; somewhat, by the peculiarly favorable natural surroundings which it had in this its first settled home while still in the formative stage of its separate race life. Whatever the explanation, the fact remains; and after all the years the heart of the world goes back to the land and the people as to the mystic charm of some old shrine, and keeps for them a tenderness, a love, such as it has given to no other among all the varied folk of the earth.

Here then, in this easing up of the struggle for daily bread, and in the leisure which thus came to men, began that development of mental life which in like manner and from like cause had come earlier to the Brahminic Aryan as he emerged from the rocky passes of the Hindu Kush upon the fertile plains of the upper Indus, and which later came to the Iranic kin as it spread over the well-watered highlands about the headwaters of the Tigro-Euphratean streams. With the Greek this mental development was no doubt stimulated and hastened by direct contact with the older and more advanced civilizations of the Phoenicians and the Egyptians. Another factor must have entered into the shaping of the type of mental life in this infant civilization which was to spring up about the shores of the Aegean. The grass belts of the world, which belong under the colder and cloudier skies of northern lands, are the natural grazing, and hence the game and meat, belts of the world. In them are especially found the fighting races of mankind, men who fight for fighting's sake, for the mere love of conflict. It was in this belt that the old Berserker, with blood heated by his strong animal diet, and fired by fermented drinks, battled for the sheer love of battling. It was only the grass-land folk who pictured a heaven wherein heroes spent celestial days hacking and hewing each other in a great Valhallic joy of slaughter, to renew their strength each night and fit for the next day's carnage by gorging upon boar's head and quaffing huge drafts of mead.

But to this man of the south came a gentler civilization; rude, primitive at first; still showing at times the slowly fading traces of the stern, turbulent Aryan blood of a harsher original homeland; yet a civilization growing gentler, kindlier with the years. Fed more upon the fruits and the grains of an agricultural life, a milder blood flowed in his veins. There was in his battling less of the mere joy of slaughter, more of pity and ruth. Even brutish Achilles could pause from the conflict to weep over the dead body of Patroklos, and with relenting heart could soften from the fury of his rage to heed the tears of gray-haired Priam pleading for the corse of his son.

We are beginning to learn, moreover, as before said, that the historic Greece we have known is only the Greece of a Renaissance; that back of this was another Greece, primitive, prehistoric; a Greece of shadowy kings of even more shadowy kingdoms. Yet that it was real is shown not merely by tradition and the spade of the antiquary, but inferentially and no less conclusively by the literary finish of Homer's work. The "Iliad" and the "Odyssey" are not the rude songs of a beginning, but rather the polished production of a culmination, the supreme literary flowering of an era. It is maturity, not youth, that they show. And the picture which Homer gives is not of rude beginnings. It is a picture of a people already far advanced in civilization, well ordered, skilled in the arts. And the Dardanian Greek is of the two the more advanced. His is evidently the older civilization. Troy is a city of no mean attainments in culture and grace. But his civilization, possibly grown feeble like that of Knossos, is manifestly going down before the onset of the newer and more vigorous Dorian blood. Yet the Dorian also was possessed already of no mean civilization. The home of Menelaus in Dorian Lacedaimon to which Telemachos comes in the quest after his long-lost father is such a home as might have been found in the stately old ranche life of the earlier Spanish days of Southern California. In many of the manners and ways, and in the kindly hospitality, the parallel is a striking one. The civilization of the Dardanian Greek went down not to rise again; for no barrier of intervening waters was to shield him from the oncoming power of Lydian and Persian who were successively to dominate the Asiatic shore.

The Homeric epics could not have stood alone as finished monuments in a desert of mental and literary life. The history of all literatures in other ages and among other races proves this. Supreme efforts are *supremus* efforts, and by their very rank imply others, and anterior, which are recedingly the *superior,* and then the maybe nearly forgotten *superus;* just as afterward in the decadence folio wan *inferior* and an *imus.* It is the same legitimate and conclusive argument which claims, and justly, that before the age of the polished shaft and the finished statue must have been, as antecedent and preparatory, the stage and age of the ruder column and the equally crude ikon. It is the story of the severely plain Dorik pillar before the more elaborate Ionik, and the ornate Korinthian with its capital of acanthus leaves. It is evolution. And it is no legitimate counter-argument to say that the history, the links, are largely lost. All human experience is one unbroken proof that they were there. In view of the perfection of literary finish of Homer, and of the startling revelations made by the spade of the antiquary concerning an older Greek life, it is, as before said, a question whether we should not revise our views with regard to the "Iliad" and the "Odyssey"? Whether, instead of the beginning, they do not mark the end of an era? Whether they should not rather take their place side by side with Tiryns, and Mykene, and Knossos, as lone surviving peaks of that submerged and long-forgotten continent of a prehistoric civilization of the Greek peoples? It would be an anomaly in the mental life of races for such finished literary work to appear unheralded and isolated and alone. Rather it would seem more probable that back of them lay the long line of a literature which had perished in the rude onslaught of the Dorian invasion; as much of Rome's literature, Ennius and the lost books of Livy for instance, perished when northern barbarism overthrew the older Latin civilization; or as the literary treasures of the south shore of the Mediterranean disappeared before the then uncultured hordes of Islam; or that of the Mayas before the bigotry of the Spanish priests. It is easier to reconcile this supposition with the literary finish of these two Greek epics than it is to suppose that they stood perfect and complete as lone monuments in a desert of mental life of a people yet in its infancy. Literatures, like civilizations, grow, and from crude beginnings. They are no exception to the general law of evolution which prevails elsewhere. Caedmon and Milton are two extremes of such a growth in one department of English literature.

And that older and largely prehistoric age was no mean period in the race life of the Greek peoples. It was that yet more ancient and heroic time of which Herodotos dimly saw the far-off fading-out, and of which he regretfully says, "All the Greeks were then free"; for Lydia and Kroisos even were not yet. This was the true age of Greek power. It was the age of Mykene, of Tiryns, of Kretan Knossos, of the Argonauts, of the wars of the Troad, whatever these may fully mean, and of the first spread of the Greek colonies. It was the age, too, of those old Theban myths which later gave, ready-made, to the pens of Alschylos and Sophokles the cycle of legends which centered about Oldipous and the Doom of Blood. It was the age of the legends of Herakles of Argolis, of Theseus of Attika, and of Minos of Krete. To it the Greek literature of that after-Renaissance, when the dramatists wrote, looked back for its inspiration and its material. Its hither verge was the days of Homer. Hesiod saw it only afar; for in "Works and Days" he even then looks back from an "iron age" to the years which were "golden." It might be termed the creative age of the Greek mind in literature. Whether written or oral, its legends were the fountain-head so far as we can trace. All after-Greek ages go back to mine among its literary creations, and to rebuild with the older material; just as the degenerate Greek of the Middle Ages builded his huts out of the marbles of the dismantled temples which his forefathers had reared. The wealth of this legendary store which furnished the very groundwork for the after-Greek dramatic literature shows a people already rich in mentality and strong in power. Apart from the cycle of the Persian wars time added little to it.

To the dying civilization of that older Greek land the Dorian invasion brought fresh blood and a new life, a rejuvenescence; just as to the failing Latin civilization of that older Rome came the wave of fresh Teutonic blood in the fourth and fifth centuries, making possible the Italy of the Middle Ages. Yet not at once in either case came the Renaissance. First came chaos. The older civilization may fall suddenly, with a crash; but the new has to grow. With the Greek no doubt, as with the Latin we know, ages of confusion and retrogression must have followed. It is the law of the mixing of bloods. And in the darkness which ensued even the recollection of the older civilization, and of the seats of its strongholds, became so dim that when out of the chaos Greek civilization emerged again reborn, historians, neglecting tradition, thought it was the beginning. The spade of the antiquary at Mykene, at Tiryns, at Knossos, has vindicated tradition.

Yet, old or new, it was a civilization kindly, sweet, light of heart, full of the cheer and the joy of life; and which looked up and was glad; and failed not to thank the gods which it knew for,

> The winds, and the foaming sea,
> And the wave-girt isles, and all
> That is fair and bright to man.

But upon the banks of the Tiber grew up a type of civilization which, while having apparently the same common race origin, was yet so different that one might almost hesitate to class it as of the same blood. And yet when we take that strain of Dorian blood which passing on to the south of the Peloponnesos isolated itself within the mountain walls of "Hollow Lacedaimon," and thus remained with least change, we can readily see the kin likeness. The Aiolik digamma of the more primitive Greek of the northern uplands and its cognate Latin V, together with a broadening of the vowels common to both as compared with the thinner vocalization of the Attik and the Ionik, and also a marked assimilation in case endings of that primitive Latin, which preceded the classic speech, to the forms of the older Greek of the Dorian and the Aiolian, to be noted especially in the nominative and dative both singular and plural; all these point apparently back to a time when the two races probably journeyed together as one somewhere on the north confines of Hellas before the Latin passed on around the head of the Adriatic, and then down the flanks of the Apennines to his final home by the Tiber. There is no evidence that this Latin man reached his home on the Tiber by way of the sea as Vergil would fain make believe; and the marked absence of maritime instinct in the primitive Latin man would also tend to controvert such a supposition. He seems first to have taken actively to the sea ages after under the pressure of the Punic wars and the keen rivalry for dominion with the man of Tyre in his newer home at Carthage. Even then, with all his fleets and his command of the sea, the man of Rome remained always in instincts a landsman. He had no love for the sea. It was the race instinct which lay back of the words of that Latin poet when he sang, "Sweet it is to watch the mariner toiling amid the perils of the deep, yourself lying at ease amid the grass upon the distant hills." He only voiced the true feeling of the Latin man. The sea was always to him a barrier and a dread. It checked the victorious march of his legions. And in his naval encounters he was always only a soldier on shipboard. Sailors he had none; all were marines. In this he and the Slav are alike. And naval tactics he had none. His sole idea was to lay his ship alongside the enemy, and over the grappled sides to fight as infantry with his foe. His fleet carried an army as its fighting force. Even his land tower was transferred to shipboard and became the *castellum* which survives in our *forecastle*.

Yet we have the apparent anomaly of an after-Italy developing a chain of maritime cities, notably Venice and Genoa, which possessed in a high degree the true maritime instinct and which, each in its turn, dominated the seas. It would be interesting to trace how far this may have been owing to a strain of coast blood which never really became Latin except in tongue, and which, repressed during the ages of Latin supremacy, afterward, as Rome failed, reasserted its old maritime instinct and aptness for the sea. That Magna Graecia which sprang up about the shores of the older Hesperia, and along the coasts of the Greek Trinakria, dotted the sheltered bays of these waters with its commercial cities. Crossing over westward from the island of Korkyra to the prominent headlands of the modern Calabria where it juts out into the waters of the Ionian Sea, the Greek peoples had gradually made their way about the Gulf of Tarentum; thence southward along the coast; and thence across the narrow strait to Sicily, and northward along the west shore of Italy; founding in their course a chain of maritime cities, Greek in population and Greek in their love of ships and of the sea. Notable among the earlier of these cities were Taras, Sybaris, Kroton, Rhegion, Megaris, and ancient Kyme in Campania. Naples, founded later, was simply Νεα Πολις, "New Town." How much farther they spread is more a matter of tradition. We know, however, that the Phokaians, of whom Herodotos speaks, sailed on northward in their "long slim ships" to the mouths of the Tiber and the Arnus, and within the recesses of the Gulf of Genoa, and thence westward to the outlet of the Rhone, and on beyond to the far land of Iberia; while boldly casting loose from the shores and trusting to the guidance of the favoring stars they crossed the open waters of the Tyrrhenian sea, and skirted the east borders of Sardinia and Corsica. Wherever they landed they established their fortified trading-posts which gradually grew into Greek cities, and remained for centuries after foci of Greek blood and Greek love for the sea. Nikaia, Monakos, Antipolis, Massalia, Panormos, as Nice, Monaco, Antibes, Marseilles, Palermo, bear testimony to their work. These are only a few of the points which history and tradition fairly locate. The evidence is that the whole coast line was dotted with their towns, while they also settled upon such islands as here and there lie off shore. There is no evidence that these cities, as they came in after-years under Roman dominion, ever lost their original Greek blood with its love and aptitude for the sea.

Upon the east side of the Italian peninsula we have somewhat of a similar tho less complete record. These same Phokaians who established their cities as far west as the shores of Spain also ventured well to the north in the waters of the Adriatic. Altho the record is less complete it would be unreasonable to suppose that they would turn away from the fertile shores and the sheltered waters of the upper Adriatic, where the rich valley of the Po has become in later times the corn-field of modern Italy, to brave the stormy vastness and the unknown perils of the Great Sea beyond; only, in the warring of races, when Greek and Phoenician and Roman battled for supremacy about the shores of Sicily and the South-Italian lands, the quieter annals of the Adriatic settlements would naturally receive less attention, and be the more apt to become lost in the lapse of the centuries.

Then, too, while the Phoenician yielded supremacy to the Latin in Sicily and about the shores of the west basin of the Mediterranean, we have no reason to suppose that he left the land. The Sicilians in fact are rather a mixed Greek and Phoenician people than Latin. In the light of these race facts it is easy to see how among a Latin-speaking people of after-times a sea aptitude is found surviving in what are really non-Latin bloods.

With the separation a well-marked differentiation began to grow up between the east and west branches of this common Graeco-Latin stock. It could not have come from climate, for climatically the home about the shores of the Aegean and that other by the Tyrrhenian sea upon the west slope of the Apennines were so nearly alike that practically they might be classed as the same. The differentiation which grew up must have come from other causes. Most potent of these would seem to have been the influence of surrounding races. And it is to be noted that it was apparently the Greek rather than the Latin to whom the change came, and who grew away from the older common type. This we may conclude from the many points of likeness which continued to exist between the Latin and that more archaic Greek man, the Dorian of Lakonia. The Ionian Greeks of both shores of the Aegean, and of the island world between, became by very force of surroundings cosmopolitan in character. Maritime in race habit through narrowness of race homeland, they were quickly and constantly brought into contact with the Semitic Phoenician of the Tyrian coast, with the Hamitic Egyptian of the Nile valley, and, through the widely scattered Greek colonies, with the barbarous races of the

Euxine and of the regions of the west basin of the Mediterranean. The very necessities of this diversified and wide-spread intercourse as traders and colonizers among so many and so unlike peoples would inevitably soon tell upon the Greek speech and the Greek character. The sentence became clear and pliant and direct; for the Greek must make himself intelligible as readily and as widely as possible to the varied peoples among whom he so largely gained his support in traffic. In reading Xenophon and Herodotos I have been constantly reminded of the simple sentences and the limpid style of Defoe.

The words also did not escape change. The eight cases of declension which the Brahminic Sanskrit retained, presumably from the framework of an elaborate common Proto-Aryan mother speech, dropped down to five with the Greek. He still kept, however, but probably for home use, and little used even there, the dual number throughout, and the middle voice. The optative mood, and the augment and reduplication, he also retained. The broader vowels and the harsher consonants, wherever possible, were softened. The archaic digamma he had left behind somewhere out upon the AIolik highlands; only, its echo is still to be faintly discerned in the scanning of Homer. The Latin retains it, but softened to V. The Greek βοϝυς-βοϝος was the Latin *bovis-bovis; the* nominatives contracted respectively by elimination to βους and *bos* to avoid confusion with the genitive. It all means an instinctive attempt to make speech easy. The tendency is especially marked in the thinning of the vowels and the changing of the harsher aspirates as heard in the musical Ionik of Herodotos him of that Halikarnassos which lay over upon the enervating Asiatic shore. It is such a change as has come to the Spanish tongue among the ease-loving natives of sub-tropic America, one of the branches of that "soft, bastard Latin" of Byron, still further softened and smoothed of its old Proto-Aryan asperities under yet milder skies. A typical illustration of the working of a broad climato-linguistic law is here to be found in the change which has come to the stately and sonorous Castilian *caballo* which softens the more difficult labial B to the dental V and drops the L sound entirely from the LL, retaining only the Y sound, while the second A melts into the more musical diphthong, giving as a result the softer and more flowing *cavaiya,* with its lighter tax upon the vocal organs.

But while the Greek was thus, through the molding influence of his surroundings and manner of life, becoming cosmopolitan in type, the Latin was on the contrary becoming more and more provincial; and he, too, because of surroundings and manner of life. Before him spread the sea, which he did not like. About him, instead of the ripened and polished civilization of the east, was that vast wilderness of western barbarism which afterward swamped Rome. And then his own land, at least for many ages, was large enough and productive enough to supply his race wants. And so, long after the Greek had become a cosmopolite, a man having lot and share in the broader race life about him, the Latin lived on in the narrow provincial ways of his forebears and changed but little.

Yet he too did change. There was a substratum of hard, sturdy common sense in that older Latin man which would not let him forever go on doing simply as the fathers had done. An evolution was coming to him also. With an even more than Dorik scorn for the superfluous he discarded from his speech the middle voice and the dual and the optative, heirlooms from the primitive Proto-Aryan tongue, while with these went the augment, and with a few exceptions, as *pependi, cucurri,* and some others, the reduplication also. Yet, with his characteristic desire for accuracy, he retained the more definite ablative, which the Greek lost. Both, however, retain traces of an ancient Proto-Aryan locative, which even in the Sanskrit was already beginning to drift from its moorings. In the face of the lack of a perfect active participle, however, he proved to be linguistically as helpless as has the English-speaking man in the lack of a common pronoun of the third person singular. His sentence, with the Latin stubbornness, retained its rigid framework. Nothing of the Greek flexibility ever came to it. Like his later military roads, with a supreme disregard of the inequalities of the way, it went on its inflexible course, up hill and down, to the desired end. His speech was lacking also in the nicer shadings and the elusive subtilities of the Greek; but then the Latin mind was not subtile, nor overly critical.

Unlike the Greek, the primitive harsh consonants of the Latin seem to have long remained with little change, until at length the softening influence of Greek culture (for Greece became schoolmaster to Rome) began to exercise a modifying and mollifying power over Latin speech. *Arx* (ks for kes) would seem to have led in sound to a genitive *arkis,* as *calx* (ks) to *calkis,* or *dux* (ks) to *dukis.* But that a change came to the hard sound of C (originally K) before certain vowels is shown by the interchangeableness of C and the Greek Sigma in the crude phonetic spelling of the early Christians as found in the inscriptions upon the walls of the catacombs. It is a softening such as came to the hard consonants and the broad vowels of the harsher old AIolik Greek, or to the uncouth sounds of the early English.

One lesson of it all, and a lesson ever to be borne in mind in linguistic research, is that we never reach the beginning in human speech. Back of the old is always a still older. Back of the Latin of Caesar, of Cicero, back even of that older Latin of Ennius or the archaic song of the Fratres Arvales, lies a still older Latin, as back of the Greek of Homer even lies a still older Greek, and as back of the Vedic hymns a yet more ancient Aryan speech; for all historic human speech is only a superstructure built upon the but half-leveled walls of some older prehistoric speech; just as Schliemann found still more ancient Iliums as the spade went deeper. Only, no linguistic spade has ever yet struck bed-rock in the speech of men.

Yet in it all that older Latin had an ear for the sonorous resonance of speech; a truer ear than his linguistic descendants. The soft Italian and the nimble French have lost this. The statelier Castilian retains a measure of it. The Roman church was wise in retaining the Latin for its ritualistic service.

Probably no other tongue could lend itself so effectively to the intoning of the lector or to the stately measures of the Gregorian chant as it echoes through the vaulted naves of dim cathedrals.

In mental type the Latin remained Dorian - that unchanged Dorian of the lower Peloponnesos. Both were of the slower, stolider type; utterly unlike the sharp-witted, volatile, laughter-loving Ionian. For the Ionian was true ancestor of the Athenian of Paul. The wit of the Ionik mind was ever like the keen thrust of a rapier, while that of the Latin never lost somewhat of the ponderous sweep of the broadsword. And the Latin never cut loose from the leading-strings of Greek literary thought. Without the "Iliad" and the "Odyssey" there would have been no "Aeneid." In fact, this dominance of Greek thought did not stop with Rome. It passed on to hold the whole West in the mental thraldom of Aristotle for a thousand years after.

The Latin man as contrasted with the Ionian Greek was singularly destitute of the poetic and artistic faculties. His whole mental strength went apparently to war and dominion, and the law-making which followed as a necessary sequence. Yet herein he showed the Dorian likeness again. He was the soldier and the law-maker of the world as has been no other man in all history. The modern army and the modern legal code go back to the Roman legion and to the Pandects of Justinian, and to that older Jus Vetus of the Res-publica, as their foundation. And he was both stern and just. When to the Jews, clamoring for the life of Paul, an untried prisoner, Festus gave answer, "It is not the manner of the Romans to deliver any man to die before that he which is accused have the accusers face to face, and have license to answer for himself concerning the crime laid against him," he only voiced the animating spirit of the whole system of Latin jurisprudence. But it was even more than this. It was West vs. East - Europe vs. Asia. It was in a more general sense Aryan vs. non-Aryan. The Roman was first to speak for the newer Aryan civilization. The emblems of Roman civilization, forerunner of the greater Aryan civilization to be, were prophetically the scales and the sword. Yet with all this stern justice, possibly because of the sternness, it was a civilization singularly lacking in the joyousness, the abandon, the childlike oneness with nature, which marked that of the Aegean. It ran in narrower and intenser lines. Its analog with the Greek lay in the valley of the Eurotas. The Roman never had a youth. The wolf-fostering of the myth ran too fiercely in his veins. His was a civilization of war, of bloodshed, of iron, ruthless and merciless. Most like him of all his children in this was the Spaniard of the fifteenth and sixteenth centuries, the Spaniard of Mexico, of Peru, of the Netherlands. Only four times in the long centuries from Numa to the Caesars were the brazen doors of the temple of Janus closed in token of universal peace. The world does not turn back lovingly across the centuries to Rome; rather with a vague wonder; for the tramp of her legions has scarcely yet died out from the troubled earth.

Yet what Latin civilization missed in sweetness it made up in strength. And the Latin stamped himself upon the world's history no less indelibly than did the Greek; only in a different way. It was, too, a civilization longer-lived in itself than that of the Greek. Possibly the strain of blood was more persistent in type; possibly the sterner battling of its early youth had strengthened and hardened it; possibly both. But the years brought no hectic, no flush of premature decay to its cheeks. It took the centuries, and old age, and the Goth; and even then the end was not. It was rather a merging into the modern life of the world. The Latin folk never became, in the same sense as the Greek, dead to the onward march of the races. It lives through its children as the Greek has not; for the Greek left no children. His widespread colonies went down before the onset of stronger peoples, losing autonomy and language. We only trace their after-life, as in the coast cities of the West Mediterranean, by the persistence of certain race characteristics. Possibly this utter dying-out of the whole genius of the Greek life may in part have arisen from the fact that the Greek, from his home upon both shores of the Aegean, always remained half-way Oriental in spirit and affiliations, and thus came in after-years to share in the torpor which settled down over the whole East after that final quick flaming-up of Mohammedanism when the Semitic Arab had his one gorgeous but evanescent race flowering; a torpor which has never lifted, but which has grown deeper as the ages have gone by until it would seem to have passed into the coma and the stertor of death.

Yet altho the Latin was himself seemingly destitute of the poetic and artistic sense, an apparent anomaly is again to be seen, as in the case of the maritime instinct, in the fact that a portion at least of the races commonly classed as of Latin origin possess these faculties in a well-marked degree. Italy, the home of painting, of sculpture, and of song, was the very center of the old Latin home life with its marked lack in these capacities.

But in explanation of this anomaly may be said that the Italian of the later years was far from pure Latin in blood. The repeated waves of Teutonic blood which swept into and remained among the Latins of the old Roman empire, have made of the modern Italians a mixed race. How much of the after-development of the poetic and artistic faculties may have been the result of this admixture, how much the awakening of a previously dormant capacity in the Latin blood itself, is a question which will probably always remain without answer. The race admixture is now too complete to allow of segregation. Then, too, it is to be remembered that the valley of the Po, which practically is North Italy, was Celtic, Cis-Alpine Gaul as the Latins themselves called it; while Southern Italy was the Magna Graecia of a people instinct with the poetic and artistic temperament. Somewhat of the same line of thought will apply also to the Spanish race, and to such development of the artistic sense as has come to it. Even yet the fair-haired, blue-eyed folk of the northlands may be found amid the darker-complexioned people of the uplands of Spain. The Visigoth is there. And Andalusia is only Vandalusia. The Frenchman, the man of Gaul, can hardly be spoken of as Latin. While using a modified and corrupted form of Latin speech, he is in blood essentially Celt and Teuton. In the south of France the old Greek towns already mentioned, and an overflow of Latin blood from Italy, give the mixed Romance population of Provence; while northward the Belgae, the Aquitani, and the Celtae, of Caesar, with the after-mixture of Gothic and Norse bloods, gave as product a population which has never been Latin save in religion and name. The "Omnis Gallia" of Caesar was no more Latin than was Ireland, that other Celtoland. Nor is it much more Latin to-day. The Breton is only the Briton a vowel changed; the man, the same. And Brittany is only a Briton land. And the Norman is still the Norseman; while the center of France is Frank; and the whole south Biscayan shore line has the blood of the Basque, whoever he may be, but one thing is sure, not Latin. It is only, as just said, in the south upon the Mediterranean littoral, that the Latin, and before him the Greek, have taken root and abide. Even the [name shows the prevailing non-Latin blood, for France is simply Frank-land, and a second Frank-land, as the Britain of Caesar became afterward the second Engle-land. In reality all southwestern Europe is much less Latin in blood than its speech would seem to indicate; for the Latin gave his name and his tongue to far more than the Latin blood.

The fact then that the Latin, a race so singularly deficient in the artistic and poetic temperament, should have left a progeny of races in whom this temperament is markedly developed, finds its probable explanation in that other fact that these races are only in part, and really only in small part, of Latin blood.

Ethnologically the question may fairly be asked, Is there in the world to-day a Latin blood in the sense in which there maybe said to be a Teutonic blood? There was a time concerning which such a question would seem strange. Back of the old Roman empire, in the days of the early kings, when the Latins lived in Latium, and even in the earlier days of the republic when the *Ager Romanus* was still an *Ager Latinus,* and the Celt still ruled in the valley of the Po, there was a true Latin blood; and it was, so far as we can judge by history, a masterful, not a fecund blood. But judging from its after-history it was not a blood which kept itself free from admixture with other, and often inferior, races; in this respect differing markedly from the Teutonic peoples. That old Latin blood would seem to have become swamped in a flood of alien bloods; within the Latin land itself in the mongrel hordes which were gathered under the corrupting largesses of food, or were brought in unwillingly as slaves, and in the alien legions of the Roman empire; in Spain swamped in the preponderating mass of Iberian blood of the native population; in Gaul swallowed up as a rivulet by a river in the great fecund stream of Celtic blood; for the Latin intermingled with the native bloods of these subjugated lands as did his mixed descendants ages afterward in Canada and tropical America. It is everywhere to be remembered that Latin speech does not prove Latin blood. Philology is of all ethnological clues the most uncertain and misleading. Of the three great divisions of the Aryan peoples in Europe the so-called Latin of to-day probably represents the most broadly mixed blood - Latin, Greek, the primitive Italic stocks, Phoenician, Iberian, Celt, Moor, German, Goth, Frank, Northman, and with him, but not of him, the Basque, that haunting shade of some long-forgotten and buried past.

In the types of civil development which came to the Greek and the Latin, altho they were so nearly akin in blood and climatic surroundings, there is a difference so marked as to call for careful consideration. The Latin developed as the key-note of his whole civil fabric the idea of centralization. Whether it were under the primitive chieftainship of a mythical Romulus, under the earlier kingships, with the so-called republic, or under aristocracy, oligarchy, triumvirate, or imperator, there could be only one Imperium; and the animating life, the political soul of that, must be upon the Seven Hills by the Tiber. Wherever might be found Roman men or Roman arms, there was only one true Roman city, and that city was the Imperium. France, in its political history, presents a curious and striking parallel. This, the least Latin of all the daughters of Rome, is yet in this respect the most Roman of all in type. Paris has been France as has no other capital in Europe been to its land. Whether under King, or Directory, or Committee of Safety, or First Consul, or Empire, or Commune, or Republic; whether under Bourbon, or Sans-Culotte, or Bonaparte, or Orleans, it is all the while Paris that rules France. The true idea of a democracy, a rule which originates with the people of a land, seems to be foreign to the whole spirit of Latin civilization. It is always the rule of one, whether king or city, over the many; the provinces always looking to the center for the initiative in all civil matters. The town meeting of New England, the village moot of the older Teuton, seems never to have existed among the Latin folk. Even republican France might be fairly described as a kingdom with a president; just as Britain might with equal truthfulness be termed a democracy with a king. In this characteristic of the centralization of power, at least, the Latin was akin to the Phoenician, for he too was a man of one city. As Rome was to the Latin, so Carthage was to the Phoenician, or that city of the older Phoenicia Tyre, upon her rock in the sea. Maybe all three had it from the Asiatic Semite, for he ever was a man of centralized power and of one city.

Yet there are hintings of a Rome - Latium rather - of the primitive days in those "antiquissimis temporibus" of the older Latin man, when the *urbs* was only the central village of the *ager,* and life was at the most only semi-urban in type. It was a land and a life of stern, simple virtues, of chaste homes, and of reverence for the gods they knew, gods of forest and field and stream, more as the Norse gods of the fjord and the woodlands. Cybele and the imported Asiatic abominations came later with the city life and the mixed bloods and the degenerate days; and with these it was no longer the respublica, but in its stead the imperium, and the arena, and the largesses; and then the Goth at the gates, and the end. But the picture which we have of that older man of Latium, before that the evil days were upon him, is a picture such as Homer gives of the earlier pre-city life of the Greek peoples in the days when Telemachos drives in his chariot across the Lakonian plains seeking for a father; or it is such a picture as we have from our own forebears of the homely, clean-hearted pioneer days of the American frontier of a century ago when American life also was as yet preurban. But *polis* and *urbs* came to the Graeco-Latin, and the simple life of the *ager* became a thing of an older past; and the man changed with the times.

Yet historically Rome, urban Rome, was, and still is, the one great, central fact of the Latin world. The Greek also had become essentially a city man; but the Greek race was a race of many cities. The Teuton, the Slav, were never city men at all. They were men of the wood, the field, the sea. The whole after-life of the Latin blood, however, centers about that one city upon the Tiber. To the older Latin Rome became the imperium about which the race life revolved; to the modern Latin it is the Imperium in imperio. It is an anchor cast into the stream of the past which holds the race fast against the current of modern life. The world can never forget, the world ought never to forget, what Rome has been to it; yet the child that remains cast in the mold of the ancestor must fail to keep pace with the march of the years. Rome has been to the Latin what sometimes a strong-minded, strong-willed father becomes to a child; the yoke is never entirely thrown off; the stamp of the parent makes thrall of the child. The stamp which the Rome of that older Latin has so indelibly fixed upon the Latin political world is centralization - the man made for the state; not the state made for the man. So deeply was the stamp impressed that it has taken the instinct of the initiative out of the individual. It has destroyed the value of the unit. Paris is to the Frenchman only a local Rome. Madrid is a local Rome to the Spaniard. From these central points the moving impulse must go out to the body politic - if there can be said to be a body politic in the without. It is because London is not Rome to Britain, Washington not Rome to America, that the English-speaking man bids fair to become the world's master; for the conditions of race supremacy have become materially changed under the stress and complexity of modern race life. It is the individuality of the unit that now counts, the initiative which begins away from the center at innumerable separate points. Modern civilization has become too vast, too widely ramified, too intricate, for the successful guidance and control of one center. It is because the English-speaking man has, of all men, most clearly realized this fact, and has based his civilization upon it, that he is so rapidly distancing all others in the struggle for race supremacy. Centralization belongs to an earlier and a lower type of civilization. The successful army can no longer be an aggregate of human machines. It must instead be an aggregate of individual thinkers. The Boer war retaught this lesson. And the army industrial now works under the same law. It is to be noted, however, that centralization and organization are not one and the same; are not necessarily even allied. Organization without centralization is one of the secrets of the English-speaking man's success. Centralization without organization is one of the secrets of the Latin man's decadence. It, with the lack of the individual initiative, is the secret of the Slav's slow progress toward a higher type of civilization.

The imperium came to the Latin race life; it never came to the Greek, altho of kindred blood. These divergences in race evolution do not come by chance. There is always a good and adequate reason. In this case such a reason may be found in the law of grades and facilities for intercommunication. The enduring empires of the world have had at least the nucleus of their power in the great plains which are to be found upon the earth. Egypt, Babylonia, Assyria, India, and later Persia, Rome, China, and in more recent times Russia, Germany, France, and America, are instances of the working of the law. It was so that the man of Mid-Latium, the Priscus Latinus, the *lowlander* of the *campus latus,* but whom we first know in his straggling villages at Alba Longa, the "Long White Town" it was so that he prevailed over his fellows, and stamped his impress of speech and tribal type upon the kindred Sabines, Volscians, Aequians, and Hernicans about him. Plain and river were the secrets of his supremacy. And the after-Rome was always and everywhere the power of the great plains. With Britain the great plain of the sea takes the place of the earth plains of the continents in the working out of the same law. Back of the fact, as its explanation and reason, lies, as just stated, the law of easy grades with the consequent possibility of ready intercommunication and of unimpeded moving of armies. Such empire may have outlying possessions in the ruggeder regions of the world, partly isolated and cut off from the main body, but they will be the last gained, will remain always in a measure alien to the center, and they are the first to drop away when any weakness begins to show itself in the central life. The saying is no less true because trite that "Mountains interposed make enemies of bloods which else like kindred drops had mingled into one." And it is in accordance with this truth that the broken mountain lands of the world give rise to small, divided nationalities, each maintaining its independence of the others, each living its own national life, each developing and perpetuating its own separate and distinct national character. If, through force of genius of an occasional ruler or conqueror, the law should at times be apparently set aside, and a broader imperium of mountain lands arise, it is only temporary; the ill-assorted kingdom is apt to perish with the death of its founder, or within a comparatively short time thereafter. It is especially the mountain lands of the world which are torn and distracted by clans and local feuds, whether it be the Epiros, the Highlands of Scotland, or the mountains of Kentucky. It is the baleful fruitage of isolation and alienation.

With the improved means of communication and transportation which have come of steam and tunnels, broader mountain empire is possible than in the ages past, and the force of repulsion is to a certain extent counteracted; yet still the general law holds good, that broad and permanent empire will have its seat in the great plains of the world, or by the sea.

The physical geography of the Greek lands affords the key to the Greek political life. Hellas, the central land of the race power, the one land to which all the widely scattered Greek folk looked, and by common consent called it Home, altho a peninsula, is like two islands rising out of the sea and joined together by a narrow isthmus. The upland region of Arcadia makes a mountain center to the Peloponnesos, while the mainland of Greece, the older Hellas, has as a similar center the broken mountain cluster of the Pindos, the Olta, and Parnassos, with Doris shut in from the sea. From these as centers numerous small yet fairly fertile valleys face out to the sea, each shut off from the others by the mountain center behind, and upon either side by the mountain spurs which, running out to the shore line like the radiating arms of the starfish, wall in each valley from its fellows. Thus shut off from each other, each Greek valley became a community by itself, developing its own separate form of government, having its own ruler, and living its own distinct civic life Attika, Argolis, Elis, Messenia, Hollow Lacedaimon, Altolia, Boiotia, and others about the two shores. Arkadia and Doris were equally isolated as inland communities occupying mountain valleys. Then came the Greek islands, scattered throughout the and along the coast of Asia Minor, and the Greek cities, dotting at long intervals the coasts of the Propontis and of the Euxine, and westward about the shores of the Italian Hesperia and of the Greek Trinakria, and the borders of the Mediterranean still farther on westward as far as the Iberian peninsula, constituting Ἡ Μεγαλη Ἑλλας of Strabo, the Magna Graecia of later writers, in contradistinction to Ἡ Αρχαῖα Ἑλλάς, the Older Greece, of Plutarch.

How were these widely scattered peoples of Greek blood to remain in any kind of manner one? In a certain sense they did not, for with the development of the separate Greek cities, which indeed seemed to be a necessity of the race surroundings, a common civic life, as already said, they utterly failed to evolve. Each became a law unto itself. Yet the kinship remained. The Greek man was a Greek man, recognized as a brother wherever he might go among the Greek peoples; easily and quickly transferring his citizenship from one to the other upon removal, as the American does his State citizenship and his local right of suffrage, upon removal from one State to another. Indeed, the analogy of American citizenship is quite striking. In the comity of the broader life of the whole Greek folk the man of Greek blood stood very much as the American does in the broader citizenship of the whole American people; only, the Greek folk stopped short where the American went on, and so failed of a legal union of the separate cities which otherwise corresponded somewhat to the American State life. Had they passed on to this, the analogy would have been nearly perfect. In all else, in readiness of citizenship transfer, in comity of race, in the quick companionship, the *camaraderie* of blood, he was simply a citizen in the general body of the whole Greek folk. When Herodotos writes his famous history, altho he is of Halikarnassos oversea in the Karian land, and altho he writes in the dialect of an Ionian of the Asiatic shore, yet it is not as a Karian that he writes, but as a Greek; and it is not of Halikarnassos, nor of Karia, nor of the Ionian, but of the Greater Hellas, and of the wars of the common Greek folk as against the outlanders, οἱ βαρβαροι as he terms them. And it is at the Pan-Hellenic gathering in Elis, where was the race shrine, that he recites the history as a common Greek epic to the assembled Hellenic folk of all Greek lands. Tho often at war among themselves, tho battling for dominion the one with the other, yet such war was always recognized as a war betwen kin, very different from war with the barbarians of the non-Greek lands. And when need arose, sinking for the time all local differences they battled as a people of one kin for all Hellas as a common fatherland, and to save the folk life from being swallowed up in the tide of barbarian invasion from Asia. Plataian, and Theban, and Athenian, and Spartan remembered only that they were Greek when the Persian crossed the Hellespont.

What influences were thus potent to keep up the kin tie in a people divided politically, and with all the dissensions which, as we well know, so often rent and tore them in internecine feuds? Among the ties of union may be cited:

1. - A common race history.

With all the divisions into tribes and separate communities they still possessed the tradition of a common origin and of a continuous kinship. It showed itself in the ready and intimate comradeship which, as before said, existed between Greek and Greek wherever they might be, and which was unlike their relationship to all others.

2. - A common language.

With all its dialects, Ionik, Dorik, primitive Alolik, and the other slighter variations, the tongue was yet so manifestly one that its unity could never be called into question. The Ionian might thin his vowels and soften the diphthongs while he avoided the harsher concurrence of consonants. The Boiotian might broaden and roughen his vowels into the full chest tones. The older and ruder Alolik might cling to its harsh aspirates. Yet back of them all were the home words, and, even in the harshest of the dialects, a liquid flow such as neighboring tongues did not have, and which was so characteristically Greek.

3. - A common religion.

Altho upon the Akropolis Athena Promachos with bronze crest and spear, towering above the city and seen of the mariner from afar, might be the guardian spirit of Attika, and as such receive local honors; and tho upon the shores of Krete might be the especial shrine of the Syrian Aphrodite; while Poseidon was to the seagoing Ionians the god most nearly interwoven -with their trading and colonizing ship life; yet all were to the folk mind only parts of a common theogony. And above all, reigning upon Olympos was Ζευς Πατηρ, the one supreme god of all the Greek kin, whom all alike worshiped. When Sophokles makes the chorus in Elektra say,

Ἔτι μέγας οὐρανῷ
Ζευς, ὃς εφορᾷ πάντα και κρατυνει,

it is Zeus, the mighty All-Father of all Greeks, who from his high seat in the heavens "looks down upon and overrules all things," of whom they speak; and it is the whole Greek kin for whom they speak.

4. - A common love of art.

The sense of the beautiful found expression in the Greek race not in music, nor in painting, but in outline. The chisel of the sculptor was to the Greek what the brush and palette were to the medieval Italian, or the director's baton to the music-loving German. Wherever the Greek man wandered he carried this love of sculpture with him; in some of the kin, notably in the Attik, developed and trained more highly than in the others, yet found in all. Wherever a Greek city arose was the temple with its statue of the guardian deity, and its carved marbles, while about were grouped the various works of art which the earth now gives up to the spade of the antiquary. And wherever the Greek man entered a Greek city these things, and the possession of the common race love of the beautiful, made him at home.

5. - A common type of architecture.

As the traveler passes up the Nile from the delta to the cataracts he sees everywhere the hand-marks of a single race in the architectural remains which line its banks. There is one common feature running through them all - massiveness. As he journeys on from the pyramids to Denderah, Karnak, Philae, and looks upon the slowly crumbling relics of men long dead, he unhesitatingly says, One race built them. So throughout the Greek world certain features are common to the architectural remains of the race. It is not massiveness. A juster sense of the fitness of things possessed this man of the Aegean. Why should he rear a pyramid? The smallest of the Kithairon hills would be greater. He had his mountains. It is the dweller upon the flat plains of the earth and in the great river valleys who strives to build above the monotonous levels. Nor was it in ponderous columns. The buttresses of the hills were stronger. In these things, however, he might exert himself, nature would still dwarf and make puny by comparison his mightiest efforts. It was in symmetry and grace that he found vent for the architectural sense within him. The Greek temples were not even large; often, indeed, almost diminutive in size. Their charm lay in the exquisite beauty] of proportion. The Akropolis with its various temples was only a contracted hill-top of a few square rods. The skilful handling of the column was especially characteristic of Greek work. Other races had it, the Egyptian, the Hindu; but with them it was simply massive. It impressed by its sheer bulk, with no especial grace or beauty of outline. In the hands of the Greek, however, it became a thing of beauty. Whether crowned with the simple capital of Doris, the spiral volutes of Ionia, or the acanthus leaves of Korinth, it was still the Greek column, and as such kept its distinctive place throughout all the centuries; and as such, together with other race characteristics in architecture, appealed to the Greek eye wherever a Greek city might be found.

6. - The common shrines - and the Pan-Hellenic councils and folk festivals.

Twice each year at the Amphictyonic council, in the springtime held at the Delphic temple of Apollo, and in the autumn at the temple of Demeter by Thermopylai, a gathering of tribes of the Hellenic homeland was called.

Each tribe was entitled to two delegates. Twelve tribes took active part upon a footing of equality, whatever their respective strength might be. A vow was taken not to destroy any town of the league, or to cut it off from running water either in peace or war, and binding not to plunder or destroy the property of the gods; and common cause was to be made against any who should do so. It was of the nature of a semi-sacred federation. At these councils, in addition to the race observance of the sacred rites of the common shrine, deliberation was held over matters pertaining to the common race welfare. Then each year came one of the great folk festivals, either the Olympic, the Isthmian, the Pythian, or the Nemean, when all the Greek world assembled to take part in the friendly contests. Every man of Hellenic blood, whether from Athens or Korinth or Sparta, or from the most distant Greek city upon the shores of the Euxine, or the far western seas, was entitled to enter the list, and stood the equal of all others. That he was Greek was the only requisite; and whether noble or humble, rich or poor, from one of the great cities of the race homeland or from the rudest and most distant outpost of the Greek kin, he had equal right and chance to compete for the victor's wreath in the contests where athlete and poet and historian and sculptor met, with the assembled Greek folk as judge. And the victors were honored alike of all Greek men, and their fame became a common heritage of all the race kin. During the month of these festivals all wars between Greeks were suspended, and peace reigned supreme.

7. - The sea.

While the mountains of the Greek homeland divided country and people into many small states independent of each other, the sea as the common highway of all Greek men served as a tie between them. This as the common highway of all Greeks knit and bound them together. It was an inseparable part of the common Greek life. To some, as the Phokaians, the shore became little more than a place for repairing their ships. Their life was upon the sea. Upon it they met in their long voyaging; and through it they made the acquaintance of the widely scattered kin of the Greek folk.

Bound together by all these ties, while there were Greek cities many, and Greek states many, there was always, and everywhere, only one Greek man.

Yet the Greek, with all his apparent freedom, and his great number of separate and distinct centers of political activity, each fixing its type of civic life for itself, failed as signally as the Roman to develop the true idea of a democracy, whether in the mother lands of that archaic Hellas or in the Greater Hellas which grew up overseas upon the coasts of Italy and Sicily, and about the west shores of the Mediterranean. The first traditions of the race are of a monarchy; the Basileus, or king, ruling by divine commission from the gods, generally himself by fable a descendant of the gods, and boastful none the less of the lineage even tho the baton sinister stretched with its betraying stain athwart the escutcheon. In this respect he was not unlike many noble families of Europe to-day. Yet whatever the lineage, it was the rule of one over the many, and so accepted,

> "The rule of many is not well; let one be ruler,
> One king; to whom the son of cunning Chronos gave
> Authority and scepter, that he might bear rule
> For other men."

Thus says Ulysses as he admonishes the brawling Thersites to cease from his fault-finding. Nor does he hesitate to lay the royal scepter athwart the back of the offender with sturdy blows as a punishment for meddling in matters which belong to his betters. Later came the oligarchies; and then the after-development into the so-called democracies. Yet, as with the Roman, the true democratic idea, the idea of "a government of the people, for the people, and by the people," this idea, without which there can be no true democracy, was utterly lacking. The people only changed masters. Thucydides is authority for the statement that in the age of Perikles, the golden age of Athens, when the so-called era of popular government was at its best, the government was virtually the rule of one man. The Ionik Greeks of the Asiatic coast never took on the democratic development. They seem always to have been overawed and controlled by the preponderating weight of the Asiatic monarchical idea. And even when Attika, which stood at the head of the democratic idea as Sparta did of the oligarchic, even when it approximated most nearly to the true democratic ideal, the tyranny of the basileus or of the oligarchy was only exchanged for the still more pitiless tyranny of the majority. The idea of a democracy in which the minority had rights that were entitled to respect, seems never to have entered the Athenian mind. And this is the fatally weak point in the Latin democracies of to-day. Aristides ostracized, Marius in exile, the proscriptions and murders of the Five Hundred and of their successors, the Thirty of Athens, the banishments and the massacres of the consulates, the dictatorships, the Triumvirate, only anticipated the days of '93 and the guillotine, and the long history of political murders, banishments, and expatriation, which mars the records of the Latin-American republics. In fact Latin republics are largely such only in name, when gaged by the Teutonic standard. It is still the imperium, and an imperium which will bear with no dissent. And it is still the central power from which all initiative must take rise. Mere labels are often misleading. The Latin republic thus far has proven to be only a kingdom under another name. The spirit of the basileus is still there, and regnant. And the *ostrakon* in one way or another still does its repressive work.

Yet it is no small debt that the world owes to the Graeco-Latin kin. To them, the first of all the western Aryans to develop a fixed civilization, it fell to bridge over the chasm between old and new. It was the Graeco-Latin who made possible the world of to-day. The Greek rolled back the tide of Asiatic invasion which threatened to overwhelm the infant civilization of the West in the fifth century B.C., and saved the mental life of the Europe which was to be from the fatal lethargy which was even then already beginning to settle down upon the intellectual and spiritual life of the Farther East. The Brahmin and the Medo-Persian succumbed to it, and sleep the sleep of intellectual and spiritual death. The Greek saved the infant West from this. Homer and Herodotos, and the dramatists, and Plato, and Aristotle, are the rich bequest of the alert, restless Greek mind to the mental life of the world.

The Latin saved the civic life of Europe from the no less deadly influence of the Phoenician Semite of Carthage, and gave law and order as the germs of western civilization; for Semitic Carthage was not law but power, despotic, irresponsible power. The Metaurus marked the beginning of the ebb of that older Semitic advance into peninsular Europe. The head of Hasdrubal tossed into Hannibal's camp was the token of the turning of the tide, and Semitic Hannibal so knew it, and began to prepare for the end. And upon the Roman military system is based the armed strength of Europe which rolled back the later barbaric waves of invasion on the plains of Chalons, and before the walls of Vienna; while upon the Pandects of Justinian, and their forerunner the Jus Vetus of the primitive Latin, is based the framework of modern jurisprudence with its safeguards of property and life. As Greece stood for mental freedom, so Rome stood for law and order law and order as opposed to Asiatic absolutism and Celtic anarchy. When Paul could say "Civis Romanus sum," the howling mob and the subservient captain alike had before them a bar they dared not cross; and when that day he stood before Festus and protestingly exclaimed, "I appeal unto Caesar," even the hand of the Governor of Judea drew back afraid, for "It was not the manner of the Romans to deliver any man to die before that he which is accused have the accusers face to face, and have license to answer for himself concerning the crimes laid against him."

Out of the womb of Roman civilization the nations of the West were born. Need it be wondered at that in the pangs of childbirth she was torn by their struggles, for it was manchild laying hold upon manchild. It was a Roman poet who wrote "Ilium fuit." Had he been a seer as well, there might have been a thirteenth and sadder book to the "Aeneid."

Upon the foundations of dying Rome a new Rome appeared. As the Rome of the Caesars failed, the Rome of the papacy began to grow up within and to supplant it. And it, too, became an imperium; and no other spiritual imperium ever had better opportunity than this, an imperium in imperio, to gain and keep universal dominion. When Christianity became the religion of the old Roman empire the Rome of the Caesars was yet strong, only beginning to die; and the Christianity of the fourth century was one. It went out from the ecumenical council at Nikaea with a united front, and the enthusiasm of youth yet upon it; and with its three great centers of power at Constantinople, at Alexandria, and at Rome. But when under the usurpation of power by the Western church it took the first step away from a true catholicity, it lost the Eastern church, and the Greek, and the Slav. Then when it ceased to be Western in spirit, and became Latin, it lost the Teutonic races, and still further narrowed the field of catholicity. And when, again, it ceased to be Latin even, and became Italian, it began to lose its hold upon Celto-Latin France. That close corporation, the Italian cardinalate, with its logical and intended corollary, the Italian papacy, is to-day the bane of the Roman church. It arouses at once race and national jealousies, and brings into a question which should be one purely of spiritual matters, issues of politics and of state. The Italianizing of the papacy, and the never-ceasing efforts after political influence in other lands, are a heavy handicap in the contest with more enlightened religions, and, if persisted in, will in the end prove fatal to all possibility of a broader catholicity, and make of the papacy only a local Italian church. There may still be, as there have been in the past, times when the present policies may meet with a temporary success; but it will only be temporary. The forces which have brought defeat in the past are the same to-day, and will continue the same in the future, for they are based upon natural law, and they will inevitably work out the same results. The Roman church will have to abandon the preponderating Italian cardinalate and cease to be national, but instead become truly Catholic as in the earlier ages of Christianity, or break again, and this time finally, with the Teutonic peoples.

Four things Romanism has incorporated into her phase of Christianity which were no part of the early church as established by Christ and as built up by the Apostles.

1. - The Papacy with its claim of spiritual infallibility and its "Holy College" of cardinals. The genesis of all this is to be found in that older priestly "Holy College" of heathenism as founded possibly by Numa, and which had also its "Pontifex Maximus" who was the ruling spiritual authority of the older heathen Rome for centuries before the Christian era, and whose word in spiritual matters was supreme. The title and the office seem to have passed down together from the older religion to the new.

2. - A practical polytheism, in its Mariolatry and its saints' adoration. The change from the polytheism of the older Rome, which found its highest expression in the Pantheon, is largely a change of name.

3. - The celibacy of the clergy and of the conventual orders. Traces of these orders, and of the celibacy, are to be found not only in the older heathenism of Rome, for it, too, had its celibates as the Vestal Virgins with their vow of virginity and their dwelling apart, but in all religions. And everywhere the thought is the same, a fleeing from the world. The monastery and the nunnery are the soul's confession of defeat in the world struggle. They are not the stronghold of the victor, but the retreat of the vanquished. They hold within their walls the weak, those spiritually unable or afraid to stand in the battle of life. Not heroes, but weaklings, seek refuge there.

4. - The temporal power.

The earthly power which Christ disavowed that day when he said to Pilate, "My kingdom is not of this world," the Roman church grasped after, and has ever struggled for. It has been the slow-working, insidious poison of that church. Centuries came and went before the full harm was made apparent, but the germs of all the subsequent harvest of evil to the church and to humanity were planted the day when the first bishop of Rome saw opened up before him the possibility of ecclesiastical domination by means of civil power. That day St. Bartholomew's and the Inquisition became possibilities; and that day the revolt of the Teutonic peoples became a prophecy, as yet far off, but inevitable. The ambition which Christ discarded, but which Gregory took up despite the virtual prohibition of the Master, has been the bane of the church, and as a disrupting force lay back of the great schism of Protestantism. A divided Christianity is the price the church of God has paid for the departure from the wholesome limitations of its founder. This departure is the more deeply to be regretted because of the great store of worldly wisdom which Rome's centuries of evangelistic work have taught her, and because of the many wholly admirable features of her teachings and her family life.

Yet the Papacy and its policies are not chance. It is the normal evolution of that episcopal system which was not of Peter, but of Paul. The Papacy is the normal evolution of the episcopacy to its legitimate end. That church represents the completed course Episcopus, Episcopus Senior, Archiepiscopus, Primatus, Pontifex Maximus. The other Episcopal churches may hardly be said to have stopped short in the evolution; they simply lack the centuries of Rome, and favoring circumstances, for the full course; but the incipient waymarks of the uncompleted evolution are to be seen. And the germ of it all lay in that old Greek Επισκοπος whom Paul ordained, but whom the church as left by Christ seems not to have known. And a heavy load has it all proven to be to the simple Εκκλησια which the Master established.

All four of these extraneous things which Rome incorporated into the Latin type of Christianity have in them certain elements of power in the immediate upbuilding of an ecclesiasticism; yet all four have in them likewise elements which, as contravening the very basic laws of man's completest spiritual evolution, must inevitably bring check, and then ultimate defeat to that ecclesiasticism both as a worldly and as a religious force. The dry rot which everywhere seizes upon the Roman type of Christianity at a certain stage of its development is no accident. It is the working out of law to its legitimate and inevitable end. For there is a law of death, as well as a law of life. These spiritual impedimenta the Latin still retains. The more robust Teuton cast them aside with the wreckage of his Middle Age camps.

The hopelessness of the Roman struggle for the position of a Church Universal lies in the fact that it is the system itself that breaks down. The older Rome, the civic Rome of the Caesars, developed the same defect; and both were built upon the same model. With both, the foundations never quite reached bed-rock. It is the old parable over again of the house upon the sand. It has been the boast of the Papacy that Rome changes not. But the world does. There is the trouble. Her *Semper Idem* is a vain attempt to withstand the current of human progress. The Vatican still dreams the dream of Gregory and Hildebrand; but the night of the dreamer is passing by, and she has failed to awake with the dawning. But the world has awakened. Pulling the curtain down may prolong for a little while the dimness of the chamber, but it does not delay the coming of the morning. Rome has repeated again that world-old ecclesiastical error of mistaking the messenger for the message, the body for the spirit. It was the mistake of the Jew before her. It is the insidious peril of Protestantism after her.

The vitality of the Latin blood seems to be again becoming exhausted. The race had a renaissance once under the revitalization which came with the infusion of fresh Northern blood from the fifth to the tenth centuries, and which was half parent to the children of Rome, the so-called Latin nations of modern Europe. What the invading stream of fresh Dorian blood did for the decadent Achaians of the Peloponnesos ten centuries before Christ, the fresh, vigorous Teutonic blood did for Rome five centuries after Christ; it brought renewed youth, energy, purity, and a new lease of race power. But even that also seems to be showing evidence of exhaustion. Spain had her culmination in the brave days of Carlos Quinto, the days when her infantry was the dread of Europe, the days when her flag waved unquestioned over the Western Continent from the banks of the Mississippi to Cape Horn, and when the Caribbean was the Spanish Main and the Pacific only a closed Spanish sea. France saw flood-tide in the earlier years of Louis XIV., before the revocation of the Edict of Nantes, and before she had in the blindness of bigotry driven out the best blood of the kingdom. Italy? - Venice and Genoa are only dreams; and the shroud of the older Rome is still wound about the Eternal City. The power to bring things to pass seems to be gone from the Latin peoples. The old man by the Tiber with his querulous "Non possumus" is no ill type of the true Latin as he stands face to face with modern civilization.

Is a new infusion of northern blood into the senile veins of the Latin again to bring back vitality and a flush of returning manhood? Time and the German must answer this question. Charlemagne and his Franks may not be so very dead after all.

And the Greek? Successive waves of fresh northern blood came to the Latin to renew again the vigor of race manhood. But no second wave of Dorian blood ever, came to bring new life to the Greek. With him the lethargy of age deepened, as the centuries went by, into the stupor of death. Yet the world does not always realize when a race has died. And the race itself may not realize that as a living force it has ceased to exist; that its heroes are dead, and the past comes not back again. Only a little while ago and the world looked on as the man of the Greek land went out once more to battle. And it was again ὁι βαρβαροι from the Hellespont against whom he went out; and again it was for the Greek homeland that he battled. And the world held its breath as it looked to see Leonidas again standing to the death at the rocky gates. It saw - a Paris dandy sprinting across the Thessalian plain before the grim lines of the Turk. And the world which had waited to cheer, turned away with a laugh; but the laugh had a tear in it; for the world does not easily give up its ideals; and it could not forget Leonidas and the Three Hundred, and how they died that olden day to roll back the tide of Asiatic invasion and save Europe from the fate of Asia Minor. The laugh had pain in it as of one who looks upon the degenerate sons of a noble sire. It is kindlier to close the book at Thermopylai and Marathon and Salamis and that old Plataian day, as we close that other Graeco-Latin book with the Goth within the gates of the Eternal City. Yet there was an afterRome at which the world does not laugh. The world has tears, not derision, for that last Constantine as he lay with dulled eyes facing the stars from among his dead in the breach of the city walls by the Bosporus. He at least knew how to die. But the Tiber had bred a sterner race blood in the after-years than did the blue skies and the lapping waves of the Aegean. Vale, et pax! O last worthy Roman!

Yet maybe Fallmerayer was right after all, and Greece, the Greece of Leonidas, died in the plague of the mid-eighth century, and this was not the blood of Leonidas, but only the mongrel Slavono-Albanian of an after-migration into the old Greek land. Better so than to believe that Greece died of the Greek.

There is one phase of that older Graeco-Latin race evolution which would seem somewhat anomalous. Side by side with a mental evolution which was marked in its attainments, we find a religious evolution which was even puerile in its essays at spiritual truth. When contrasted with that of the Indo-Aryan or the Irano-Aryan it seems almost childlike. Indeed, childish would be a fitter word. Yet, such as it was, it was his, and has left its imprint upon the type of his after-Christianity. While the type of his material and intellectual civilization was higher, the religious faith which the Graeco-Latin developed was distinctively lower in type than that of either the Indo-Aryan, the Irano-Aryan, or the Teuton; for while lower in spiritual insight and grasp of religious truth than the faith of Indo-or Irano-Aryan, it was lower in morality than that of the Teuton. Yet it was not all darkness. There was light, even tho dim. Men did see more than Olympos - some men. When Sokrates, in a faith which somehow took hold upon the unseen, stood facing the mystery beyond, it was with a deeper prescience that he unfearingly said, "Know of a truth, That no evil can befall a good man either in life or after death." Yet the mystery was still there, unsolved, unsolvable; for as he receives the unmerited sentence to death, he turns with the old, old puzzle still upon him and says to his judges, "The hour of the parting has come and we go our ways, I to die, you to live. Which is better only God knows." But in it all was the confidence and the hope. In this at least he stood upon a plane that was as high as the halting incertitude of Christian Hamlet.

Yet while the faith of Sokrates was a faith such as the philosopher might cling to, it was also one in which the unphilosophical, unreasoning mind of the populace had no part. The Underworld of the Immortals, that old A-ιδης of Homer, the "Unseen" which yet Sokrates by faith somehow takes hold upon, is the world of Orpheos, of Hesiod, of Homer, of Palamedes, and of Ajax and the heroes of that mighty past of which Herodotos dimly hints, "When all the Greeks were free," and when great deeds were yet done of men. And so it was with Marcus Aurelius; for the plane upon which he lived was not the spiritual plane of the Roman people. These heights were for the learned. In matters of faith there was no common ground for peasant and courtier, for philosopher and dullard. For the one, the juggling priest, and the superstition, and an immorality revolting in its grossness; for the other, the cold, solitary heights of a morality which, while better, was yet unfruitful and repellent in its frigid agnosticism.

And yet the Indo-and the Irano-Aryan with all their deeper spiritual insight failed as signally in their purely intellectual development as did the Graeco-Latin in his spiritual evolution. These one-sided failures and one-sided successes of both cases would seem to be anomalous, yet a reason may be assigned which would apparently throw at least some light upon the point, aside from any consideration of variations in type through difference in natural endowment. And again it is the working out of the law of environments. The broken, irregular seacoast regions of the world through their very variety of physical and climatic features, and through the more diversified material interests to which they give rise, lead to a more varied intellectual life, and especially in its practical and scientific aspect. The mind is kept active, alert, and tends to become objective rather than subjective in type. The interiors of the great continents are the opposite of all this. By their very sameness, the simplicity and monotony of natural features, and their less varied material interests, they turn the mind away from the external world inward upon itself. Men become contemplative and introspective in character. No maritime nation has ever given birth to one of the higher, more spiritual types of religion. And no mid-continental nation has ever evolved an intellectual life which has left a deep or lasting impress upon the general mental life of the world. One who has never known the life of the mid-continental uplands can hardly realize their molding power upon the men who dwell there. It must be felt to be understood. Two years of my own life spent in the loneliness of the mountains and the deserts of the mid-continent stand separate and apart from all the other years. As the long months went by the world seemed to drop away. The older life became a dream. The intangible things were become the real. A new sense seemed to arouse to life; a sense which somehow had power to take cognizance of things before unfelt and unseen. One day I especially remember, when this new sense seemed to overpower all else. I was at a military camp in the north of Arizona awaiting an escort across the Indian country to the post to which I had been ordered. Wearying of the sameness of the camp, I took a man with me and we rode out some miles across the mesa looking for game. Finally telling the man he might return without me, I rode on alone, keeping close watch, for it was a dangerous country. Out upon the dry mesa stood a lone live-oak tree. Riding under the low, wide-spread branches where I was hid as by a screen, I stepped from the saddle to one of the great boughs and tying my horse to it I sat for an hour. It was an early summer day, but already the atmosphere was wavering with the dry heat. Not a breath of air broke the hush of the desert noon. Not a sound of a bird, the howl of a coyote, not the whir of a rattlesnake. Even my horse slept in the fierce heat. It was the utter hush of the desert noon. But as I sat looking out over the brown, dry plain to the simple outline of the far-off mountains a strange sense of a new life seemed to come to me. It was no longer the desert, lifeless and still. I somehow seemed, as with a new-born perception, to awake to a sense of life about me. Intangible, unseen, but life. The whole air seemed to throb and palpitate with life - life that reached out beyond the desert, beyond the distant rim of the bare, sleeping mountains, on and on into the infinite. I seemed somehow to have stepped out of the old narrow bounds and bonds of the flesh and to stand within the portals of a new and broader existence. That day I awoke to the desert. From that day it had for me a new meaning. Nearly forty years have come and gone since the hour when I sat amid the branches of the oak alone with the Spirit of the Waste. My life has been so ordered that I have never revisited the desert. But its power is upon me still, after all the years, as it was that day. The old longing for it has never died out. It brought into my life possibilities which otherwise never would have been existent. It aroused capacities and a spiritual sense which would otherwise have remained dormant. It made of me a different man. It has for forty years made to me the city a desert, the desert a place of abounding life. Our complex, high-pressure, materialistic civilization, with all its comforts and its intellectual activities, yet brings with it also a curse of spiritual poverty to the souls of men. It is the doom of Israel over again, "And he gave them their request; but - but sent leanness into their soul."

We have lost something since that day when our far-off forefathers turned from the highlands of the desert mid-continent away to the sea, some deeper spiritual sense. Can we ever find it again? - or is it the heritage of the desert peoples alone?

Yet the debt of even the Teutonic world to the Graeco-Latin is no small one. To them came a work to be done for all after-ages, and they did it well. The Graeco-Latin era was one of humanity's great deciding epochs; possibly, indeed, the most pregnant in its after-results of all the great determining epochs of the world's history. It settled the question of the world's future as between Asia and Europe, as between old and new. As Greece saved Europe and the germ of modern civilization from Asia in the fifth and sixth centuries B.C., so Rome saved a later Europe and its nascent civilization from Phoenicia and the Semite seven centuries after. The battle which Greece fought with

Persia, and the battle which Rome fought with Carthage, were our battles as well as theirs; for to us has fallen the heritage of the results. These battles settled for all time the question whether Europe was to be Europe, or only Asia over again. Settled it, altho the battle is not yet entirely closed. It still has in some way, by arms or by arts, to be fought to a finish with the lands north of the Volga. Greek philosophy and the intellectual freedom which it involved, Roman jurisprudence and the rights of the individual which it built up and safeguarded, could not have been had Asia won. And they could not continue should Europe fail in the twentieth-century battle with the Asia north of the Volga.

Another work the Graeco-Latin did for the world. To him it fell as human instrument to decide, not simply whether Asiatic polytheism, but whether European polytheism as well, should survive, or be relegated to a buried past. He made his decision by receiving and acting as evangel for Christian monotheism; and Moloch and Astarte, and Zeus and his alias Jupiter were put aside to be shelved in the theological-curiosity shop of man's infantile beliefs side by side with countless other steppingstones of humanity's spiritual nature in its evolution upward. Yet man never wholly frees himself from his past. As Protestant Christianity shows still the plastic fingermarks of its predecessor, the old Teutonic theogony, so the Graeco-Latin types of Christianity show even more broadly the molding and shaping influence of the polytheism which preceded them. There is a suggestive significance in the fact that the Pantheon yet stands upon the Campus Martius as in the days of pagan Rome. Only, now in this the images, as the ikons in the Greek cathedrals, have taken the place of the idols. It was not so much of a transition after all from the many gods of the older altars to the adoration of Mary and Joseph and the saints innumerable; only, there was the germ of better things in it all. Despite the lingering polytheistic taint, however, Rome kept through the long night of the Dark Ages much of the true message of Christianity to the human soul, and men and women found peace, and the world still had the light, a light that could guide to better things even with the pagan admixture.

What the Latin peoples might have been without even this mixed form of Christianity to aid them, no man can say. That it did aid them, no man can question; for the life and the dim light of the old heathenism were rapidly dying out even before Christianity came to fill the void. The Meditations of Marcus Aurelius and the speech of Sokrates before his judges show the light which the philosophical mind found under the old; but the untrained and untaught masses found little to guide. The change from this to even the mixed light of Roman Christianity was to them as the change from night to day.

If only Rome had stopped there! But there came a darker day to Latin Christianity. It came when Rome, no longer content to guide, claimed as divine the right to drive. The bringing in of force and of the temporal power marks the true day of Rome's spiritual decadence. And the Latin peoples have paid the penalty. The Inquisition burned the heart out of the whole

Spanish peninsula. The Auto da Fé became to it instead an act of race death. It was more than the martyrs that perished at the stake. It was Spain herself that went up in the smoke of torment from the fagots of the martyrs' pyre, the light, the hope, the future of the Spain which might have been; just as St. Bartholomew's slew France, the fair, God-fearing France which might have made '93 and the guillotine impossible. Will the world ever learn that old, old Bible lesson, that it is the killer, not the killed, that is really slain? It is a strange problem this, as. to how much the Inquisition had to do with the failure of the Latin peoples to hold their own in the keen rivalry for world dominion which came to the nations. It was not simply the lives sacrificed. Other nations have from other causes lost far more heavily. Germany at the close of the Thirty Years' War had lost, through battle, famine, and disease, half her population. The twenty millions had become only ten millions. Cities were burned; farms abandoned; the land desolate. Tilly and Wallenstein had done their work of ruin only too well. Yet they had failed. This was the price Germany had paid for freedom of thought. True, the settlement spoke of other things; but that war, like the war of 1812 between Britain and America, settled some things not stipulated in the bond. And under the stimulating atmosphere of free thought Germany soon made good her losses.

It was not in the mere numerical loss of the thirty-two thousands burned at the stake in Spain alone that the great harm to the Latin peoples came; or in the two hundred thousands of Spain's best citizens sent to the dungeons; or in the other thousands of victims in Portugal, and Italy, and France, or in the thousands of the Huguenots who fell in the religious massacre of St. Bartholomew's day. These, and the Te Deum of rejoicing ordered in the churches by Pope Gregory XIII. over the massacre could be passed by. For these, hideous as they were, torture, and massacre, and blasphemous rejoicing, were possibly a part of the age of cruelty in state and church to which they belonged. There was, however, an insidious and far-reaching harm done in it all to the Latin peoples which only time revealed. Pope Gregory's Te Deums might better be called the passing knell of Latin greatness. It was not simply so many thousands of the best blood of the Latin race that were murdered in the name of religion; it was freedom of thought among the Latin peoples as well that was slain. Herein was the deadliest harm. And herein lay the retribution. For with the direct loss to the race of so large a portion of its best mental life, and with generations of repression of the very faculty of independent thought, the Latin became by heredity, as well as by training, unfitted to compete with the keen-witted, self-reliant Teutonic mind in that battle for the world dominion which was even then already upon the nations. The Latin church helped to the Latin undoing.

It is also a question of maleficent import, what the spectacle of all these generations of ecclesiastical and judicial cruelty must have done toward brutalizing the Latin peoples. The spectacle of thousands of their neighbors and fellow countrymen burning at the stake, with civic official applying the torch, and ecclesiastic standing by to witness and give the seal of approval of the church, was not one to humanize or soften the brute side of man; nor the spectacle of Henry IX. firing from his palace window with his fowling-piece at the fleeing Huguenots in the streets of Paris. When we see the brutalizing effect of the stray cases of negro burning by the mob upon the local communities of the border States of America in the nineteenth century, we may understand what must have been the effect of the spectacle of the thousands of cases of legalized burning and torture upon the people of the Middle Ages. Are we to look back to the Auto da Fé, and the torture chamber, and to St. Bartholomew's for the genesis of Robespierre and '93, and of the reconcentrado policy in Cuba? And it was all done in the name of Him who said, "Blessed are the merciful, for they shall obtain mercy." It is a hideous record to answer for; and sore is the penalty the Latin peoples have paid.

Yet this was not all. The persecuted sought safety by tens of thousands in flight, especially from France. The expatriated Huguenots helped to build up the industries and to increase the population and raise the average prosperity of the Latin man's rivals. They swarmed across the border to Germany, over the Channel to Britain, beyond the seas to America, everywhere carrying with them industry, thrift, intelligence; for they were of the best blood of France. They were especially the classes of France who represented her great economic and productive industries. These they took with them to build up the manufacturing and commercial greatness of the Latin man's rivals. And they never went back. All this expatriated current of population was to the Latin peoples as the cup of water spilled upon the ground, which can never be gathered up again.

It is estimated that during the hundred years which have St. Bartholomew and the revocation of the Edict of Nantes as their central events, France lost through religious expatriation a million of her people. And, as just said, these were not the vicious, the ignorant, the idle, but the moral, the intelligent, the industrious. Especially did she lose in artizans and craftsmen. And these, who were the best trained and most skilful of the artizans of Europe, carried their great industries with them to the Teutonic lands which, until then lagging behind in the industrial race, now under the stimulus of this influx began rapidly to forge ahead of the Latin peoples in all mechanical pursuits. It is an interesting problem, How much of that vast mechanical and industrial league of Mid-Europe which overthrew Napoleon, and finally broke the French power in both the old and the new worlds, owed the possibility of its existence to these unforeseen results of the bigotry of the Roman church. Even the far-off banks of the Yadkin, the Ohio, and the Cumberland and Tennessee, had the blood of the Huguenot exiles of France flowing in the veins of their pioneers, and their names are found upon the polling lists to-day. In the irony of retributive justice they helped to wrest from Roman Catholic France her vast possessions in the New World and to give over to the English-speaking Protestant all the broad lands of the West. Rome missed her opportunity when instead of going on she stood still. And again it was "The traditions of the Elders making the Word of God of none effect." If Rome had faced the world and gone out with the open Bible she might have become what Israel failed to be, The Messenger. But, instead, she closed the Bible and chose the "Writings of the Fathers." It was the turning-point in Rome's history as a spiritual leader; and again the message-bearing had to be given over to the Gentiles.

There is a curious parallel between the first and the sixteenth centuries. History, even spiritual history, strangely repeats itself. Rome just before the Reformation stood where the old Jew had stood at the opening of the New Covenant era. To each came a supreme testing hour; and it involved the possibility of a future such as comes only once in the life of a race or a religion. But with the Jew the teachings of the Elders had largely supplanted the spirit of the Old Covenant, and he was blind to the possibilities it had held out. With Rome the Writings of the Fathers had largely supplanted the spirit of both Covenants, and she, too, was blind to the possibilities held out to her. And when the supreme hour came each drew back, and failed. When the Jew had failed of his opportunity as the message-bearer of a broader covenant to the world of all men, Rome was called. And for a time she proved faithful. But as the ages went by she too, following in the footsteps of the Jew and forgetting the Book of the Covenant, began to build upon her "Traditions of the Elders," the Writings of the Fathers, making the Gospel of no effect; and then, to cover up the inconsistencies of her position, made of the Bible a sealed book to her people. And again, a second time, it was to the Gentiles that the message was given over. The Teuton took up the work which Rome laid down.

When the Jew, forgetting that broader prophetic promise of the All-Father to Abraham, drew back within himself and became only Jew, he failed of becoming leader of the greater Israel of God. When Rome, forgetting the true catholicity of the message to all men, drew back from the wider possibilities which lay before her, and became only and avowedly Latin, she failed of becoming the Church Universal. And these two do not stand alone. It was so that English Episcopalianism two centuries later failed of her opportunity and let Methodism, with its fiery zeal and its intense propagandism, go out to carry the message which she failed of. And again it was because of the Traditions of the Elders. That day when to the caviling of the Jews that the disciples "walked not according to the traditions of the elders," Christ made reply that the Jews "made the Word of God of none effect through their tradition," he touched upon the danger-point not only of Judaeism but of all ecclesiasticisms as they grow old. History repeats itself even in religions. It again becomes the "Teaching for doctrines the commandments of men." All religions seem to reach the time in their spiritual and ecclesiastical life when they can no longer unload the burden of tradition; and men can only become free by moving on and leaving both church and tradition behind. Again it is the incubus of The Writings of the Fathers - Ante- and Post-Nicene, and Medieval - of

Calvin - of Jonathan Edwards - of Wesley. And again, as of old, it becomes a burden greater than men can bear.

Yet the second Rome, like the first, dies hard.

What is to be the Future of the Graeco-Latin Peoples?

To at least the one-half of the question the answer would seem to be plain. Judging from a political standpoint the future of the people who now dwell in the Greek land would seem to lie in the hands of either the German or the Slav. That they possess either strength or ability to maintain an independent race life in the coming battle of giants is entirely improbable. More probably [the Greek land will go as a collateral in the closing out of the landed estate of the Turk, when the time of his political demise shall have come. Even more, it will surely so come to pass, unless the sentiment of the world shall agree to hold the Greek land for the sake of its past as the Greeks themselves in the olden time held the little territory of Elis, as something sacred and apart from the strifes and ambitions and jealousies of warring peoples, a spot of peace whither men may come as to a shrine, and forget the years as they discourse of the ages.

With the Latin it is different, however. His is a broader land; and even in his decadence a sturdier individuality sets him apart from the Greek. The Latin dies hard. But then he has been a strong man among the nations. Yet nations, as individuals, die; and the nation, as the individual, if it die not out utterly as a race from the earth, must live its life over again in its children. But the curse of miscegenation is upon the Latin wherever he has gone to colonize. He has left progeny, but it is by the bondwoman. In these lands there is no Isaac to keep up the line of promise. It is Ishmael who holds the birthright - and Ishmael is the wild man of the nations; and his hand is still against every man; and every man's hand must perforce be against him, for there is the ferment of unrest and violence in his blood. Abroad, the Latin has tried and has failed. He has no future there. Two thousand years have settled that. But in the homeland his family history has been different. While there has been mixing of bloods, it has not been miscegenation. Here the blood has mingled, not with alien, but with kindred bloods. Here it was Isaac who peopled the land, and the mother of his children was not the alien bondwoman, but came of his own kin. There is a mingling of bloods which is miscegenation, and which brings with it race deterioration and premature decay. But these are the evil fruitage of the crossing of bloods widely variant from each other. It is shown in the mulatto, the mestizo, the Eurasian. But there is also a mingling of bloods which is not miscegenation in this evil and disastrous sense, and which instead of deterioration and decay brings vigor and renewed youth. It is the mingling of kindred yet separate bloods. It is Isaac and Jacob going back to their kinsmen in the land of Haran for wives. This is the race remolding which made Britain, which is making America, which remade the dying Greece of the pre-Dorian days, the Greece of Knossos, of Mykene, of

Tiryns, and which once before, in the days which followed the Caesars, saved Rome from political death, and made possible Italy, Portugal, and Spain. Judging from the past it might safely be said that only the transfusion of new blood into the senile veins of the Latin can save the race from the decay of age which is upon it; and that new blood, if it comes at all, must come from that same Teuton who, still vigorous in the normal climatic belt of the Aryan peoples, has never, as the Latin, lowered the primitive race vitality by migration south of the normal Aryan race habitat. It must be such a reinforcing of race vitality, only to a less noticeable degree, as is given to the English blood upon the plains of India by the constant influx from the homeland of Britain. The difference is this, that the decay of race vitality which the climate of India brings about in one generation, the less alien climate of the Mediterranean littoral requires many generations to work out in the more northern Aryan blood. Yet the law is there, and the end the same. But who can do this work of race rejuvenescence for the Latin? The limitations which come of mere geographical lines answer the question even before the asking. It must be, as said, the same man who did the work once before, the Teuton of Mid-Europe.

The best hope of the Latin lies in a renaissance which shall both politically and spiritually go back of the Roman imperium to the Latin Res-publica. It is the days of Cincinnatus, not the days of Caesar, the days of the Ante-Nicene Fathers rather than the days of the "Holy Fathers," that the Latin peoples need. For there were days at the first of a spiritual Res-publica also. They were when the bishop of Rome was only bishop of Rome, as the bishops of Alexandria, of Carthage, of Constantinople, were each bishop of his own diocese only. The Caesars built upon the foundations of the old Res-publica; the primitive church upon the foundations of the Ante-Nicene Fathers. To these early beginnings the Latin nations must go back if they would again touch the fountains of their pristine vigor. Can they do it? Their future hinges upon the answer. If they can, well. If not other men in the ages to come will possess their lands, and again build homes over the graves of the dead, as the Latin did before them. For the Latin, too, was a supplanter; and the law of the supplanter still has not worked out the fulness of its will among the races of men. Under its remorseless fiat the supplanter who stops short in the way, or who fails in the keen competition of races, becomes in turn the supplanted. It is again the survival of the fittest; and man, and beast, and plant alike go down, helpless in the presence of the law, when the hour has come.

What Have Been the Contributions of the Greco-Latin to the Mental Life of the World?

For the Greek, chiefest of all the answer might be summed up in the single word, Beauty. To the Greek, more than to any other of the Aryan peoples, came the evolution of the idea of beauty, finished, symmetrical beauty; but beauty rather of form and of outline than of color. His architecture was not dependent upon size for its impress. The massiveness, the gross massiveness of the Ganges and the Nile lands he discarded. With him the idea of mere bulk dropped away. The idea of symmetry took its place. Instead of the gigantic figures of Karnak and Denderah, and of the primitive Indian Cave Temples, were the almost dainty creations which crowned the Akropolis. Yet the Greek land also had known its days of childhood Cyclopean crudeness; but it had evoluted beyond these, while the others stopped and stood still. To the Greek came the evolution of form and outline which the others failed of; and this he left as his legacy to the world. In his literature the same characteristic is manifest. It is the finished beauty of the Greek epic, the Greek drama, the Greek historic narrative even, which has made of Greek letters the mental training-school of after-ages. Add to this keen sense of beauty a certain alert quickness of mental make-up, and a vivant, inquiring mind which passed on through the Greek literature as a ferment to quicken the half-dormant mentality of the medieval ages, and to hasten the coming of a renaissance, and the mental work of the Greek for the world is fairly rounded out.

But the work of the Latin was different. He was the foundation-builder for modern civic life. Law, order, and law and order through the might of arms, were his legacy to the ages. And he builded strongly and well; and Celt and Teuton are his joint heirs and debtors together with the semi-Latin races of the Mediterranean shore.

Chapter Nine - The Celto-Aryan

The Teuton was not, apparently, the first Aryan man to reach the west shores of Europe. The Celt seems to have preceded him; a man only presumably Aryan because of his speech; for the route, or even the direction of his migration is largely a matter of conjecture. When the Teuton came to the shores of what is now known as the German ocean, he found dwelling upon the islands beyond him, and in the lands southward, this man of Celtic speech. We speak ordinarily of the Celt as we speak of the Teuton, as a man of one folk blood. Yet it may be well doubted whether he really is such; whether back of the apparent kinship of allied speech there be not, in reality, a composite blood of diversified and unlike peoples. For we must ever bear in mind in these race investigations that kinship of speech is only presumptive evidence of kinship of blood, nothing more. The Celt of Britain has lost his own tongue, and now speaks English, yet he is Celt. The Basque has in a measure lost his native tongue and now speaks French or Spanish, yet he is Basque, the Israelite of the Gentile world as the Zigani is its Ishmaelite. And so the negro of America, to whom the English language is now mother tongue, yet he is ever African, the Ethiop of old. This change of race speech which we see going on everywhere even now, was probably much more frequent in the past under the stress of race conquest. In the light of this fact we are justified in the supposition that much of the now so-called Aryan blood of the world may after all only be Aryan in speech. Physical and mental characteristics are possibly a more critical and reliable test. Yet even these are no tsure. From the same loins and out of the same womb came Reuben, unstable as water; Issacher, the strong ass crouching down between two burdens, content to serve; and Judah, the lion's whelp, and the scepter-bearer. There is need of caution in this whole subject of race investigation.

There would seem to be fairly clear evidence of at least two distinct men making use of the Celtic speech, and passing by the name of Celt; one tall, blond, dolichocephalic, as the Scot of North Ireland and of the Highlands; the other short, dark, brachycephalic, as the South Irish and the Welsh; the one the true Celtic blood, the other an older subjugated race which only took on the Celtic speech. It is so there were two Latins one born of Latin blood, the other subjugated peoples of acquired Latin speech With the Celt it may indeed even be questioned whether we have not to do with a whole group of races now classified under the one common name of Celt Scotch, Irish, Welsh, Gauls, and what more no man can say, for the Celt never kept his blood pure. The fatal Celtic facility for miscegenation, then as now, has proven his race undoing. And then of all these types which was the real Celt? Was it the sober-sided, canny, unimaginative Scot? the stolid Welsh and Cornishman? the vindictive, dark-skinned South-of-Ireland man? or was it the mercurial, nimble-witted, light-hearted, sunny Irishman as the world has learned to know and to love him? Probably the latter; for so is he across the Channel in the France of modern Europe, the Gaul, that central Celto-land of Caesar, the land and people of whom he says, "*qui ipsorum lingua Celtae, nostra Galli, appellantur.*" And this is the man who, in the English and French peoples, has given of his sunshine and cheer to lighten up the somber, rather stolid character which is normal to the Teuton; for the Englishman is mainly Teuto-Celt, the Teuton predominating; the Frenchman, Celto-Teuton, the Celt predominating, with a veneering of Latin in speech and type of civic life. And the Scot? - may be Norse. And the Welsh and Cornish man? - Possibly the autochthonous Iberian of the yet older days.

Yet in it all this much would seem to be clear, that to a primitive folk of Southwestern Europe, one in race blood or many, the Celt came in some prehistoric time as conqueror, and remained as a dominant race at least long enough to fix his speech upon all, time and the subject tongues working out in the respective cases the various dialectic types which we afterward find. And the Celt was thus already divided up when historic record begins; for Caesar's "*Omnis Gallia in tres paries divisa est*" meant more than mere territorial lines. It was a division manifestly of race lines as well, for "these all differ from each other in tongue, institutions, and laws," he further says. And then the Celts upon the islands across the Channel - these too "differed from each other in tongues, institutions, and laws."

Yet the process of unification for the Celt is again going on, but it is a unification which means obliteration as a separate and distinct race. South of the

Channel, Latin, Frank, and Norseman have done the work. Upon the islands it has been the English-speaking man.

But with all its self-destructive facility for miscegenation and race-merging with other types, the impress which has been left upon the other races of Western Europe by the Celtic blood shows it to have been possest of a strongly individualistic race type of its own, and full of vitality and power. It has merged, but it has not been lost. Spiritually it may be questioned whether the primitive Celt with his Druidic oaks and his mistletoe was not a nobler figure in history than the priest-ridden Celt of later ages; for his faith, and his priests, were at least his own.

How did this Celto-Aryan man reach the west shores of Europe? That he too was not autochthonous, but was at one time an outlander to his present home, is shown by the prehistoric remains of a yet older folk life which manifestly preceded him in the land. He, in common with the other Aryan peoples of Western Europe, was an intruder in the land which he now calls home. Some light is thrown upon the question of the line of race migration by taking into consideration the location of the lands in Europe which were occupied by the Celtic folk at the beginning of the historical era. Men sometimes think of the British Islands as the central home of the Celtic blood. Instead they were only the outlying posts of a far broader Celtic land. The true Celtic homeland in Europe, the center of the power as a race, lay southward. The Celt was near neighbor to the Latin. The older Celto-land is known to have been in Southwestern Europe. And it was no narrow home that they held. They, and not the Latin, were the early masters from the Adriatic to the Atlantic. The Latin as he first appears upon the stage is not a Cis-Alpine, but a Cis-Apennine man, having only a narrow foothold by the rim of the sea. The Trans-Apennine land was Celto-land. The upper coasts of the Adriatic, and the valley of the Po, were not Latin, but Celtic. Yet this was only the smaller portion of Celto-land. As there was a Cis-Alpine Celtoland, so there was a Trans-Alpine and far broader Celtoland. The center of it all, the great hive of the Celtic peoples, was the land bounded by the Rhine, the Bay of Biscay, and the Mediterranean. Of the people dwelling in this land Caesar says, "In their own tongue they are called Celts, in ours, Gauls." From this central home a spur of Celtic blood flanked the Pyrenees into what is now Spain. Another spur followed the valley of the Rhone eastward into Switzerland, the Helvetia of Caesar. Still another, crossing the narrow waters of the Channel, found lodgment in Ireland, Wales, Cornwall, and upon the smaller Channel Islands and over to the Highlands of Scotland. They were, as Caesar says, a people divided into tribes which differed from each other in language, institutions, and laws, and were ever shifting and at war with each other. It was into this hive of restless, warring tribes that the disciplined armies of Rome drove as a wedge; and where the armies had opened the way the superior organization of Latin civilization followed to possess the land and abide. To the encroachment of this more highly organized Latin civilization the Celt made brave yet only ineffective resistance. His fatal weakness lay in his lack of co-operation; for the Celt was then as now a wrangler and a quarreler with his own kin. It was tribe against tribe, village against village, neighbor against neighbor. Donnybrook Fair is Celtic, not' simply Irish. It was this race spirit of dissension, and its opposite, Latin unity, rather than any superiority in Roman valor that gave to the Latin control of Southwestern Europe. The Celt had the broader land and the greater numbers, yet he succumbed to the superior organization and the more tenacious purpose of the Latin, even tho the Latin was a man of narrow homeland and of comparatively limited numbers. Is anarchy the fatal birth-mark of the Celt? It would even seem so. Gaul and Irish and Scot, they have had the mark alike upon them. And again the question arises, Is this Celtic instability, this race inability to cooperate with each other in any common race policy, only the ferment and unrest of mixed bloods of widely variant types? It works so elsewhere among the peoples of the earth. It is the key to the chronic unrest of Eastern Europe. The so-called "Eastern Question" is only the ferment of mixed bloods of widely unlike type; and therein lies its hopelessness.

Yet the Celtic blood of West Europe survived. In one sense it proved to be stronger than the Latin. It received the Latin, but it absorbed him. Altho the Latin came as conqueror and remained as ruler, and tho his civil rule impressed his speech and his civic institutions upon the Celtic peoples of the mainland, yet the blood, the race characteristics, continued Celtic, and are so to this day. The French man is classed by speech and institutions with the Latin folk. Yet in all but speech and type of political organization he is, as elsewhere stated, not Latin but Celt, Celt and Teuton, with possibly an Iberian substratum and only a Graeco-Latin veneer. His true kin are across the water in Ireland, Wales, and to a less extent maybe, in the Highlands of Scotland, and among the Teutons of Mid-Europe and the British Islands and of the greater Teuton land which is growing up oversea.

With the great bulk of the Celtic peoples thus found in the earliest historic times in south and not in north Europe, and extending backward to the headwaters of the Adriatic, and with the further fact that no trace of the Celt is to be found eastward along the Mid-European lowland, it is probable that the original line of migration was by a southern rather than by a northern route westward to the sea, and that he was follower in the track of the Graeco-Latin rather than of the Teuton. That he did not precede the Latin would seem to be shown by the fact that we find the Latin man crowded on before him down into the Italian peninsula, whereas had the Latin been follower he would have had to fight his way through the great body of the Celts in the valley of the Po and northern Italy to his home by the Tiber, which with the feeble numbers of the early Latin and the preponderating strength of the early Celt is not probable. It is to be remembered that the Gauls first stood as conquerors within the walls of the earlier Rome; and that it was nearly three and a half centuries later before Caesar and his legions fought their way as conquerors within the bounds of the great Celtic homeland. The main body of Celtic migration may have come by the way of the open lands of the lower Danube, and through the low passes of the Julian Alps to the head waters of the Adriatic, some small offshoots wandering on by the valleys of the upper Danube and across to the Swiss lakes, as Herodotos would seem to indicate, unless the latter branch was a recurrent flow of the wave which had flanked the great Alpine center of Europe by the southern route. It may possibly also have been the lateral pressure of this same westward after-wave of Celtic peoples that forced the Dorian Greeks southward upon the earlier and decadent Greek civilization of Mykene and Tiryns and Knossos, and brought to it in the vigor of its fresh blood the renaissance of the second Greek civilization.

The Celt is of a type peculiar to himself in the family of the Aryan peoples. Rhetorical rather than logical in mental make-up; discerning his points more by intuition than by the slower process of reason; quick to see, yet infirm to hold; possessed of a warm and lively imagination; and withal of a vivacious temperament which enjoys life because it is life, enjoying intensely; yet it has been his doom to become a feeder to the race life of other peoples rather than to develop and retain a race life of his own. He has merged his own life into the life of the more sturdy stocks about him. The reason for this seems to lie in a peculiar instability of race character which has ever made him unable long to remain united with his own folk in any common race policy. It is the old doom of Reuben over again, "Unstable as water, thou shalt not excel." It was this race instability rather than the might of the Roman arms which made the Celt of Gaul fall so easy a prey to the legions of Caesar. Individually brave; collectively helpless. It is this peculiarity of race character which has helped to make the after-life of Gaul so full of unrest. It is this that has been the fatal weakness of the Celt of Ireland, and was of the Celt of Scotland until the mutual hatreds and the feuds of Highlander and Lowlander made the Scot a victim to the not braver, but more united, English-speaking Teutons. Of all the primitive peoples of Europe the Celt had apparently the best chance to survive, and to maintain his race power among the nations. He was the most numerous, had the choicest location and the broadest lands; yet of all he has left the least impress of his own race individuality upon the ages following. He held North Italy, that Trans-Apeninne, Cis-Alpine region of the Po, the richest and broadest portion of all the Italian land; he held, as Caesar tells, Helvetia and all Gaul; he held the British Isles. Yet to-day, while the Latin has left his impress upon all Southern Europe, and while the Teuton holds all central Europe and the British Islands as his own, and has reached out beyond all the seas, the Celt as a separate race is only a name of the past. As a people among the nations he lives only in history. Even his legends in that Arthurian cycle which seems to have been the common possession of all the Celtic folk of West Europe as the Nibelungen was of all Teutons, have passed on to enrich the race literature of the English-speaking Teuton who has appropriated them as his own.

The Celtic blood as a distinct strain is disappearing from among the races of the earth. The race speech long ago died out in the land of the Gaul; it is gone from the land of the Cornishman; it is unspoken in the Channel Islands; it is a rapidly dying speech to the Celt of Ireland and Scotland and Wales. The race identity of the Celts who yet remain distinct as a people seems fated to be soon lost in the sturdier folk-life of the English-speaking peoples. Yet the Celt has had a work to do; and he has done it well. It has been said that the work of the Norman in Britain was to tone up the sluggish Saxon blood. So the work of the Celt may be described as that of lightening up the somber gloom of the Latin, and of the English-speaking Teuton with whom he has mingled his blood. His sunny temper, his cheerfulness, his elasticity of temperament, have seemed as the bringing in of the sunshine to race lives that were not sunny. He has been to the Teutonic race life what Baldur was to the Teutonic theogony, the coming in of the light and gladness of the morning. That old English and Norse blood was not a cheerful nor a kindly blood. It was strong, but it was harsh and hard. The strain of Celtic blood has helped to humanize and sweeten it. It has been as a leaven which has left its trace in the literature, the race constitution, the daily life. And now as the kindly rain which has watered and quickened the earth, and then returns again to be lost in the waters of the sea, so the Celt, his separate race life lived out, his work done, goes back whence he came, to be again mingled and lost in the blood of the broader folk-life of the Aryan peoples.

And the French man, that Celto-man of the "*Omnis Gallia in tres paries divisa est,*" the man of whom Caesar said, "Who in their own tongue are called Celts, in ours, Gauls," what of him and the future? for, as elsewhere said, he is not Latin. In his Latin surroundings this modern man of ancient Gaul is out of his natural affiliations. He is in blood almost purely Celto-Teuton, with only the Latinized speech and the Latin imperium. In temperament he is as unlike that somber, heavy-witted, grim old Latin of the Ager Romanus as can well be conceived. In blood he is probably nearest to the English man, for the English man is Teuto-Celt without the Latin veneering. He had it once; but sloughed it off ages ago. Englishman and Frenchman are largely one in blood, the difference lying in the predominating strain. To the Celt of Gaul came the Teutonic Frank as invader, colonizer, and ruler, just as farther east came to the Celtic man of the Valley of the Po the Teutonic Lombard, each giving name, and rule, and mingling his blood with that of the subject race. To the Celt of Gaul came also, but later, the Norse man to still further Teutonize the blood.

The civilization of the West owes two great debts to that older Frenchman. When Charles Martel - Karl of the Northland battle-ax - with his Teuto-Celtic forces at the battle of Tours turned back the tide of Asiatic invasion in the eighth century and thus saved Western Christendom from the Mohammedan overflow, he saved it also from a mongrel race disorganization such as for a thousand years has kept Eastern Mid-Europe in the throes of unceasing warfare. That victory made possible Western civilization. It was such a work of defense upon the south line of assault in the eighth century as German and Pole did in the seventeenth century in Mid-Europe, or as the Greek of the fifth century B.C. did upon the shores of the Aegean. It was the work of saving the young civilization of Europe from the mental and spiritual stagnation which has fallen upon the Farther East.

The second great debt which the civilization of the West owes to this Celto-Teutonic man of France is the bringing of order out of the chaos which followed the overthrow of the Roman Empire. When Charlemagne of the French, that Carolus Magnus of the Holy Roman Empire, with his Teutonic Franks built upon the ruins of the old Celto-Latin provinces of Gaul the Teuto-Celtic kingdom which within the forty-six years of his reign had spread its borders from beyond the Pyrenees to the shores of the Baltic and down the Italian peninsula to Rome itself, he laid the foundations of law and order for the new civilization of the West. And the Frenchman of to-day is in blood and succession the lineal heir and devisee of the name and the glory of that older kingdom which did its work for humanity when the Frenchman was as yet the Teutonic Frank-man. And a gallant and chivalrous blood it has ever proven to be, whether as battler upon the plains of Europe, or as explorer and rival to the English-speaking man along the great waterways and amid the deep forests of the New World.

But Charlemagne left in the very framework of his dominion the germs of its own undoing. When he made alliance with the papacy and received from the hands of Pope Leo the crown of the Holy Roman Empire, he left a legacy of discord and dissensions to the after-ages; for therein lay the inception of those claims to the temporal suzerainty of the papacy which have for a thousand years proven the bane of the nations of the West, and a nemesis to the papacy itself. The overmastering personality of Charles kept the harm from being felt within the times of his own life; but from the day of his death it may be traced in an ever-broadening stream of intrigues, dissensions, and battlings.

But despite the historic Caesar and his legions, and the ages of Latin rule, and a reactionary Roman church, the Frenchman felt the ties of consanguinity, and began to share more and more in the race evolution of his kin, and to take part in the newer Teuto-Celtic life which was growing up upon both shores of the Atlantic. It was the kin blood turning to its own again. In America the Frenchman, except where held aloof through ecclesiastical influence, merged into the common mass of his Teuto-Celtic kin within a single generation. I have, myself, Huguenot blood in my veins. The whole mid-line of America is tinged with it. And it was much the same in the older England beyond the sea, the Huguenot there also becoming one with his nearest of kin.

And then came the reaction in the Frankland, and the revival of the old Latin idea, and the turning away again back to a traditional, yet largely fictitious past. Much of this revival of the Latin idea in France had its birth in the fertile brain of Corsican Napoleon, who fostered it for a purpose. To the Napoleonic mind the whole spirit of Teuto-Celtic freedom was foreign and antagonistic; while the Latin imperium was congenial and accordant. Born of revolution, the mind of Napoleon was yet a mind essentially imperialistic and Oriental in type. And the Concordat with Latin Rome was the price Napoleon paid at the spiritual and intellectual expense of the French people for papal recognition and support in his aspirations to found a dynasty and to enter the charmed circle of European royalty. Its repeal signals the emancipation of France, and the final downfall of the Napoleonic idea. This Latin idea, and the Napoleonic tradition, have been largely instrumental in withdrawing Celto-Teutonic France from her natural affiliations with Celto-Teutonic West Europe, and have been the shackles which have bound her to a mighty but a dead Roman past. The Latin-Napoleonic idea was a distorted and spectacular revival of the Charlemagne Holy-Roman-Empire idea of the eighth century; only Charlemagne and his Franks were the masters, while Napoleon and his French were not, for Rome has dominated.

This manufactured Latin tradition, together with a semi-Latinized tongue, and the adoption of the civic idea of the Roman imperium have diverted and perverted the whole after-life of the French peoples, and made them unnatural exiles from the race life of their blood kin. The repeal of the Concordat, with its attendant and logical cutting loose from the Rome ecclesiastical, and the growing spirit of oneness with the evolution of English-speaking men as members of a common family, are the most significant and hopeful signs of race regeneration in the decadent French blood.

And Corsican Napoleon himself, with his oval face, and his olive complexion, and his "star of destiny," and his fatalism, and his cold-blooded disregard for human life, and his dream of universal dominion - was he, back of the centuries really not Aryan at all, but Semitic, and kinsman in blood with that Punic Hannibal whom he so admired and emulated? His whole type of mind was Oriental and antique, not Western and modern. His prototype is to be found, not in Occidental Caesar, but in the conquerors who flamed up as the bale-fires of that ancient half-forgotten world about the waters of the Euphrates and the Nile. He was in spirit a Rameses, or a Sargon, or a Shalmaneser, born out of his due time; for the ages were ajog, and the old came back once more. It is to be remembered that the centuries of Phoenician colonization and domination had filled the islands of the west basin of the Mediterranean with a population which was not, and which never became, Latin in blood, but a people whose kin and whose homeland lay far in the East about and beyond the Syrian shore.

The Latin tradition, and the Roman ecclesiastical domination, have kept Celto-Teutonic France alien to her blood kin. Will she find her own again?

Chapter Ten - The Slav

Of all the Aryan kin folk, certainly of that portion which made its way westward into Europe, the branch which retains in the most marked degree the Asiatic stamp is the Slav. So marked is the difference in race characteristics between the Slav and other branches of the European family, that were it not for a fairly clear history and philological proof, one might almost doubt whether this man really is Aryan. The kinship has in fact been disputed. This does not apply, however, to the ruling and titled classes, for through long-continued intermarriage the ruling families of Europe, Hapsburg, Bourbon, Hohenzollern, Romanoff, Guelph, and their numerous progeny, titled and untitled, who so largely constitute the ruling and official classes, are essentially one in blood, a race separate and apart from the great, toiling masses. But these, the toilers, and not the rulers, are the race. It is to them, the peasant behind his plow, the workman at his bench, the herdsman afield, that one must look for pure blood and race characteristics; and these, rather than a ruling class or a family, will ultimately settle the race destiny. And with all the corruption of Russian officialdom, the Slav home and the Slav family life seem to be sweet and true; and herein, and not in the titled classes, lies the future of the Slavic peoples. Neither in studying the race future of the Slav must we look to the mixed blood of the Baltic provinces, or to that fringe of mongrel Slavic peoples which is found well south in Central Europe, and which in its boisterous self-assertiveness might unguardedly be taken as the true exponent of the Slavs as a race. We must look back of these to the great, silent, self-contained masses of the Volga, the Don, the Dnieper, and of the black lands which overlap into Asia, Greater Russians, Little Russians, White Russians, sixty millions of them, and multiplying as is no other race in Europe. This is the Slav. This is the man with whom Europe and Asia have to reckon in the future. What is *he* going to be and to do, is the question - this silent man who has not yet found voice? The others, the vociferous Slavs of the south, are only as street brawlers by the side of him. No stir of intellectual activity has as yet broken the dull sameness of the Russian village life which, like the steppes and tundras of their subarctic home, goes on and on in dull uniform monotony. While the Teutonic *vik* and *tun* have become the modern city and town with all their intense stir of mental life, the Russian *mir* remains as it was ages ago with still the village narrowness and torpor. One must not mistake the half-German officialdom of Russia for the Slav race life. It negotiates and plans and intrigues; but the great placid Slavic mass of the plains and the steppes goes on, living its race life as a thing unheard and apart. It knows the White Czar as Egypt knew the Pharaoh, or the Peruvian knew the Inca, and asks no questions. There is something strangely pathetic about this silent, uncomplaining man, more Asiatic than European in type, content as yet with his black bread, his caviar, and his vodka. Will he remain content? Will he remain voiceless? Or will he awake? He is beginning to stir in his sleep.

Granting the kinship, that this man is really Aryan in blood, several reasons might be assigned to account for the variation in type.

1. The isolation of his rigorous, subarctic home, which in the absence of ready means of communication has kept him for ages apart from the vivifying current of European race life. Then, too, civilization is of slower development under the inclement skies of the north than under the genial and favoring warmth of a southern sun. The stir of its vivifying impulse came first in Europe to the semi-tropic Mediterranean shore; then to the harsher Mid-European lands; now it begins to arouse the subarctic plains of the Volga and beyond.

2. The great Mongol invasion of the thirteenth century which swept over Northeastern Europe, only to be checked at the banks of the Danube, and which dominated the northern Slavs as a subject race for more than two centuries, leading presumably during that time to a more or less extensive mingling of bloods, certainly to an impress upon institutions and people which time has never effaced. It is this which has made the Slav of all men of the West the most successful in his intercourse with the races of inner Asia. To them he is somehow less alien than the Englishman, the German, or the Latin. He instinctively understands the Asiatic; the other men of the West do not. Mid-Asia prefers his despotism to other men's freedom. They soon harmonize their ways with his. To other men they remain alien. It is not mere tact that thus puts the Slav in touch with the, Turanian of inland and upland Asia. In his intercourse with other races he evinces the possession of no such capability. It is something else; something more. Blood only can account for it. The Slav of all the Western peoples is most Asiatic in his ideas of government. He is Asiatic rather than European. To him despotism seems normal and natural. He seems scarcely to dream of aught else. It is Asia in the blood.

3. His religion. This came to him from the Greek. But it was from that orientalized Greek who in his religion as in all else never quite escaped from the dominating spirit of Asia; only it was Semitic, not Turanian, Asia. The Greek phase of Christianity was less racial in type than the Roman - more cosmopolitan; yet not cosmopolitan in the broadest sense of the word, for that older Graeco-Roman Constantinople was a cosmopolis of the Asiatic world rather than of the world of East and West. The West had never much influenced the current of its Oriental life. To what extent the borrowed Slavic Christianity became still further modified by an injection into it of the older Slavic heathenism, it is difficult now to say. Yet that it would be so modified we have reason to infer from what we know of the modifying influence of the older heathenisms of Latin and Teuton upon their phases of Christianity, as shown in the better-kept historic records of the West. Possibly also this Slavono-Greek phase of Christianity did not escape some further change in the long Mongol domination. Slavonic fatalism and Mongol fatalism are curiously alike; and neither has touch or kin with the spirit of Western race life. Calvin and Jonathan Edwards might theorize of predestination; and men might give

intellectual assent to the doctrine; but neither they nor their people ever really accepted and lived its practical corollary of fatalism as do Mongol and Slav.

4. Possibly some primary difference or variation in race type; for the various branches of even a common kin will differ markedly in their after-development, just as the children of one parentage prove to possess different and unlike individual characteristics, and go out to an adult life of unlike types of manhood.

Whatever the cause, the fact remains that of all the so-called Aryan peoples of Europe the Slav most widely departs from the common family type. He has developed less of the individual personality and initiative, less of the family mechanical skill, less of the restless intellectual activity, more docility under the hands of his rulers, and with it all, as said, a practical fatalism which is more Asiatic than European in type; and which is possibly the stamp of the Mongol upon him. Is it to both a heritage from the fixed and unchanging monotony of the great, unending plains upon which man is only as a helpless atom in the grasp of space? For the years come and go; and the generations fade away; but space, and the far horizon line, and the ever-recurring stars, change not.

The Slav has developed another trait which is also more Asiatic than European in type, a passive endurance which in time of reverse or disaster enables him to take what comes, yet survive. Should it be defeat, like the Mongol of Asia, hedge-hog fashion he rolls himself into a ball, takes his wooling, and when the conflict is over uncoils and goes his way little the worse, while it is the other battler that has the spines in his mouth. And the Slav is most dangerous when retreating. He does not stampede; but goes on fighting just the same. And when there is no further retreat - the time to beware of the bear is when his back is to the rock. The first lesson Napoleon learned at Borodino; the second at Moscow. It is this passive endurance, this capacity for taking punishment without being vanquished or even seriously crippled, which more than any other trait makes of the Slav the menace he is to Eastern Europe. Seldom successful in battle, he is yet, at least in certain directions, ever advancing. He presents the paradox of winning success through defeat. He generally retreats forward. For two centuries the Slavic power has hung as a storm cloud in the north, having in its black bosom unknown possibilities of conflict.

Yet with it all the Slav is, and for centuries past has been, actually retreating from Western Europe. His advance is in other directions. Once he dwelt upon the shores of the North Sea and held all the land as far westward as the mouth of the Rhine. From that river eastward the whole shore line of the Baltic was his. He held the Saxon valleys. Now only a thin wedge of Slavic blood reaches the sea along the line of the Neva to the Gulf of Finland; for even the Russian provinces of the east shore of the Baltic are not Slavic in blood, nor will be; and Finland is only another, tho smaller and weaker, Poland. The flag may for the time carry with it race supremacy, but only blood will perpetuate race dominion. And the Slav is making no headway to regain his lost land. The Teuton has supplanted him; and as of old it is the supplanter that abides. The retreat of the Slav has been as the recoil from the over-compressed spring. The Teuton, wedged in between the Latin and the sea, has turned backward upon the Slav, and repossessed himself of the Baltic shore and the river valleys of Mid-Europe. Even the Baltic provinces which the Slav still holds are, and probably will continue to be to him, only a frontier; if indeed he continue to hold them; for the east shore of the Baltic despite the years of Russian domination is in blood and sympathy German and Finn, while across the narrow water is still the Norseman. The whole power of Slavic Russia has failed to make the Baltic shore Slav, or to force a western outlet to the sea. With the Teuton holding the islands and shores, and commanding the narrow channels about Zealand and Funen, the Slav only reaches the open sea by permission. That barred outlet is to him upon the west what the Dardanelles is to him upon the south; only, upon the west he can have no hope of changing the control for the whole strength of the Teutonic nations lies across the pathway, and they dare not let him gain possession. It would mean the turning of Asia loose upon the Atlantic, for the Slav is Asia. It may well be questioned whether Russia would not be to-day more powerful, further on in the work of national upbuilding, if Peter the Great had never selected the swamps of the Neva for his capital, but had remained in the old race home by the banks of the Moskwa. For two hundred years the strength, financial and of blood, of the whole race has gone into the attempt to battle against nature, and in the clashing with the Western nations which has come of entering the list with the European powers. The true field of the Slav has always been eastward rather than westward. Asia rather than Europe holds his future. Altho he forced his way into Europe he has never become European. The whole genius of his institutions, the whole spirit of the people, is Asiatic. He has himself instinctively recognized this fact, and in all his westward aspirations has never ceased to steadily reach out to the east. Behind the wall of desert and mountains, saying little, making no parade of plans, allowing no press dispatches or special-correspondent reports, he has pressed on and on, down the Volga to the Caspian, about its shores, across the upland plain to the Aral, back along the long-forgotten course of the Amu-, and the Syr-Daria, up to the Pamir, that Asiatic "Roof of the World," and now over the ridge pole he looks down upon British India. By a more northerly line he has reached the great fertile river valley of the Amur, and will yet have his hand, the iron hand and the iron will of Peter, on Mongolia and Manchuria, and reaching further on for Korea. And there despite any temporary reverses he will abide, for into and over it all he is carrying the Slav family. And this he can do, for it is all within the climatic belt of his normal race home. In this fact lies the assurance of his permanency. He enters, not as a sojourner, but as an abider. He is only repeating what the English man did in America. Should we, of all men, find fault with him for following in our footsteps? This broad Asiatic upland, with its as yet but vaguely apprehended possibilities of race support, is to be the Greater Slav Land as America is already become the Greater Engle Land. While Europe has been quarreling over dynasties, the Slav has been quietly seizing land. He, too, has the Earth Hunger; and he has learned the secret of the English man's power. Need we blame him for being an apt pupil?

It is no chance that has thus turned the footsteps of the Slav eastward to Asia rather than westward along the rim of the sea, or southward to Mid-Europe. Back of the fact lie readily discernible and adequate causes. The resistance of an already existing and dense population in Western and Southern Europe would tend to check his progress in those directions, and to roll the tide of race advance backward upon itself; and race growth, other things being equal, will by a natural law be along the line of least resistance. But back of this lie other and deeper, yet likewise readily discernible factors, factors geographic, climatic, and racial in character. As the tide after passing the flood will return by the channels whereby it came, so the line of retreat for races which have reached the flood of advance in any given direction will, unless the way be blocked against them, naturally be backward along what had been the line of advance.

Take the map of Europe and Asia. Geographically the Slav faces, if the solecism may be pardoned, backward upon Asia, not toward Europe. The Volga, the one great river of the Western Slav, which has its headwaters almost upon the shores of the Gulf of Finland, turns inland and after a navigable course of over two thousand miles, with fourteen thousand miles of tributary navigation, empties into the Caspian, a Mid-Asiatic sea with no outlet to the ocean. This fact means that the basin of the Caspian extends to within a hundred miles of St. Petersburg. And it further means that even Western Russia is, geographically considered, Asiatic and not European. The waterway of the Volga is the key alike to the Slav line of advance into Europe and to the Slav race policies, and holds in it the prophecy of the Slav future. It is not probable that the future of the Slav will lead him southward to the Bosporus. Whatever he might succeed in gaining in that direction would probably only be for a time and not as a permanency. While probably no other race of Europe is so well-fitted by race constitution and temperament to act as nurse, priest, and undertaker to the so-called sick man of the Bosporus as this half-Asiatic Slav, yet it is doubtful whether Europe will ever permit it. And then why should he desire this office? or to become heir to the sick man's estate? for whoever may inherit it, it will always be, in the multiplicity of interests involved, a disputed succession, only to be held *vi et armis* as against all others. Russia could well afford to give up all claims to a reversionary interest in the estate of this sick man of Europe in exchange for a free hand in the estate of another sick man, him of the Southern Caspian. And at least some of the nations of Europe, enough to break the concert of the powers, would be willing to assent. Disputed and divided outlet to the sea by the Bosporus and the Dardanelles might well be traded off for sole and undisputed outlet to the sea by the way of the Caspian and the Persian Gulf. It opens up the Indies to Northern Europe by a new interior route. Trace the line of the Volga and its navigable tributaries. Sixteen thousand miles of waterway as a distributing channel in the heart of Northern Europe; then eight hundred miles of sea way by the Caspian; then only five hundred miles of railway; and the Indian seas are reached at the headwaters of the Persian Gulf. All this, and the Persian Gulf only a Russian lake; and the fertile Euphratean plain, and the valley of the Tigris, the seat of the world's early civilization, as tributary territory. It is a prize worth the price of the Dardanelles. The outlet by the Persian Gulf means of course a powerful fleet; but then Russia is a powerful nation. And it means a great Slavic wedge driven in between East and West. It is a Slavic outlook upon Europe's highway to India and China at the half-way point. Britain has already recognized the possibility and the danger, in the notice of "hands off" which she so promptly served upon Russia with regard to the shore line of that gulf.

Yet it is not so much a line by the Bosporus or the Caspian southward, as it is the great land line eastward which is to settle the future of the Slav. Russia's future as the one great Slavic power lies eastward rather than southward or westward. Her true empire is on the broad steppes, by the inland seas, along the northern rivers, with just and reasonable outlet upon the shores of the Pacific. Here she may be all-powerful, with no rivals. It is empire broad enough to satisfy any ambition. A frank recognition of this fact by the Slav, and a race policy shaped in accordance therewith, would do much to diminish the possibility of future clashings with the nations of Western Europe and to disarm hostility to Russia's continental development. There is justice in the position of the Western Powers in the stand they have taken. The Slav's attempt to force a way westward or southward is an attempt to intrude into the recognized homelands, and into the essential and already preempted fields of influence, of these nations; while the whole north half of the continent eastward is conceded by them as legitimately within the field of development of the Slavic peoples; and no one claims right to interfere. The clashing upon the Pacific shore, time will adjust. More vitally important to the Slav than the westward outlet or the line to the Mediterranean or to the Caspian, is the land line across the great northern plain of Asia to the valley of the Amur. It is more important because while the line southward or westward means only outlet to the sea, the line eastward means also homes six thousand miles of unbroken and unassailable Slav homeland. And it is the Slav's home climate. The isothermal line is the inexorable line of race development. Races may conquer northward or southward, but they will develop by east and west lines. It is the climatic belt which settles race destiny. No other race of the world to-day possesses the possibility of one unbroken homeland equal in area to that of the Slav. Harsh in climate much of it; inhospitable to feebler bloods; monotonous in its vast expanse of subarctic plain - yet by its very sameness, its lack of variety, its monotony, and because of these, all the more fitted to become the future molder of a homogeneous people who, with no natural dividing line, are the more apt 'to remain one in sentiment and nationality. The very isolation of that great northern plain, shut in by icy seas toward the pole, walled apart by the long mountain back-bone of Asia upon the south, touching the open seas only at the extreme ends, will still further tend to the development of a race life, a race future, apart from and unlike all others of the world. Even the great waterways of the Slav tend to encourage race isolation. As already said, the Volga, the one great river of the Western Slav, which has its headwaters almost upon the shores of the Gulf of Finland, turns inward and after a navigable course of over two thousand miles empties into the Caspian, a mid-Asiatic sea with no outlet to the ocean. The Dwina, the Obi, the Yenisei, the Lena, all classing among the great rivers of the world, drain to the unnavigable arctic waters; the Ural, to the Caspian; the Amu- and the Syr-Daria, to the Aral in the heart of the continent. The Amur, with its twenty-four hundred miles of navigable length and a river basin of over seven hundred thousands of square miles, flows to the wintry waters of the Tartar Strait in the lonely north Pacific. Of all the Slav's far-reaching water system only two streams of commercial importance, the Don and the Dnieper, gain available exit to the ocean, and these two have the Turk, backed by all Western Europe, sitting as doorkeeper between them and the open sea. Thus shut in, the Slav through his one representative power bids fair to become the hermit of the nations. But it will be a hermit giant.

But, indeed, the Slav scarcely needs outlet to the western seas. With the internal growth and the mechanical development which will come through the exploitation of the vast agricultural and mineral resources of his hinterland, the heart of Asia, he can as a race live largely within himself; his market, China and the East. The true front of the Slav is by his back door upon the Pacific. There he reaches out to the tropical products of the East Indies; and there he stands face to face with the one man for whom he entertains sincere friendship, and with whom he has no real rivalries, the English man of America. The fellow feeling which has always been so marked between these two has back of it good and sufficient reasons. It is no mere sentimental feeling. Each recognizes in the other youth, a vigorous race life, and that which is best expressed by the somewhat derided yet pregnant phrase "manifest destiny." And each has faith in itself. Temporary misunderstandings may come at times, as they will come between friends. And the man of America may not be in sympathy with all features of the governmental life of the Slav, and may at times so express himself; yet this does not mean enmity, or even loss of friendship. It was a king who wrote, "Faithful are the wounds of a friend; but the kisses of an enemy are deceitful." The Slav in the governmental throes of race regeneration will sooner or later see this, and understand what may seem hard to him in an hour of pain. Maybe also the hand of the friend has not been as tenderly considerate as it might have been in the wounding. If so, his is the regret; and he will remember in sorrow. Then, too, there is a wide difference between a people and the officialdom of a people. All peoples have need to learn this lesson. It will help to save many a race friendship.

It has become customary in certain quarters to speak of the Russian advance upon Manchuria and the Pacific shore line as evidence of race greed. The future with a wiser insight will call it race need. It is only the old English common law over again - the right of free and unobstructed way to mill and market. And why should not what is good and just common law for the English man be good and just international law for the Russian? What other great power would quietly consent to remain ice-bound for half of each year; her ports frozen up; her navy useless; her commerce having outlet only through courtesy of other nations? It is this great unrighted wrong of the Slav that makes him most dangerous. And there can be no permanent peace until it is righted. His very necessities make him, willingly or unwillingly, a continuous menace to the peace of the world. Europe has hardly been fair or just to the Slav. Is not he also a man? Has he not also a right to live and to make the most of his opportunities? If the Western powers for racial reasons deny free outlet to the Atlantic and the Mediterranean, they can scarcely with good grace try to bar the way to the Pacific also. The Slav is in much the same position that the American would be in if free access to the sea were barred except by way of Hudson Bay and Alaska. Yet with the ports of the whole Atlantic seaboard open and in his sole possession, the English man of America claimed, and virtually seized, outlet to the open sea for the country west of the Alleghenies by way of the Mississippi. He is prepared to fight, if need be, for control of the West Indies for the same reason. Has not the Slav an equal right to outlet to the sea? Any other race in Russia's position would do just as Russia is doing, and would allow no permanent peace until the right was conceded. And it is a right because it is right. This is the pregnant thought for Europe - Pent-up Russia is dangerous Russia. And Europe is, by her present policies, sitting down upon the safety-valve while the pressure of the pent-up steam is steadily rising. With the present policies unchanged it is only a question of time for the explosion to come; and the longer the delay, the more violent it will be. It is not a dynasty that is shut in, but a race. It is the wrong done to the Slavic peoples that arms Russia. Better give to her her race right, and then fight her if fight there must be. It would be easier. It is hard to fight a man or a nation that has an unrighted wrong as ally. And then maybe with the race right conceded there would be no fight; for the Slav also has reason and justice in him.

Of all the races of Europe the Slav has best learned the value of patience, that all things come to him who can wait. He bides his time. There is a Slav proverb that the past belongs to the Latin; the present to the Teuton; the future to the Slav. Certainly Russian patience is the antithesis of the French impatience. But then the Slav as a race power is young; and youth means the possibility of growth and ever-increasing strength; while the Latin - it is the story over again of forty and the wrinkles. Or is it sixty, and the gray hairs? and the vanished youth which comes not back again? Looking to the future there are only two great powers to the world, the Teuton and the Slav; for both are young; the Slav with a youth undeveloped; the Teuton with a youth renewed by migration and new lands. Between them they practically possess the yet unpeopled and habitable portions of the temperate zone; and they are able to hold them. Herein is the guaranty of the future. Even the myriad Mongols have not this. But the Teuton holds also the sea.

There is, however, still another, and as yet not fully developed factor to the problem. While the Slav has shown faith in himself, and the power of cohesion and unity of purpose, he has not thus far shown the mental alertness and the individual initiative which are characteristic especially of the English-speaking Teuton, and which are essential to the highest grade of race success. Whether the capacity is simply dormant in the Slav, and with suitable opportunity will arouse to active exercise, is the question. A strong argument in the negative is the fact that while these traits in the English Teuton seem always to have been active, even when his civilization was still as infantile as that of the Slav, yet the Slav shows no signs of their existence in him to any effective degree. The fatal weakness of the Latin is also apparently the weakness of the Slav, a failure to recognize and develop the individual man as the basic unit of race progress. The result is a lack of the capacity of the initiative in the individual man. He always waits to be led in religion - in politics - in war, whether martial or industrial. And it is the opposite of this that gives to the Teuton, and especially to the English Teuton, his power. With him the individual does not have to be led; each man is born a leader; they only have to combine. And it is to be remembered that the army industrial is with each year becoming more potent in the contest for race supremacy than even the army militant. And it is also to be remembered that in the army industrial the successful captains come up from the ranks. In the war militant the Russo-Japanese conflict reveals the disastrous effect of generations of mental repression in the Slav. It has revealed also the awakening influence of even a single generation of mental freedom in the Japanese. The progress of the contest has shown more clearly than ever before that it is not so much the difference in arms and numbers as it is the difference in quickness and alertness of thought which is to decide the issues of modern warfare. The Slav forces have been comparatively helpless in the presence of the complicated problems of modern militarism. Upon the water, the fleet of the Slav has been an unmanageable machine in his hands. The nimbleness and the alertness of the Japanese mind have outranked him. His ponderous slowness has been helpless before the more agile and ready foe.

Neither has the Slav thus far shown signs of possessing the mechanical and scientific aptitudes which have become modern essentials to the higher type of race success; and without these elements of race constitution he has little chance in the modern battling for race supremacy. His success thus far has been the success of the Persian or of Genghis Khan; but the time is rapidly nearing, if not already upon the world, when a Darius or a Genghis Khan is no longer among the possibilities. Mere brute force has had its day. An army of witless Samsons would be helpless in the hands of a force of schoolmen. The soldier, whether of the army militant or the army industrial, must now think. It is brain, not brawn, that is to decide the modern race battle. The Slav has brawn. Has he also the brain? - the Western brain; not the Oriental? Upon this question much of his future as a race hinges.

There is, however, yet another element of uncertainty in the future of the Slav; and it is one over which he can in the very nature of things have no control. The Graeco-Latin migrated south of the normal race habitat of the Aryan stock. Twice has he shown the resultant race decay. The first time an infusion of kindred blood coming fresh from the normal climatic home of the Aryan peoples saved him from apparently impending extinction. The second decadence, setting in as the southern climate again began to undermine his original northern vigor, is now upon him. The Slav, upon the contrary, has moved northward of the normal Aryan habitat. And much of the Slav homeland of the future lies still farther toward the north. From a dweller in the mid-temperate zone he has become an inhabitant of subarctic lands. What is to be the ultimate effect of this radical change of climatic homeland upon the stock? for excess of cold is no less inimical to the development of the higher types of civilization than excess of heat. There is a northern as well as southern limit to the climatic belt of civilization. The subarctic climatic belt has never yet given rise to an indigenous civilization. Can it even succeed in perpetuating the higher type of an imported civilization? How much of the un-Aryan mental slowness and torpor of the Slav may be due to the influence of an unfriendly climate, how much to the historically presumptive admixture of the stolid Mongol blood, is a question. Through inability to contend with the rigors of the harsher northern climates the earliest successful efforts of primitive man to rise from barbarism were necessarily restricted to the regions of the subtropics. A growing knowledge of the mechanic arts, and the consequent increased ability to battle successfully with nature, moved the possible climatic belt of civilization ten degrees northward from the subtropic shores of the Mediterranean to the more rigorous regions of Mid-Europe. Will increasing knowledge make possible a further extension to the subarctic lands of the inhospitable north? Time only can decide. Yet the probabilities are against it; for an abundant and nutritious supply of food, easily obtainable, is essential to the development and continuance of civilization; and food production is dependent, not upon mechanical, but upon natural laws. The mid-temperate climatic belt will probably remain, as it ever has been, the great meat- and grain-producing belt of the world. And here, in this milder, more equable mid-temperate belt, not only is man at his best both physically and mentally, but here also the summer's toil yields a surplus of production beyond the winter's needs; and it is this surplus which makes possible that stored-up capital which is one of the elements of advancement and power.

The Slav of Russia can hardly be said as yet to have found himself. He was exploited as a people first by the Swede; then by the German; not yet by himself. His own time is still to come. And even in the exploiting there has been an arrested evolution; for the Slav stood once where the Englishman stood before the days of King John and Runnymede. He, too, had his feudal days. The autocracy was not always an autocracy. The Romanoff was elected to office, and was limited in power by restrictive oath of coronation. In the year 1613 the Boyars, those Slav barons of the older Russian empire, sent out a call to the clergy, the nobility, and the citizens of the Russian land to convene by deputies in the ancient capital, Moscow, there in national assembly to elect a new Czar. It was the last time the popular voice was heard in the government of Russia. Michael Romanoff was chosen; not as first choice, but after withdrawal of other names. And Michael, the first royal Romanoff, was required to take oath of office, as were the old English kings, swearing "To protect religion, to declare amnesty for past political offenses, to make no new laws nor to alter the old ways unless dire necessity made imperative, and that in important causes he would decide nothing by himself; that the existing legal forms should remain in force; that he would not at his own pleasure make either war or peace with other nations; and that he would hold no lands or estates in himself." It is much such an oath as that exacted of those early kings of the English land, "To govern well, and to abide by the ancient ways"; only it is even more restrictive of the royal power. Yet out of it has come the absolutism of the Romanoffs of the last three centuries; and this is not the "ancient way" of the Slav. There was an older and a freer way, as there was an England of an older and freer way before the days of King John; but the Russian Boyars failed to call for an accounting; and the Russian land has in its history no Runnymede, and no Magna Charta such as the stern-willed Barons wrung from autocrizing John. This was where medieval Russia stopped short in her national evolution.

And then came the retrogression to the Asiatic type; for even medievalism died with the Boyars; and that ill-laid, old despotic ghost of the two and a half centuries of Mongol domination came to life again in its stead. Maybe the lingering tradition of the Mongol rule of the thirteenth and fourteenth centuries only hastened the retrogression; yet, whatever the more occult causation, this much is clear, that with the coming of the Romanoffs to power the older, freer Russia died, and in its place grew up the autocracy and the absolutism.

Will the Slav of the Russian land find himself again? Much of his race history in the future hinges upon the answer which he may be able to give to the question. Ages of oppression and of repression have rendered largely dormant the race capacity for organization and cooperation; but judging from the history of the other branches of the Aryan peoples who have emerged from the age of repression, the capacity is only dormant, and will, with opportunity, arouse to activity. And if ages of oppression and of repression have been doing the harm, it need not be wondered at, if years, maybe generations, are needed to undo it. It was so with the Teuton; and the Teutonic peoples surely may be patient with their brother, the Slav, if the throes of his regeneration travail should prove to be tedious. It is so that liberty is born. And true liberty is born; not purchased with a price, or granted as a favor. It is free-born Paul versus the *freed* Roman captain over again.

Chapter Eleven - The Teuto-Aryan

It has been the custom with many writers to designate the great wave of Aryan blood which swept over Western Europe north of the Rhine, as the Germanic wave. Yet the unfitness of thus designating the general wave by a name ordinarily given to only one, and that probably a later, stream of the common folk blood, is apparent upon even slight research. Even the word itself is an alien to the folk speech, a Latinized word of possibly Celtic origin applied by the Romans to the border tribes which lay nearest to them on the north shores of the Rhine. Teuton, the Latinized form of an older folk name, is better, as it has by custom taken upon itself a wider signification than the "German" of later writers. For this Aryan folk of the midwest was not German. Flowing westward as a common Aryan current it, as the ages went by, differentiated itself into the separate peoples who came to be known through after-times by such names as Norse folk, Jutes, Danes, Saxons, Germans, Dutch, Engles (English); but in the speech of them all was a folk name of common root origin which in Gothic became Thieuda, in Anglo-Saxon Theod, in old High-German Diutisc, in modern German Deutsch, and which in the Latinized form comes to us in modern English as Teuton the primitive root of all meaning the *folk,* or *people.* It is this name which was thus common to all that is best suited to become the common race designation.

With all the differences of climate and of many of the physical surroundings, there is yet in some respects a striking analogy between the first home of the Teuton by the western sea and that of his Graeco-Latin kinsman upon the south. Take a map of Europe. Mark the Aegean land, with its clustering islands filling the narrow seas even before one comes to the mainland of Greece. Invert it and place it beside the clustered islands and the mainland of Denmark. They are not dissimilar in area and grouping; the one jutting southward into the outflow of the Black Sea; the other northward into the outflow of the Baltic; each backed up, the one upon the north, the other upon the south, by the great Alpine center of Europe. Trace the waterways. From the Aegean lead out northeastward the water roads of the Black Sea and of the Azov. From the Danish shores reach out toward north and east the far-spreading waters of the Baltic and its branches. Westward of the one is the broad expanse of the Ionian Sea; to the west of the other the broad waters of the German Ocean. Skirting the shore northward from the one lies the narrow strait of Otranto; and looking across one sees the hills of the beginning of Magna Graecia, and of that other Graeco-Latin land which in the ages after was to be Rome. From the strait opens out the long reach of the Adriatic. Skirting southward from the other, one looks across from the shores of France to the white cliffs of Dover where was to be the Rome of the Teutonic man; and yet southward is the long line of the English Channel; and across the Irish Sea that other Sardinia of the Teuton. It is, to say the least, an interesting analogy this between the first lines of settlement of the two great westward currents of Aryan blood, the Graeco-Latin and the Teuton - these two which the testings of time and stress have shown to be abiding parent streams; for all other peoples within their borders are disappearing before them, or else may be classed as offshoots or descendants from them.

What was it that made these two homelands, which are so strikingly alike in physical outlines, the starting-points of two civilizations which were destined between them to give shape and tone to a world? Was it the stir, the variety, the broader possibilities of existence in these island domains that aroused the only half-awakened race bloods to a keener throb of life? The answer may possibly be found as we trace the successive steps of the race development amid these new environments. Yet there were differences, marked, radical differences, as well as similarities. The analogy holds only partly true. The climatic characteristics of the Aegean and Italic centers have already been discussed. The differences will appear in the answer to the question –

What Did the Teuton Find in His New Homeland?

The shores of the Baltic were probably the first continued halting-place of the Teuto-Aryan in his westward march from his primitive homeland. Geographically he has gone 12° of latitude north of the presumptive original race home in the farther interior of the continent. Climatically, however, owing to the tempering influence of the great on-shore air currents of the Atlantic, which carry the mildness of the ocean inland over Western Europe, he is still upon his native isothermal line of 50°. Only, there is this difference, the climate is more equable.

Instead of the fierce, parching heat of the inland plateaus beating down from the midsummer sky, the summer sun now is tempered by the mists and the vapors of an air heavily charged with moisture, and is thus robbed of a portion of its power. It is the softened sheen of this excess of moisture in the skies which gives so much of what artists call "atmosphere" to the landscapes of the Dutch painters, an effect lacking in the work of the Mediterranean schools. Instead, also, of the keen, dry, winter air of the continental uplands he now has the damp chill of the sea. He has left a homeland of light summer rainfall and has come where the summer sky drips with the condensed moisture from off the northward expansion of the Gulf Stream. He has left behind him the clear skies of the interior; he has come to dwell where the sun looks out feebly through the thick vapors and the drifting clouds of the low west coasts. He has come from an average annual rainfall of possibly twelve to fifteen inches to a yearly precipitation of from thirty inches upward. He has left the elevated plateaus and mountain slopes, and has made his home in lands hardly safe from the overflow of the high spring tides. But he still dwells in the land of the beech, the oak, the apple, the pear, the cherry, the hawthorn. He still as of old cultivates the wheat and barley, tho less successfully, but finds in the rye and oats a tolerable, even if coarser, substitute. And even more than of old is he in the grass belt, and is becoming a pastoral man and a dairyman. The *duhitar* of his olden Proto-Aryan tongue is now become the *milkmaid* of the new.

In the long migration across the midlands of Europe with flocks and herds, and through the range of the deer, the elk, the bear, the wild boar, he became of necessity, as already stated, more of a meat-eater, less a consumer of grain and fruits. This change of diet has been favored by the strong appetite and the vigorous digestion which would come of the outdoor, migratory life; just as the emigrant upon the plains of the Humboldt or the Columbia loses taste for the more delicate vegetable foods of a settled civilization, and craves the more nourishing diet of pork and beans which constitute the favorite fare of the plains. To the diet of meat he now in the home by the sea adds fish; for the waters of the deep become to him a new and exhaustless source of food supply. The damp chill of the newer seacoast home, with its call for the generation of increased bodily warmth to resist that rapid abstraction of vital heat which comes with a chill moist atmosphere, has helped in the change; until now, under this strong stimulating diet, the spare, rather thin-blooded man of the higher, drier inland plains has been transformed into the full-blooded, more fleshy man of the seacoast. And now after the long march of centuries he settles down once more in a fixed home. The waters of the ocean put a check to the migratory life. Hamlet and village and town spring up amid the openings of the beech-woods, and along the shores of inlet and river, with the forest line of the "Mark" between. And now also a new factor enters into the race molding of this branch of the westward-moving Aryan folk, as it had come earlier to that other branch which moved westward along the more southerly line.

For the first time in his long migration, in fact, for the first time in his history as a people, the Teuton becomes a dweller by the waters of the sea, and under conditions similar to those which made of his Greek kinsman a man of ships and of seafaring. He, also, this man of the Baltic, has found dwelling-place upon the shores of a partially sheltered inland sea, dotted with islands, amid whose quieter waters he would be tempted to launch his first rude crafts to reach the islands beyond, and to add to his food supply from the fisheries which he would quickly discover within the sheltered channels. It is well again to consider that of all the Aryan folk who have reached the waters of the sea only these two, the Englo-Norse amid the sheltered islands of the lower Baltic, and the Greek amid the equally sheltered islands of the Aegean, have ever developed the true seaman instinct. To all others, the Hindu, the Roman and his descendants, to the German even, the sea has always been only as a foreign realm upon which they have never been entirely at home. Tho they have after a fashion taken to the sea, yet it has always been to them as an unnatural thing. They have remained always essentially landsmen. The Roman fought his fleets as he would have fought a legion of infantry. His descendants never have met the Englo-Norse man upon the sea on equal terms, whether in the old Viking days, or in the waters of the English Channel, or off Trafalgar, or at Santiago or Manila. The German even, he of the midlands of Europe, has only thus far taken to the sea as a second nature, and reluctantly, as one who is not there at home. Is this apparent absence of the sea instinct in so many branches of the common Aryan blood to be attributed to the lack of a suitable training-field for the race while still in its infancy, when its habits as a race were yet forming? The ponderous sweep of the surf, rolling in from an ocean whose horizon is unbroken by island or sheltering port, would not tempt the frail craft which must be the first ships of primitive man. Rather, in despair at the immensity beyond, he turns back to the plains and the solid hills which stand fast, and which he knows, and so remains a landsman. But with the branch of the race which came upon the comparatively sheltered waters of the Danish archipelago, as with the Greek of the Aegean, it would be different. The still waters would not frighten him back from launching his rude boat, while the numerous islands dotting the sea within sight of the shore and within easy distance of each other, with the refuge of their sheltering ports, would ever tempt him on until, growing bolder with each new venture, the sea habit would become fixed upon him, and be passed on as a transmitted instinct to his children. Then, too, as already said, it is only in the sheltered and shoal waters of these inner seas that the primitive man found the fishing-grounds which supplied him with new and valuable sources of food. The shell mound and the kitchen midden are to be seen everywhere about the shores of the Baltic, never upon the shores of the open Atlantic.

In this new home the true development of a separate and distinct folk life began for the Teutonic peoples. A deep-seated climatic prompting possibly had guided them in the line of migration and the selection of a new race home; possibly race pressure from peoples preoccupying the lands had deflected and forced them along the lines of migration which they followed; and then the law of grades, and of food supply. Whatever the underlying causes which led or forced them to the Baltic shores, they there found a soil suited to the development of the peculiar type of the Teutonic mind. Life upon the shores of the Baltic was for primitive races a different thing from life about the shores of the Graeco-Latin lands of the East Mediterranean, and it could not but leave its impress upon the type of man to whom it became a permanent race home. The Graeco-Latin found sunny skies, an atmosphere not surcharged with moisture, a warm welldrained soil, friendly to the plant life of fruits and cereals. In it he quickly grew and developed, as a flower transplanted to the favoring influences of genial surroundings. To him the race life became a daily joy and gladness. The Teuton, on the contrary, found an inhospitable shore, overcast through much of the year with somber dripping skies; a soil ill-drained, cold and sour through excess of ground-water and unfavorable to the growth of fruit and grain, covered with dark forests, the haunt of wolf and bear; and before him a cold and rigorous sea. To him life, the race life in the new home, was a battle; and the physical battle and the race environments left their trace deeply stamped upon the race type. The gloomy skies, the roar of the November gales, and the hoarse bellowing of the seas as they roll inland and break upon the sullen coasts, are factors in the race evolution which have left an indelible stamp. It shows itself in the somber undertone of tragedy which is so markedly characteristic of the Teutonic mind, a tragedy finding relief from its depressing gloom at times in the broad humor which has in it ever the echo of a sob. There is, indeed, an underlying vein of tragedy in the whole Aryan blood; in some strains lightening as the ages go by; in some only deepening to a more somber gloom. It is especially in the line of the spiritual nature that this is to be traced in the various branches of the kin.

Every religion may be viewed as composed of three elements:

1. The special revelation or teaching upon which it is based.
2. The modifying influences of race character and race environments.
3. The coloring or warping which comes of previous beliefs.

In making a study of comparative religions this last is always to be taken into account and allowed for. As an instance may be cited the modifying influence of Judaeism upon early Christianity as shown in the disputes and contentions of the Judaeic and Hellenic disciples in the primitive church. The whole after spiritual life of the Aryan peoples is tinged and modified by an element of tragedy born apparently away back somewhere in the obscurity of the common Proto-Aryan origin. It is shown in that old Graeco-Latin myth of the Fates, the Erinyes of the Greek, the Norns of the Teuton - in all, a doom that is stronger than men, stronger even than the gods; and which in its stern demands is never satisfied until the full tale has been paid, and which knows nothing of gentleness and mercy and truth. It is fate, hard, inexorable, and which crushes alike under its remorseless feet evil and good; in whose power man is a helpless victim, and who even if forewarned can not escape the doom which is upon him. And the doom is irrespective of merit or demerit. Possibly, probably, back of it all lay a nature-myth, the slumbering memory of the time when primitive man, untrained, unskilled, unarmed, was as yet helpless against storm and flood and famine and savage beast; and "one event came alike to all." The writer of Ecclesiastes that day of soul despondency only voiced afar the inarticulate cry of the ruder primitive folk.

In the Greek mythology the working of this doctrine of fate, inexorable, unchanging, is best shown in the legends which cluster about Thebes with Oedipus as their central figure, and in the series of calamities which close down as a black cloud upon the doomed family, a doom in no way connected with moral questions, or guilt upon the part of the sufferers. Laios, king of Thebes, is warned by the oracle that if he beget a son that son's hand shall slay him. Oedipus being born to him, he exposes the infant child in the forest to die that the doom may be averted. The child, found by a woodsman, is carried to Korinth, and there reared by King Polybos. Grown to manhood, and stung by questions of his birth, he consults the Delphic oracle about his parentage, but only to receive the misleading reply, not to return to his native land as he is destined to slay his father and marry his own mother; but with fateful cruelty the warning words give no intimation of the true land of his birth. Filled with horror at the thought of what is predicted, and believing Polybos to be his father, and Korinth his native land, he strives to escape the doom by fleeing to Thebes. Thus in his anxiety to escape the impending doom, and to avoid the commission of the crimes, he blindly pursues the surest course to the fulfilment. Upon the road in a quarrel he slays a man who, unknown to him, is the king of Thebes and the father the shedding of whose blood he had been striving to avoid. Proceeding to Thebes, in return for a great public service, the slaying of the Sphinx, he receives in marriage the hand of the queen, his own mother, and is made king. And now the doom thickens. Because of the slaying of King Laios and the incestuous marriage, pestilence desolates the land; and again the oracle demands that to stay its ravages the murderer of King Laios must be found and punished. In the search which follows, the whole hideous array of facts is brought to light. Queen Jokasta, in horror at the marriage with her own son, hangs herself. Oedipus, unwilling longer to see the pure light of day, puts out his own eyes, and expelled from the city by his sons, becomes a wanderer, cared for in his helplessness only by his two faithful daughters, while the sons, apparently under doom of a curse from the father for their unnatural deed, yet really under the still uncompleted doom of the fated family, fall by each other's hands in a fratricidal struggle for the possession of the city, the city itself being finally taken by foes and razed to the ground. It was the Fates - the Fates that are stronger than the gods, and that change not.

A legend somewhat similar in its fateful ending hung over the early history of the Teuton, passing on as a common heirloom to the various branches of that folk; and this came of the slaying of Otter, not by men who become the innocent sufferers, but by the gods. In this case the doom was connected with the curse of the dwarf Andvari upon the hoard of gold of which he is deprived by the gods in order to pay their ransom of blood money for the offense of the slaying; and from thence forward the curse carries doom and death to the possessor of the hoard, however innocent or unconscious of his fate. And by a baleful doom all men covet the hoard. But the curse never lifts until the hoard is forever sunk beneath the waters of the Rhine; and not then until the strength of the Nibleungs, its last possessors, goes forth to its final doom in King Atli's land. And back of this, too, lies Fate - Fate that is stronger than the gods, and that changes not.

This somber cloud of fate seems to have hung over the spiritual sky of the whole Aryan kin back in a common race home, for it left its legacy to all the scattered branches, tingeing and shading their whole after religious life. With some the cloud seems to have lifted earlier than with others. Under the sunny skies of the Mediterranean, as man became more and more master of his material surroundings, and as life grew easier to the toiling race of men, the cloud lightened until the Christianity of the southlands, as spiritual successor of the older faith, cast aside the inherited soul gloom and took upon it a more hopeful cast. The Teuton, on the contrary, with his harsh, rigorous clime, his inhospitable land, and stormy seas, helpless for so long in the hands of nature, was slower to cast off the incubus of the old myths; and the stern, inexorable Norns, to whom even the gods were subject, passed on to deepen the gloom of Puritanism and to give shape and color to the fateful doctrine of predestination. It is a curious thought, how far the doctrine of predestination as found in the creed of the Calvinist may be only the lingering survival of that older Teutonic myth of the Norns - fate that is stronger than the gods. It is a strangely curious thing, too, how these old soul battles of the primitive fathers reappear in the spiritual struggles of the far-off generations of the children. Was Calvin only the lineal descendant spiritually of that older ProtoAryan man in his despairing efforts to solve that still unsolvable question of the unending battle between good and evil? The myth of the Fates was the common Aryan confession of failure in the presence of the great unsolvable mystery. Is the later doctrine of predestination only the same confession over again? And is the hard, hopeless, merciless theology of Jonathan Edwards only a far-off echo of the hopeless death-song of Gunnar in the adder pit?

At the root of it all is fate; fate stronger than the will of man; fate stronger than the kindly mercy of God; fate, in whose hands man is only as a hapless, helpless atom in the grasp of a power that is inexorable and remorseless as tho he were not. In the vain struggle to reconcile these, the irreconcilable, fate and the abounding mercy of God, the Puritan soul writhed in an agony of self-torment which killed out the joy and the gladness of life.

Yet back of the tragedy in the Aryan soul was a saner, truer germ which ever in the end reasserted itself; and it came from his close touch with nature. As that older Teuton felt the stir of the green-wood and the thrill of the morning breeze enter into his being, and as the broad sweet life of the material world about him dawned upon him and the struggle for daily bread became less crushing, there began to grow up within him hope, and a brighter faith. Balder the Beautiful, the Northland Apollo, god of the northward coming sun, and of the springtime, and bursting blossoms, and of the glad glint of the sunlight afar upon the seas, came to the Teutonic soul to soften and humanize that stern old pre-Christian belief, as the wild rose twining about and shedding its fragrance over the gnarled and twisted trunk of some ancient oak. And then back of the Aesir, back of Balder, back of the Norns even, ever smoldered as an undying ember the hinting of Ragnarök, and the wreck of all things that were, and then the coming somewhere out from the depths of space of "All-Fader," with whom there is neither pitiless fate, nor "variableness, neither shadow of turning," but who is the bearer of "every good and perfect gift"; and he would right all wrongs, and make all things new in a new heaven and a new earth free from evil or stain. Ragnarök was the Northland Apocalypse. It is the primitive monotheism of the Proto-Aryan reasserting itself after the ages. The Puritan for a little while forgot Balder and "All-Fader"; his children are beginning to remember. Like the echo of an old, long-forgotten song float back to them the words of one who, ages before Jonathan Edwards and Calvin, had said, "Like as a father pitieth his children so the Lord pitieth them that fear him. For he knoweth our frame; he remembereth we are dust"; - and those other words of one who said, "For God so loved the world -"

But scarcely yet, in the noonday light of the twentieth century, is this soul struggle of the Aryan man over; for bewildered and helpless in the midst of the only as yet half-comprehended machinery of a civilization which is become his master, the individual turns startled, despairing, as his fathers did of old before the forces of nature. This Aryan man stands to-day awed in the presence of the powers he has conjured up. The far-reaching, elusive forces of the civilization he has builded are become to him as the shadowy forms about Faust. Whether, as Faust, he shall cower before them; or whether, as Manfred, he shall go down crushed, yet defiant; or whether he shall become their master, and hold fast to the old faith in "All-Fader," and the ultimate triumph of good, is the mental and spiritual problem of modern civilization as it stands face to face with the future.

The after-development of the spiritual life of the Teuton will be taken up in the race history of the Engle folk to whom it came as the common Teutonic inheritance. Yet this might here be said for all the Teutonic peoples in common: The men of the North, the Teutons of Mid-Europe and the Baltic and Atlantic shores, never at heart accepted Christianity in its Romanized form. Their faith always held in it the possibility of Protestantism and the Reformation. It only required time, and the occasion, to make of the latent possibility an accomplished fact. And time and the occasion came to what were only smoldering embers; for the old fires of the free primitive Northland faith had never quite died out. It was the Christianity of Woden and the All-Father casting off the Christianity of Jupiter and the Pontifex Maximus. For Teuton, Latin, Slav, have each taken the Judaeic Christianity, and with the older faiths as starting-points have made of it a religion patterned to the needs and the genius of their separate peoples. In this racial fact lies the hopelessness of the struggle which the Roman spiritual imperium is ever making, yet ever unsuccessfully, to regain that medieval catholic power which it apparently lost, but which it never really possessed. The deep-rooted law of race types is against Rome. The Teutonic temperament has never taken kindly to the imperium whether in state or church. There is always the spirit of protest against overlordship whether in religion or politics. Teutonic Rolf the Ganger spoke for soul as well as body that day upon the waters of the Seine when to the inquiries of Latin Charles he made reply: "We have no master. We are all equal."

If the race lines could be yet traced it would be a matter of much interest to know whether the little groups of South-European non-Catholic communities which, despite ages of persecution, have always retained their own separate race and religious life, are not really only isolated remnants of the north blood still retaining its purity from the times of that Teutonic invasion which overthrew the civil power of Rome. If not, we have presented to us the anomaly of small and feeble groups of a common blood contravening the race law by establishing, and age after age maintaining, a community and religious life separate and distinct from that of the common kin. Is the blood of the old Woden-worshipers flowing in the veins of the Waldenses? and are they blood kin to the Puritan? Their faith is the faith, not of the Latin, but of the Northland?

Chapter Twelve - The German

In Mid-Europe is the Germanic Teuton standing like a great rock rising out of the sea. The waves of the nations have beat upon it, often dashing over it, sometimes apparently submerging it, yet as the years have gone by the waves have retreated and still the rock has stood. In the way of all races, a bar across their paths, his lands have been the battle-ground of the centuries. Often overrun, he has never been subjugated. That old wail over the lost legions of Varus has never quite died out on the air of the ages, and may go up yet again over other legions. The necessity which made of the Germans who stood across the pathway of the Caesars a nation of warriors makes of the Germans of to-day a nation of warriors still. No other race of Europe occupies a position at once so masterful and so vulnerable. If the German is not shut in, neither also is the foe shut out. Open upon all sides to attack, with no natural boundaries or lines of defense, constant watchfulness and an ever-readiness to repel invasion are the price of safety. But the same conditions which make him so peculiarly vulnerable make him also equally a menace to his neighbors. The mere fact that thus exposed, and often overrun, the German has survived and held his own, is proof of the inherent vitality and virility of the race.

Rapidly increasing in numbers, and even now cramped for land, whither is the German going? The fifty-six millions of the German Empire will soon have the ten millions of Germans in the Austrian Empire added to them.

About these, so nearly allied in blood and thought that their race destiny must be the same, are ten millions more. Possessed of high mechanical skill, having the capacity for organization in a marked degree, full of confidence in themselves, beginning again to show a race unrest which is one of the portents of the times, the German peoples to-day are in much the same condition as in the fifth century, when they overflowed into the fertile plains of upper Italy. But whither are they to go this time? Lack of land has always been the weakness of the German. It is his weakness now. There was a greater Latin land; there is a greater Slav land, and a greater English land; but where is there a possibility of a greater German land? Not tributary territory, but homeland. Germany as a consolidated power came upon the scene too late in the era of discovery and settlement to secure available territory for colonization. The desirable regions of the temperate zone, such as might have been made a homeland for Germanic peoples, a greater German land, had already been monopolized by other nations. Colonization into such new and unoccupied lands is no longer possible to the German upon any extended scale, for the untaken lands which he may yet secure will not breed Germans. The Teutonic climatic belt of the outer lands is now in other hands, and hands able to hold it. Is Germany fated to be, like Ireland, only a feeder of other races, sending out ever a stream of emigration which is lost, not simply to the fatherland, but to the German peoples as well? It is the history of her emigration in the past. That Germany should save her emigration to the Germanic peoples it is absolutely necessary that she should secure a new homeland for them, a land in which they would neither be absorbed by another race, and so lose their identity as Germans, nor through unfavorable climatic surroundings become so modified in type as to be no longer German in race characteristics. The ultimate and enduring factor in the problem of race power is the home; not what can it conquer, but where can it abide, and fill the land with its homes? - this is the vital question. It was the lack of homeland that was the fatal weakness in the Phoenician domination.

But where is such a land to be found for the German? The Monroe Doctrine bars the way in the Western Continent; neither is the temperate region of South America unoccupied, even if the Monroe Doctrine were not in the way. Russia controls Central and Eastern Asia. Africa has little to offer. The islands of the seas which might be secured are tropical. Down the valley of the Danube to the sea is a backward road not impossible to him, yet there are many obstacles, for there lies that mixed population of Eastern Europe which, whatever else it may be, is not German, not even in sympathy, Slav rather. Even the Turk is at heart kindlier to the half-Asiatic Russian than to the European German, and would more readily and willingly submit to him as master. When the sick man of Europe dies it will be found that, so far as the Turk had power, the Russian is the preferred heir. The Russian of all European men best knows how to manage the Mohammedan and the Asiatic without antagonizing them. Asia Minor, with its sparse population and its not too enervating climate, and its rich possibilities of soil and commerce, might serve as a new German homeland, but between are still the Slav and the Turk. And then with the Black Sea practically only a Russian lake, and the Caspian entirely so; and with Russia already south of the Caucasus .and the province of Trans-Caucasia in her possession; she will have an active voice in the disposal of that portion of the sick man's estate when the time of his demise shall have come. Eliminate Russia from the problem and the solution would be easy for the German; but whether, with her organized forces to head the battle, any combination will prove able to keep back the Slav from forcing his way by sheer bulk out through the Dardanelles and over the lands of Asia Minor, is an open question, with the chances ultimately in favor of the Slav.

And then no other great power of Europe is so debarred from expansion beyond the seas as Germany. Her hands are tied by the vulnerability of her home position, and her environment upon all sides by rival and hostile nations. The thought of her own home safety will not let her become involved in any serious complications afar; there are .too many close about her who are watching for, and are only too ready to take advantage of, such a mistake. Her expansion must be in the future, as it has been in the past, close at home, and upon continuous lines, absorbing and assimilating as she goes, with continuity of territory unbroken, so that the strength of her whole army may in case of necessity be quickly rallied at any danger-point for home defense. To depart from this policy is to invite disaster.

If the valley of the Danube had drained southward to the Adriatic instead of eastward to the Black Sea, the problem of the Germanic race future would have settled itself long ago. Yet, despite mountain chains, the railway and the tunnel, and the shorter line to the high sea, together with the feebler race resistance, will probably take him southward, for the Alps are less formidable than the Slav. And then there is that slow but sure influence of a climatic longing which is ever at work drawing the races of the earth away from the rigors of the north to the milder skies of southern lands. Whichever way the German may spread, he must dispossess or absorb those who lie before him, or be absorbed. The German has been in the valley of the Po and about the shores of the Adriatic before; he will surely be there again. Then he found Rome; now there is no Rome. His second march southward may be by the peaceful conquest of overflow and gradual settlement; it may be by the more sudden conquest of war. There was a Cis-Alpine Gaul. Why may there not be a Cis-Alpine Germany? The Latin is approaching a standstill in population; even beginning to show signs of dying out; the German rapidly multiplying; and the roads of the Caesars to Mid-Europe have been traveled backward before. They may be again. And then the Latin is at last taking race hold upon North Africa. To that older Latin of Rome it was somehow an impossible race home; to the modern Latin it seems less so. He is beginning to migrate to it. Race pressure from behind, that *vis a tergo* of the schoolmen, might hasten the process and leave a clearer field for the German upon the north shores of the sea. It would only be repeating an old happening in the race history of the Aryan peoples. It is largely the history of the Celt before the Teuton. It is to be remembered also that while the older Latin had the Phoenician before him upon the African shore, there is no Phoenician now. That masterful sea-lord left only a progeny of petty pirates. He, too, felt the debasing and undermining curse of mixed bloods.

The *ausgang* of the German of the twenty-first century is a possibility not simply by way of the eastern roads of the Caesars over the low passes of the Julian Alps, but by the western roads as well. "Die Wacht am Rhein" may again become "Die Wacht am Rhone." It was so in the fifth century. History has recorded stranger cycles. And the German will yet again rest one arm upon the North Sea and the Baltic and the other upon the Adriatic as master. He will again bisect Europe. Not necessarily in this generation, nor the next, but in the times to come. Poland was the sick man of Europe of the eighteenth century; the Turk is the sick man of the nineteenth; Austria will be the sick man of the twentieth; the Latin - he may not wait for the twenty-first, for the pace of the nations is accelerating.

Napoleon's dream of a second Roman empire failed because there was no second Roman people. The race blood was exhausted. The intense life and the vices of that older Roman empire had consumed it. A second German empire, however, is a possibility, because the half-barbaric yet moral and wholesome stir of national life in the first great German empire did not exhaust the race. It became as the premature swelling of the buds of an early spring, only to be checked and set back by the chill of the Middle-Age darkness, but now again to expand and have fruitage in the midsummer of modern civilization. Charlemagne may yet again sit upon his throne. Yet the fact that the German is largely barred from the broader world-field, and can only gain further homeland by wresting territory from, or absorbing, his neighbors, means a comparatively slow growth, with a constant loss by emigration to non-Germanic lands. Outside of Europe, and especially in America, his future apparently is to be bound up in the broader race life of the whole Teutonic peoples, the German to become only one of the component parts of the stronger life of the greater Teuton land. Because of this the German bids fair to lag behind the Slav and the English man in a distinctively national growth.

The future of the German is not without peril, moreover, even in Europe. An ever-present danger is upon him. The Slav does not love him; for the German power more than any other stands across the pathway to Constantinople and the open sea. And the Latin hates him; race instinct will not let the offspring of imperial Rome forget Charlemange, and that early Germanic empire which seized upon the domain of the Caesars and ruled the Latin land from the Tiber to the mountain wall of the Pyrenees. In these two facts lies the secret of the Franco-Russian alliance. It is not that France and Russia love each other. Moscow, and the tramp of Alexander's Cossacks through the streets of Paris, are not so very far back in the past. The French Revolution and Russian Absolutism joining hands! - the very unnaturalness of the alliance betrays the powerful motives which must lie behind it. It is an alliance of France's seeking; and she sought it, not because she loved Russia or had race sympathy with her, but because she hated Germany, and would have revenge. And despotic Russia consents, not because she has friendship for republican France, but because it gives her a checkmate to German power in her plans for expansion in Southern Europe. And between the two the German is as the grist between the upper and the nether millstones.

Germany has before her the most difficult problem of all the great nations of Europe. Surrounded by hostile peoples, with no natural lines of defense, overcrowded, no longer able to feed herself, she must to insure safety keep an army as strong as any possible combination against her, while to insure food supply she must be able to command freedom of the seas; and her resources are not, and can not be made, equal to this double task. Britain, with all her vast resources, has had only the one necessity upon her, for the Channel is her army of defense. Behind it as a safeguard, as Tyre upon her island stronghold, she has been able to throw almost her whole strength into her navy. It has made her mistress of the seas. The command of the seas by the English peoples is Germany's constant menace in times of political combinations; and it is an insuperable weakness, for whatever might have been the German hope of overthrow of the power of the English man of Britain, the rise of the Greater England beyond the seas has effectually and for all time made it an impossibility. Germany's one hope, her only ultimate safety as against Latin and Slavic Europe, is in alliance with the other Teutonic peoples of West Europe, notably the English-speaking people, and through these with the Greater England beyond the seas. Without this close alliance with the Greater Teuton land she stands isolated and restricted in sphere of influence; with it, she shares in the larger race destiny and has Mid-Europe from sea to sea as her own. The fleet of Britain is even now, altho German pride is loth to recognize the fact, Germany's greatest safeguard against the continental perils which beset her. But suppose Britain also hostile - what then?

But in it all is another and more subtle danger to the German future from which even tardy alliance with her kin can not save her. How long can the German people endure the strain of even her present enormous and disproportionate armaments without exhaustion? The overmilitarism of Germany is as the overtraining of the athlete; for the time there is an excessive development of muscle and apparent vigor, but it is at the expense of enduring vitality. It is invariably followed by premature exhaustion. France under Napoleon is an instance to the point. No race, no nation, can habitually go beyond the limit of its normal strength without impairment of vitality and inevitable reaction. There is a danger line to race life, and that danger line is crossed when the drain begins to exceed the normal powers of recuperation. A nation or a race is as a man; the morning must find the waste of the previous day replaced, or deterioration quickly sets in, and decadence soon follows. The trouble is that both men and nations are apt to see this too late. A man came into my office one day for medical advice. He was possibly twenty-five or twenty-six years of age and with the frame of an athlete; yet he was a mere bodily wreck. "Three years ago," he said to me, "I was stroke oarsman of one of the British university teams." Over-training had killed him. It kills a man; it will kill a race. If Germany dies, it will die of the German army. The France of the Republic, which was able for a time to defy Europe, died of Napoleon's army. Germany in her enormous and disproportionate armaments is doing what Napoleon did, discounting the future. But the bills have to be paid. With the nation as with the man, it is the pace that kills.

Yet to insure his national existence the German is forced to make of his homeland a vast military camp. And this necessity brings him, as said, face to face with the problem which has been the undoing of so many races - How to keep militarism from sapping the strength and vitality of the race? No nation has yet succeeded in solving the problem alone. Germany can not; for to the single nation the problem is unsolvable. If the German shall be compelled to keep up his present disproportionate armaments, the strength of the race will be gone before the days of its greatest possibilities are upon it. There is only one way of escape - alliance with his kin. The German is not Slav. He is not Latin. He is Teuton. Neither is he a race by himself; he is only a portion of a race. The natural alliance of the German is with the Teutonic peoples of Western Europe. They are his kinsmen. The blood is the same; the speech allied. The race development is along similar lines. They look to a like future. The race clashings of the future must inevitably force the Teutonic peoples of Western Europe closer together, rather than apart. With Briton, Norseman, Dane, Hollander, German, one hundred and twenty millions of them, united for mutual protection; and with the command of the European seas which this would give; the vast armaments which separately each must now carry may be safely diminished, the burden of each lightened, and the race vitality economized. With them united the Baltic and the North Sea become only Teutonic lakes, and the Slav question in the West is settled once for all. Such an alliance means more to the German than it does to the Briton or to the Norseman, for without it he stands alone amid foes. Can he continue to stand alone? And if he can, must it not be with a race future restricted and dwarfed? For the Slav has flanked him upon the east; is pressing him from the north; and upon the west is the sea.

Is this a possible forecasting of the future? Western Russia is Teutonic rather than Slav. The Slav is working eastward and southward to Asia and the Black Sea. His capital will not remain upon the Neva; it will follow the migration of the race. It is even now in an alien land. Draw a line northward from East Germany to the White Sea; westward are largely Teutons. Germany, Germanic Russia of the Baltic shores, Sweden, Norway, Denmark, the Netherlands, Britain - is it to be a confederation of kin? Is Knut's eleventh-century dream of a Teuton land which should take in all the shore peoples to come

122

true in the twentieth century, only as a still broader Teuton land which shall take in as well the Mid-European Teuton? If Knut's dream had been realized as a permanency in the eleventh century, St. Petersburg would never have been upon the Neva; and the Slav question would not be hanging over West Europe to-day.

Yet any expansion of the German folk must, as before stated, be southward. That is the line of least resistance. Northward the German can not go. There the Slav, with a race vitality at least the equal of his own, holds the land; and the Slav's retreat toward Asia is too slow for the rapid increase of the German population. Eastward the same Slav as surely shuts off the pathway. A successful colonizer afar the German never has been. And then, as has been asked, where are the new lands suited to his race constitution? The English-speaking man has been before him, and holds them. One thing, and only the one, seems possible. Southward the German must go to find room, or else continue as he has been only a feeder to other peoples. The fact that once the Rhine was not his southern boundary, neither the Alps; and that the valleys of the Po, the Rhone, the Loire once before knew him as conqueror, and that there he abode; these facts throw much light upon the possibilities of the future. Who shall say that he is not to repeat the past and again to abide there? this time maybe as a peaceful conqueror through the mastery of superior race vitality, for the mixed Latin is in this respect far from being his equal. Is time thus once more to undo the work of Caesar's legions? For fifteen centuries the German has been revitalizing Southern Europe, just as the Dorian in the fifteen centuries preceding had revitalized Southern Hellas; and German has toned up Latin just as the Dorian toned up that older decadent Greek, or as the Norseman toned up the Celt and the Saxon.

The first great wave southward from the banks of the Rhine half-way Germanized Southern Europe. The next may do more. And history is curiously repeating itself in another thing. It was the pressure from behind of still more northerly races which forced those older Germans of the second to the sixth centuries southward upon the Latin. It is the pressure from behind of the northern Slav which is again forcing him southward, for the German is again entering upon the stage of expansion. The homeland which proved too narrow for the steadily increasing numbers of that older German, and from which he was forced by lack of bread to overflow and go out, is again proving too narrow for the homes it has to furnish and the mouths it has to feed. It is Ariovistus with his landless hordes *redivivus*.

Is it to be Kaiser, or Imperator, or Kaiser and Imperator with the Alps between, or is it to be neither, but only the *populus* with its *res-publica*? Whichever it may be, one fact will stand out above all others, that it is still the stronger northern blood fresh from the normal climatic home belt of the primitive Aryan folk bringing again renewed youth and vigor to the failing folk blood in a climatically alien land. Turn back the picture three thousand years; it is only Krete, and Argolis, and the Dorian, over again. And both are only Solomon's vision of "The thing which hath been is the thing which shall be" with the added light of thirty more centuries thrown upon it. And then, after it all, history will no doubt yet again repeat itself in the other centuries still to be; for the working of climatic law upon race bloods is as that old law of the Medes and Persians, and changes not, but will, age after age, work on to its predestined and inexorable end. As the new years go by the past will be lived over again; for it will again be southland and northland as before; and the Alps still between. But railroads and mountain tunnels and the more constant mingling of bloods of modern life will be countervailing factors at work to prevent the recurrence of the long isolations of the earlier ages, and the wide divergences of type which resulted therefrom.

There is still another factor in the German problem, and as yet it remains a disturbing factor of undetermined value. The German never has been one as the English man is one. His weakness has always been that of the Celt, dissensions and divisions. It was his weakness as against the Roman; for the Roman, whatever else he might be, was united. Here was the fatal weakness in the Prankish empire of Charlemagne, which quickly fell apart after the strong hand of its founder was gone. It was the German's weakness in the Napoleonic wars. It is in the blood. The bewildering multiplicity of tribes of Tacitus, ever wrangling and quarreling with each other even in the presence of the common foe, often indeed siding with the foe in battle array against their own kin, had their lineal descendants in the petty feudal baronies of the early Middle Ages, and in the Free Cities, each a law unto itself, and in the Hanse Towns and the guilds of the age that followed, and even only a generation ago in the numerous insignificant duchies and principalities which made the map of Germany look like a patchwork quilt, a chronic horror, and a nightmare to the suffering schoolboy. It was this weakness of the German people that the elder William and Bismarck saw when they struck down with apparently ruthless hand the petty states of a disunited German fatherland and forced a union. It is this which Wilhelm, Kaiser and War-lord, is trying so indefatigably to drill out of the German kin. Will he be able to do it? This is not the least of the problems of the German future. In fact, all else hinges upon this. There is a lesson and a warning also to the German from that old Greek race. Greece could overcome the Persian; she could not overcome herself. It is self that nations as well as men have most to fear. Greece died of the Greek. All Germans permanently united, and upon terms of friendly alliance with the other Teutonic peoples of West Europe, means sooner or later an All-Germany from the Baltic and the North Sea to the Adriatic, and possibly to the Black. All Germans not so united means at the best only the empire of Charlemagne over again - and then again chaos. Which is it to be? The future of Mid-Europe hangs upon the answer. Disunited, the German folk may still serve as a bumper between Latin and Slav. United, they will press both back and enlarge their borders. Other empires have disintegrated when made up of alien and unlike bloods. Germany disintegrated while made up of only the one blood. Have the German folk at last, after two thousand years of bitter experience, learned political wisdom to stand together? Time will show; time, and those upper and nether millstones, the Latin and the Slav.

That there are to be ultimately only three Teutonic nations upon the west shore of Europe, German, Scandinavian, and Englishman, is becoming increasingly probable. It is thus that the natural boundary-lines divide the Teutonic kin. The process of absorption, which in the course of race evolution seems to have become the underlying law of modern national life, would seem destined to go on upon the mainland until Belgian and Hollander and Dane shall disappear as separate nationalities and merge their political existence into the broader race life of the German, constituting together the greater kinfolk of the East Teutons whose land shall only cease with the shore line of the English Channel and the Skager Rack. The mere and sheer bulk of the German peoples will almost inevitably bring this about, impelled as they are by the necessity of securing a sea frontage commensurate with their rapidly growing numbers; while the increasing disabilities and dangers which are incident to the separate national life of the weaker peoples will as inevitably force them as a matter of race preservation to seek safety through union with their stronger kin. The Scandinavian is set apart as a nation by the water-lines of the Baltic and its outlet; but there is no strength for two. Norwegian and Swede by the necessity of a like struggle for existence as against the Slav will be more and more forced together into a common national life; and even then it will be the stronger arm of their Teutonic kin, German and English, that must save them from the fate of the Finn. Finland is the ever-present death's head of warning before them. It is only when the Slav is convinced through Teutonic unity that the contest is hopeless, that he will at last give up the struggle and turn back upon Asia. And then, and not until then, will the peril of the Norseman be over. Britain is set apart as a nation from the Teutonic peoples of the mainland by the waters of the English Channel and by the strong tie of blood and speech with her kin beyond the Atlantic.

The German, like the Celt, has been fated to be a feeder to other races rather than an expanding race-builder within a nationality of his own. He has gone on through the ages ever multiplying yet never increasing. Those of his race who have pressed southward, either peacefully or in war, have become Latin in speech and affiliation. The great and unceasing stream which has for centuries flowed westward has become English. Lack of new homeland of his own in the climatic belt where Germans might breed Germans and remain unchanged in race type has held him back in the race for dominion. No new Americas, or Australias, or New Zealands, or South Africas have opened up for him fresh lands for race increase. And now the lands are gone. With all that the German may do, and surely will again do, in Southern Europe among the Latins, his own race life so far as can be now seen must be lived with and through his own kin. As Britain must live her life over again in the broader life of the whole English-speaking peoples, so Germany must live her life over in the greater life of the whole Teutonic peoples. As there must come a Pan-Engle-land so there must come later a Pan-Teuton-land as opposed to a Pan-Latin-land and a Pan-Slav-land.

But do the other Aryans of the West, Latin, Celt, Teuton, realize what they owe to the German? Coming last in the wave of westward migration, he has for ages stood as the rear-guard of the Aryan peoples against the onsets of all subsequent race advances. He has been to Western Europe since the fall of the Roman Empire what the Greek was to all Europe before the Roman Empire was - a bumper race to receive and ward off the assaults of Asia from the lands which had shelter behind him. Against Hun and Mongol and Turk he has had to bear the brunt of the battle. And he has always stood, and never flinched or given back. Is it much wonder that in the struggle of centuries he had small chance for the building up of self? He stood guard while others built themselves up. But it is a sore price the German has had to pay for this security to others. The constant warring and battling kept Germany herself politically in a state of arrested development. It is a case of the Middle Ages lapping over into the twentieth century. She has stood still while others have gone on. And the end is not yet. History repeats itself. The old battle of Herodotos is to be fought over again. Again it is to be Europe as against Asia - for the Slav is Asia; and the valley of the Volga, not the Ural Mountains of the atlas, is the dividing-line between East and West; and it is no longer the Bosphorus that separates the rival forces; and the German now stands, as the Greek did of old, in the forefront of the battle. But he can not stand alone.

The German is Teuton; yet he is not English; neither is he Norse. He is less like either than they are like to each other. He stands apart from the other Teutonic peoples in a class by himself. He mingles more readily with non-Teutonic bloods than do the others of the Teutonic kin. He is less scrupulous of purity of race blood. He shows mental characteristics unlike in type to the other Teutonic peoples. His political trend is different from that of his kinfolk. There must be a reason for this. It can not be ascribed to chance; for chance does not enter as a factor into the problem of race evolution any more than it does into the evolution of a star or of a solar system. And then in a higher sense there is no chance; for chance so-called is only causation as yet unseen.

One reason for these differences may be found in the fact that the German is less purely Teutonic in blood than his kindred. Whatever may have been the historical correctness or incorrectness of the view of Tacitus when he says of the early German peoples, "I have deemed the Germans to be native to the land, and very little mixed by immigration (*adventu*) or temporary sojourns (*hospitiis*) of other peoples," he gives an opinion which if true was probably truer then than now, for the ages when Mid-Europe, the German land, became the battle-ground and the mixing field of Latin, Goth, Slav, Hun, and German, were yet to be, and the German may well have dwelt as yet in the land "little mixed" with alien bloods. That time, however, passed by; and with the vast land migrations, of which Tacitus in his thought of the sea as the normal highway of shifting peoples seems to have had so little prevision, the old isolation of the Germans ceased; and for fifteen centuries, from the Hun in the fourth to the Franco-Latin in the closing of the eighteenth, he has had to battle with invasion of alien bloods, and to suffer from inevitable ad-mixture. While he has in the main thrown off the alien wave, it has not al-ways been at once, but often only after a while; and even then there have been isolated fragments, as the Bohemian, the Moravian, the Wend, the Lith-uanian, remaining in his midst, subject yet there, to mingle their blood with his, while others, as the half-way Mongol of the Hungarian plains, the Slav of all the northern border, the Turk upon his east, and all the half-Mongol peo-ples of the East-European lands, and the Latin upon the south, have been neighbors to him and have to some extent during all these centuries crossed their stock with his and thus rendered less pure the current of his primitive Teutonic blood. Whether as invader or invaded, or whether as neighboring races dwelling side by side in peace, the crossing would go steadily on. The English man and the Norse man, with the German standing as a rear-guard between them and the non-Teutonic peoples, and with the added safeguard of the sea to shield them, escaped all this; and thus it came that they were saved from race admixtures and have kept up the purer Teutonic stock. This varied and extensive admixture with alien bloods, and the close contact and constant intercourse with neighboring peoples of unlike type, continuing through so many centuries, could not but have a modifying influence upon the primitive race character of the German peoples.

A second factor at work to differentiate the Teutonic peoples of Britain and the Norse lands from the German has been the influence of the sea. The Eng-lish man and the Norse man early became seafarers; while the German re-mained, through limitations of his Mid-European home, largely a man of the land. He missed the education of the sea. And this was no small loss to a race in its infancy, the time of race life when race types are formed and fixed. For the period of the segregation of the Teutonic peoples of Western Europe from each other forms a new starting-point which to them, as they look back and compare themselves the one with the other, is a Teutonic race infancy from which divergences of type begin; just as the crossing of the Atlantic by a portion of the English kin is a new starting-point to them whence the minor variations of the English-speaking peoples may be traced.

With each added century the divergence between the East Teutons and the West Teutons became more marked. The West Teutons reached out to the broader life of the seas and of the new worlds. The East Teutons, on the con-trary, lived their race life with the life of the inland peoples of Mid-Europe and the Farther East. Under the spur of the spirit of personal freedom and the individual initiative, which came back as a returning current from the new race homelands oversea, the West Teutons tended more and more toward a democratic type of government. With the East Teutons it was different. No healthful stimulus of race expansion into new lands served as a spur to race spirit. No refluent currents of kin blood, revitalized by the fresh life of new homelands oversea, helped the parent land to stem the tide of European monarchism. Under the stress of the rivalry and battling for existence with the powerful and alien races about it, the German homeland drifted naturally and inevitably toward the ultramonarchic type of government. For it is to be remembered that in times of sudden danger the concentration of power in a monarchy is the better suited to insure quick and effective action in national defense. The "War-lord" is a prompter military factor than the "Folkmoot." And the stress evolves the warlord. Germany, in the defensive necessity which has never lifted from her borders, has developed other Fredericks. Britain in the security of her island home has evolved no second Elizabeth, that last and greatest of the Tudors, the woman who behind the mask of a flirt concealed the mind of a man and the courage of a war-lord. And Britain has had no need; for the Armada was the last serious attempt at an invasion of an English homeland; while Germany has had Napoleon the Great and Napoleon the Little, and always the ominous shadow of the Slav and the Turk.

The East Teuton never cut loose from Rome so entirely as did the other Teutonic peoples. The Reformation left large numbers of the Germanic kin who still looked to the papacy for spiritual guidance. The Puritan was English; not Teutonic even in the sense of a common race product.

In speech, the German has displayed less ability to free himself from the cumbersome grammatical trammels of the inflectional stage of an agglutinative past than even the Latin. In this respect he affords a marked contrast to the more practical and more self-helpful English man who long ago left these things behind together with the other rubbish of youth in the lumber-room of that outgrown past.

In his mental make-up the German has an element of dreamy mysticism not found elsewhere in the Teutonic blood. How much of this may come of a strain born especially in the blood of that particular branch of the Teutonic family; how much may be due to an incorporation of some foreign blood; how much to the morbid workings of a mind driven in upon itself for generations in the despondency of adverse warrings and battlings; it would be difficult to say. Only, this may be said, that since the German has through unity gained strength to stand as one among the nations of the world and no longer lives in dread, there seems to be less manifestation of this rather morbid tendency in the working of the race mind than when, torn by contending factions, the fatherland stood helpless as the martyr of the nations.

In the final summing up of the race work of the German two facts thus far stand prominently forth: That he has ever been the rejuvenator of the Latin; And that he has been the rear-guard of Teutonic civilization behind which, as a secure shelter, it has had chance to develop its characteristic type and build up unmolested its world power. The German has made possible the Norse

Chapter Thirteen - The Norse Man

On the rim of the northern seas another branch of the Teuto-Aryan family made its home. Least in numbers among the Teutonic peoples is the Norse man. For this the Norse land, cold, inhospitable, and only to a limited extent tillable, may be held accountable, for in race vitality he seems to be in no way inferior to his more fecund kin. That in restless energy he has been in no way inferior, is well testified by the old Viking records, and the voyages of Eric the Red, and Lief Thorwaldson, in their open boats over wintry seas to the shores of Greenland and America ages before Cabot and Hudson ventured westward from the known waters of the European coast. Snow, and ice, and the sea have made the Norse man different from his kin. The deficient food supply of an inhospitable homeland forced him to eke out his living from the waters of his fjords and inlets, and then, as these became insufficient, he boldly put out to the well-stocked waters of the island channels, and north-ward to the Loffodens, and then to the open sea beyond.

A rather curious division runs through the blood which we ordinarily class as Norse, separating it into two well-defined stocks. So noticeable is this that only a difference in the direct line of Teutonic ancestry will adequately ex-plain it. Dane and Norwegian in affinity of speech and in race characteristics are apparently much more nearly allied to each other than is either to the Swede. Dane and Norwegian class more nearly with the English speaking peoples; the Swede certainly would not be so classed. A possible strain of Gothic blood may explain this. South Sweden, the province which contains the greater portion of the Swedish peoples, and which from climatic reasons we may assume to have been their first point of settlement upon the Scandi-navian peninsula, is still called Gothland; altho it is only fair to state that the etymology of the word has been disputed. Race character, however, is a bet-ter guide than speech in the search for race kinship. The volatile, somewhat fickle, heady, and quarrelsome Swede is little like the set, patient, more peaceable Dane or Norwegian. Bishop Ulfilas of the Goths, when in translat-ing the Scriptures for his people in the fourth century he left out the Book of Joshua with its vivid account of the Canaanitish wars, saying that his people were too fond of fighting already, might almost have been speaking for the medieval Swede. Viewed from the standpoint of race characteristics it seems hardly going too far, indeed, to classify the Swede entirely apart from the Dano-Norwegian and to rank him as the lineal descendant of that restless, battling Goth of the fourth century whose after-power reached across Mid-Europe from the Black Sea to the Baltic, and whose blood upon the south runs in the veins of Italian and Spaniard and Gaul. He has not inaptly been called the Frenchman of the North. Reckless, dashing, spectacular Charles XII. was a typical Swede; and he might as fitly have been Celto-Frank.

The lowlands of Denmark may be looked upon as the first race home of the Norse branch of the Teutonic family upon the sea. From this point the natural spread would be, by the law of successive overflow, into the adjacent islands of the West Baltic, and across the narrow channel of what is now known as the Skager Rack to the coast rim of South Norway, and on along the coast line, insular and peninsular, of the Norwegian lands far to the north. Walled off from the interior by the long snow line of the Dovrefjeld Mountains, and with a narrow rim of land facing out upon the sea, which as he went northward grew ever less and less capable of affording a subsistence from the frosty soil, this branch of the Teutonic family was forced to become maritime in habits and type of life. Then came the time when not even land and sea gave adequate support to a population which despite adverse surroundings steadily increased; and then this man of the inhospitable North began his series of raids southward along the more fertile shores of Britain and France, and on, until his piratical fleets became the scourge and the dread of even the inland waters of the Mediterranean. Whatever lust of conquest grew up within him afterward, the primary moving force which impelled him out from his Northern home was hunger, his fields and his fisheries not yielding food sufficient for the mouths to be filled. As he learned new wants amid the luxuries of the southland he became less content with the simpler ways of the old Northern home life, and the discontent led him on and on, and ultimately made of him a permanent conqueror and an abider in other homes far to the south.

In Teutonic Britain both the original direct wave of Norse invasion of the ninth and tenth centuries, and the reflex wave from Normandy of the eleventh century, became quickly merged into the kindred blood of the new home, losing tongue and separate race identity. In Celto-Latin France he has left name and race characteristics. Normandy, the French Normandie, is only North-man-dig, North-man's-land, the *Terra Normannorum* of the old Saxon chronicles, but to the Celto-Latin in the bitterness of his harrying, *Terra Piratarum*. It is the old Norse blood of Normandy, of Bretagne, of Channel Islands, and of the seacoast towns of the Biscayan shores which has largely supplied the fisher folk and the seafaring men of Atlantic France, as it is the Greek blood of the old Hellenic colonies of the south coast of France which has supplied the seafaring men of the French Mediterranean shore; for the Latin, the Celt, and the Iberian, whether separately or mixed, have never to any marked extent become men of the sea. It was this Franco-Norse blood which gave to the English-speaking man his one rival upon the cod banks of Newfoundland, a rivalry which still leaves its lingering traces in the islands of Miquelon and St. Pierre, and in the ever-present fishing dispute between Britain and France. And so it is the Franco-Greek blood which goes out from Marseilles and Toulon and the Mediterranean coast villages to the tunny fisheries of the Sicilian and Sardinian seas. It is these men, not the Celto-Latin bloods, who furnish the seamen for the French civil and naval marine.

There is, however, to the student of that race life which is deeper than the mere record of deeds done, an interest in this Norse man that is out of all proportion to the place he fills in the world history of to-day. It lies in this fact, that his is the strain of the Teutonic blood which brought the old pagan life of the fathers down into touch with modern history. Through him we know how our forefathers lived; what their thoughts were of the mystery of life; what they knew, or believed they knew, of the hereafter. The Sagas and the Runes of the northland have done for the Teutonic branch of the Aryan peoples what the Iliad did for the South European branch, the A vestas for the Iranic, or the Vedas for the Brahminic. Shut off by his icy seas and his wintry skies from that earlier outgoing of Christianity which so quickly over-ran the Graeco-Latin, and only a little later the Celt and the Southern Teutons of Mid-Europe and the British Isles, he carried the older pagan life of the Teu-tons well on toward the Middle Ages, with all its store of old pagan folk-lore and folk-belief, and, especially through the Icelandic off shoot, preserved the-se in written record. In these Sagas and Runes and Chronicles we have op-portunity to study the race life of our common blood as it was before Christi-anity and civilization had touched and changed it. It is the youth of our folk life revealed - the after folk life in its formative stage. No race study of the Teutonic peoples is complete, or is even measurably satisfactory, without this as its starting-point. It is the law of heredity invoked to help explain the race character of to-day. Indeed, even the Celto-Latin blood of Southwestern Europe can not be fairly understood without a race study of the Northman, for in that restless swarming of the Norse folk southward during the Viking age not only his Teutonic kin of the British Isles received the remolding stamp of his strong race personality, but the whole Atlantic and Mediterra-nean seaboard of the Celto-Latin, and even Graeco-Semitic Sicily also, shared in the impress. The race study of Southwestern Europe which leaves out of the count the Norseman of the Baltic shores and of the fjord-indented and island-fringed Norwegian coast beyond, must of necessity be radically defec-tive and incomplete. And it is upon the Sagas and Chronicles of this northern branch of the kin that we must almost entirely depend for our knowledge of the primitive folk life of the whole Teutonic peoples, for the earlier literature of the other branches, included practically within the "Nibelungen Lied" in its Germanic versions and the "Song of Beowulf" in the older English, is so lim-ited in scope, and so tinged by the medieval monkish atmosphere through which it has been filtered, that it has lost the freshness, the ingenuousness, which must always make the chief value of such records. The side-glimpses which we obtain in the pages of Tacitus are of value; yet they are the race life as seen and told by an alien, and from afar, not the living picture as painted by the race itself.

What Manner of Man then was this Primitive Norse-Aryan, so nearly as we May be able to Reconstruct Him from His Own Records?

A strong, self-reliant, simple-hearted man of forest and field and sea. Half-farmer, half-fisher, wholly battler whether with his own kin or with the stranger afar. Seldom long at peace; looking upon a quiet death at home in his bed as unworthy of a true man; esteeming death upon the battle-field or in tempest and storm at sea the only fit ending of men. In body tall, muscular, active, complexion fair, eyes blue or gray, hair reddish or flaxen. In temperament restless, adventurous, ready to launch his frail boat upon the waters of the sea whether for a fishing trip or a voyage of exploration across the trackless wastes of the unknown ocean of the west or to sail upon a piratical expedition to the shores of the southlands. In habits of food simple, an eater of fish and of animal food rather than a grain-eater, possibly as much because of the ungenerous soil of his homeland as through natural taste; yet finding in the rye of his northern climate a passable substitute for the wheat of his southern kinfolk; a consumer of milk and cheese from the kine which made so large a portion of his wealth. He was a healthy man, not morbid mentally or spiritually apart from that one strain of fatalism. Free from any inherited taint of an older civilization, for to him civilization had never yet come. Free from the corrupting influences of city life, for cities he had none. He was a man of the farm and the woodland village. It is the *bonder,* the husbandman, that is the *civis* of the Northland. And it is to the Northland *bonder* as it is to the German *bauer,* the Dutch *boer,* the Russian peasant, or to the American farmer and frontiersman, and not to the city man or to noble, that we look for the purer and more characteristic race types. This Northman of the farm and the woodlands seems, of all the kin of the widely scattered Aryan folk, to have remained most like to the man who sang the hymns to the Maruts in the mountain-passes of the Hindu Rush; that is, he of all had changed least from the primitive Aryan of the continental highlands, that ancient Proto-Aryan forefather of all the widely scattered Aryan stocks. There is the same close touch with nature; the same exuberant overflow of sheer animal life; the same glad abandon and oneness with the material world about him. He, too, has in him the terebinthic flavor of the mountain pines; but added to it, what that older Aryan lacked, the tang of the salt spume of the sea.

The same self-respecting personal independence marked the older Norseman that marks his descendants to-day. He would be no man's servant. As a roving band of piratical Vikings sailed up the Seine the envoys of the king of France hailed them, asking who was their overlord. "We have no lord over us; we are all equal," was the sturdy reply. Charles the Simple, of France, had a lesson of the same sort from Rolf the Ganger. Having given to Rolf the province of Normandy as a bribe to keep the peace, he demanded that Rolf should show the usual sign of fealty by kissing the royal foot. "I will never bend my knee before any man; nor will I kiss any one's foot," was the haughty reply. And Charles had to let it go at that.

Yet with all these masterful characteristics, the Norseman has never built up an abiding dominion of his own. His work has been rather to touch and tone up other bloods than to build up dominion for himself. Why has it been so? There must be an adequate reason for it. His homeland tells the story. Cold, bleak, picturesque, but inhospitable, while it has made the race character it has unmade the race power. The normal increase of population has only served to swell a tide of emigration which has simply added to the numerical strength of other lands, and increased their power. While the Dane has had to migrate because of narrowness of homeland, the Scandinavian of the opposite peninsula has had to migrate because the homeland is so largely untillable; in each, the working of the same causes has led to the outflow of the Viking age, lack of food for an ever-increasing population, and lack of opportunity for broader race life. And as in that older migration so now, the overflow has never been that of a stream coming from a fountain-head strong enough in numbers to take and hold a new homeland to itself, and so to preserve the identity of speech and institutions. The Northman in Sicily was soon lost in the greater preponderance of the Graeco-Semitic blood into which he had, by force of race character, thrust himself. The Northman in France lost speech and civil institutions in the passive resistance of the denser Celto-Latin mass which surrounded him. The Northman in Britain, after two separate periods of overrule, is to-day only the English man in speech and race life. In each of the foregoing cases the stream, while strong enough in personality to leave an abiding impress upon the land to which it has passed, has not been strong enough in numbers to possess the land to the exclusion or absorption of other races; and the fountain-head has been numerically too feeble to adequately reinforce the first outflow; and so it has come to pass that each wave of migration has been ultimately lost to the Scandinavian race, and has only served to strengthen and build up other bloods. The mental and spiritual life of the Norseman, and its impress upon the thought and the beliefs of the world, will be considered more fully under the topic of the English man, to whom he furnished so strong a strain of race blood, and in whom the continuous spiritual evolution of the Teutonic kin can be traced most completely.

What is to be the Future of the Norseman?

That in the larger movements of modern race life he can alone long maintain his separate national identity, is not probable. To the Slav, if he is to continue his efforts to become an Atlantic power, Scandinavia is a necessity. Of all the great races of the world the Slav is most shut in. His large rivers, the Obi, the Yenissei, the Lena, the Amur, all, with the exception of the Volga, drain to icy seas, ice-locked through the greater portion of the year; and even the Volga giving no ocean outlet, but emptying into a Mid-Asian inland sea. His two ocean ports, Vladivostok upon the Pacific and St. Petersburg upon the waters of the upper Baltic, ice-bound for so many months of the year, are no adequate outlet for a nation of one hundred and twenty millions of people. The Black Sea is to them no free outlet, for across the Dardanelles the

Turk sits as a warder whose main duty is to hold back the Slav from the open sea; and all Europe is at his back. The same necessity which has forced Russia to reach out after Manchuria and the open-sea ports of the Liao-Tung peninsula, and which will admit of no permanent peace until she has them in undisputed possession, likewise impels her to reach out for Scandinavia and the open seaport of Christiania. Peter's work was only half done when he seized the mud flats of the Neva and built thereon his capital city and his naval headquarters. Probably Peter foresaw this himself, for Peter was a seer; but then it was all that was possible in his day; and the Muscovite had already learned to bide his time. It has, however, been a long wait, for ice and the Teuton still bar the way to the clear waters of the open sea. The narrow outlet of the Zealand waters is to him upon the west what the narrower waters of the Dardanelles are upon the south; and, across the way a worse than the Turk stands guard - the whole Teutonic power of Western Europe. In the face of this opposition the only possible chance for the Slav is to flank the entrenched force and gain outlet beyond. This he can not do upon the south shore, for there is the German, fifty-six millions strong and rapidly increasing in numbers. The only possibility is upon the north. The fate of Finland, first independent, then tributary, now to be Russianized or obliterated is only a forewarning of the fate in store for the Scandinavian peninsula, unless the Norseman shall find help from without himself. With the north shore of the Baltic outlet in his possession the Slav may claim equal right to it as a highway to the open sea; and he will be in position to enforce the claim. And this will be no conflict at the farther end of five thousand miles of poorly constructed single-track railway, and with a foe who has the advantage of battling at his own doors. This time the Slav will be at home; and in a homeland where nature largely does for him the work of an army of defense. No nation since Napoleon's time has cared to repeat his experiment of following the Russian within his own land. The lesson of Moscow and the northern winter has not been forgotten. Should Europe be inclined to forget, that monument standing upon Russia's southern border with the terse inscription upon the one side, "This way Napoleon passed with four hundred and ten thousand men," and upon the obverse that suggestive after-reading, "This way Napoleon repassed with nine thousand men," is an ever-constant reminder.

In the clashing of these larger interests the only hope of the Norseman will lie in alliance with his kin. He is too feeble a folk to make the battle alone. And when the time shall come they will help him, for his battle is their battle. The Teutons, by a common race instinct which is deeper than the considerations and ties of mere dynastic lines, claim the waters of the North Atlantic as their own; and they will fight to the bitter end to make good their claim. Under the pressure of this race feeling the future is therefore more apt to see the Slav receding from a hopeless contest with all Teutonic Western Europe, and withdrawing eastward and southward away from the Atlantic shore, especially as the law of grades and of inland water carriage of his land is away from the sea eastward toward the heart of the Continent. Had the waterway of the Volga drained to the Baltic instead of to the Caspian, the whole after-history of Western Europe would have been changed; for so does the law of grades make or mar history. The Baltic is by right of population a Teutonic sea. Not in the selfish sense of a Mare Clausum as against all others; but still by preponderance of influence a Teutonic sea. The Teuton lines its shores upon the north, the south, and the west, and stands as an insular power and bar across its outlet. Upon the east the Teuton and the Finn constitute its preponderating littoral peoples; for Russia's Baltic provinces are largely of Germanic blood. Russia only touches the Baltic along the line of the Neva with the tapering point of a thin wedge of Slavic peoples, protruded between Teuton and Finn; and this, not as a line of self-supporting and indigenous population, but as aliens and exotics, transported thither by imperial ukase to found a city and to essay an imperialistic policy. It was so the old Babylonian monarchs founded cities. It is Asia. The present status can not, as a race question, permanently continue. The Slav must either multiply and spread or else ultimately disappear from the shores of the Baltic. And Britain and Germany can not allow him to spread by the acquisition of the Scandinavian lands and the exercise of an overlordship of the Scandinavian peoples. And then it may be questioned whether such expansion would in the end prove to be a wise thing for the Slav himself. Acquisition of the Scandinavian lands without assimilation of the Scandinavian peoples would bring weakness rather than strength to the Slav. Mere extent of dominion is not in itself strength. It may upon the contrary prove to be weakness, fatal weakness. Acquisition without assimilation is not growth; it is only added burden. Alien in blood and spirit of race institutions, disaffected, separated by the waters of the Baltic from the centers of Slavic race life, easy of attack but difficult of defense, the holding of the Scandinavian lands and peoples would prove to be a constant and exhausting drain upon the resources of the Slavic lands. Then, too, time, with the ever-growing bulk of the Slavic peoples eastward, will ultimately pull the Slavic race capital inland, away from the Baltic. When it does, the thin wedge of Slavs will normally recede from the line of the Neva under the lateral pressure of German and Finn; for the end is not yet to the Finn; a ukase does not settle race problems or change race blood. Poland has taught this lesson. Peter attempted the impossible for his Slavic empire. Blood and the centuries are against him. The Baltic will again become only a Teutonic lake.

Some light might be thrown upon the probable future affiliations of the Norseman by noting his affiliations in the past. These have always been with the older branch of the Teutonic peoples as represented by the English-speaking man, rather than with the younger, as represented by the German. The blood of the Norseman, the Dane, is found by the banks of the Humber and the Thames, not upon the Rhine. No Knut ever sat upon a German throne. No Norman Senlac ever came to Germanic shores. The *Long Serpent* and the *Dragon* have their successors in the *Benbow* and *Victory,* not in the *Kaiser Wilhelms* of the German waters. And the Scandinavian and the Dane are now to be found by the tens of thousands in new homes all over the great American Northwest, with an ever-increasing stream of immigration. Their children speak English as their native tongue, but the older home-ties reach back to the Norse land across the Atlantic, and help to bind it more closely to the English-speaking lands. Norse family names are found in the halls of legislation of all the English peoples. In the light of all these facts it is evident that the future of the Norse lands of Europe will naturally be interwoven most closely with that of their nearest of kin, the English-speaking peoples. Knut's dream of a federation of the Norse and English peoples of Western Europe may yet be more than a dream.

If the question were asked, What has been the especial contribution of the Norseman to modern civilization? the answer would possibly be, The preservation and the passing on to its civic life of that spirit of personal independence which under the repressive influences of medieval political forms had become less marked in the other branches of the Aryan peoples. Rolf the Ganger and his kin of the fjords and ice-fields have left their mark indelibly stamped upon the whole after-life of the West Teutons. It is found alike by the banks of the Thames and by the banks of the Ohio, and over the broad plains of the Farther West. And there is contagion in it.

Chapter Fourteen - The English Man

The name Englishman has become a family name. It has gone through the same process of amplification as that which came to the race names Teuton and Aryan before it. There was a time, millenniums ago, when there was only one Aryan people. Now there are many; and the name Aryan, which once applied to the one exclusively, now belongs equally to all; for they are all alike only the widely scattered children of the one long buried but common Aryan forefather. And there was a time also, but not so far back in the past, a space measured by the centuries rather than by the millenniums, when in the multiplication and subdivision of the Aryan peoples there was no doubt one, and only one, Teutonic folk. Now they also are become many; and the name Teuton has become the family name of a whole group of kin peoples. In like manner was there a time, but again still nearer, when in the subdivision of the Teutonic peoples through separation and isolation the one branch from the other, there was an English people who first were only one. Now they, too, have multiplied and subdivided and drifted apart until they also have become many peoples. Yet as, despite the years and the separation, Aryan is still Aryan, and Teuton still Teuton, so despite the lesser separations and the fewer years the English peoples are still English peoples - English, and nothing else. This amplification of name among the races of men is the same as that by which in natural history the name of the single family ceases after a while to belong to and to designate only the one, but becomes instead the common designation of all the members of the evolved and subdivided group which has origin therefrom. It is the process which is ever going on in all nature; and through the working of which the name of the single species becomes after a while the name of a family or group. And as this process goes on the different individuals or the smaller groups of the family take on through necessity special names to distinguish them the one from the other.

In this process of race subdivision and separation the family name often suffers somewhat of change in form, yet still as a general thing preserving enough of the original consonantal framework to enable us to readily trace and identify it through all the alterations. The process is the same as in the changes which so often come to the name of the individual man. It is as in case of the Smythe who is now not of the smithy, but whose restored name goes back to that first Smith who was of the smithy with its anvil and its flying sparks; or the *Wab*ster who is now not of the loom with its warp and woof, but who belongs in name with that first *Web*ster who was of the loom. The Aryan who is no longer always of a race of tillers of the soil, fisherman now maybe and man of the sea, yet goes back for his race designation to that primitive Aryan who was an *arar*-er before all else. The term Englishman like the term Aryan, or the term Teuton, has become a family name. The time was when if the term Englishman was used every one knew just who was meant, and where he had race habitation. Now one stops to inquire, "Which English man? and in what land?" The name has become generic, and is no longer special in application.

It is of that older time, however, that we now come to speak; the time when the name still designated only the one people; the time when men did not have to ask inquiringly, "Which English man? and which English land?" There was such a time; "and there was such a land and such a man; and all three date back for their inception beyond the British Isles; for there was another England before that of Britain, and another Englishman before him of the island home. The lands of that older England lay about the south shores of the Baltic; and the name was then not yet English, but Engle, or Angle. Both forms have been used, but the consonantal framework is the same. We retain the one in the fuller word English; the other in the compounds of Angle, as AngloSaxon, Anglo-American. And that older English man of the mainland was not some one else. He was himself. He was not Saxon. He was not Jute. He was simply and purely Engle. The others were kin; and evidently near kin; but that was all. And of the family he proved to be the stronger, and in a common migration to a new land soon absorbed the others. It was so that the man of Latium absorbed Sabine, and AEquian, and Hernican, and Volscian, and that older Etruscan, whoever he was, and out of them all was only the Latin man. No little confusion has arisen through looking upon the landing of a body of Saxons and Jutes at Ebbsfleet on the south shore of Britain, supposedly in the year 449, as essentially the English invasion of Britain; ignoring or overlooking that far vaster yet less heralded outpouring of the Engle, or English folk, upon the long line of the whole Northumbrian coast from the Scotch border southward to the Thames. This race-crossing oversea of Engle, Saxon, and Jute was similar in character and outcome to that after English, Dutch, and Swede invasion of the New World. English, Dutch, Swedes, crossed over the broader waters of the Atlantic and made lodgment upon the American shore from Boston Bay to the Floridas. Yet it was the Englishman who held the land and gave type to the new race life. So it was in that earlier migration from the mainland of Europe to the island home in Britain. Here, too, it was the Engle, or English man who gave name and type to the new home and its people, and who absorbed the others. The Engle or English man absorbed the Saxon, absorbed the Jute, but himself remained English. And he made English men of the others. There is as good reason to use the term Anglo-Dutch as the proper race designation for the American as there is to employ the term Anglo-Saxon as descriptive of the Englishman of Britain. That there were Dutch and Swedes participating with the English in the settlement of America, is historically true. That there were Saxons and Jutes taking part with the Engles in the settlement of Britain is equally a matter of history. But it is also historically well established that in each case the dominant blood proved to be the English; and that the others lost race identity and became merged into the stronger English blood.

And that older Engle land about the shores of the Baltic was not Saxon land nor Jute land, but Engle land. The Saxon and the Jute had their lands also, but they were not Engle land. A marked line of anterior division is shown in the significant fact that while Saxon and Jute crossed the Channel together, and under common leaders, the Engle man crossed alone, thus showing a race strength which had no need of allies. And while Saxon and Jute seized upon a small portion of South Britain, the Engle boldly invaded the whole east coast and made it his own. And he not only gave his own name to the whole British land, but left it fixed even upon the waters of the narrow sea itself.

How long the Engle folk had made race home upon the shores of the mainland before they crossed the sea to Britain, no man can now say. Yet, reasoning from the laws which lie back of race migrations, we might fairly say, from times before the German had settled home in Mid-Europe; for it would seem to have been the crowding of the German from behind which forced them on westward to the rim of the sea, as it was probably the further pressure of the ever-increasing population of the German peoples after their settlement in the interior, added no doubt to the growing numbers of the Engle folk themselves, which finally drove them to seek broader homeland across the water in Britain. It is safe to say that need of land rather than lust for land lies back of most race migrations as causation.

It is this older Engle land we are now to consider; the Engle land which was before that other and later Engle land of the British Islands.

Chapter Fifteen - Engle-Land and the Engle-Man

Between the waters of the Baltic and the North Sea, in the low flat lands of Sleswick and Holstein, and southwestward through Hanover and about the mouths of the Elbe and the Weser, and even as far as the mouth of the Rhine, another division of the Teuto-Aryan peoples found a home. This man of the Lowlands was not German. The German seems to have been a later comer to the European lands. He was not Norse. The Norse man possibly preceded him; more probably is only an offshoot from him. Both belong to, and together make up, that older Teutonic wave which was pioneer upon the shores of the Atlantic. In the confusion which came of subsequent race migrations some obscurity grew up for a while about this man, and his earlier homeland upon the Continent, and the essential unity of the folk which was still known as between themselves by the minor tribal names of Engle, Saxon, Jute. It was such obscurity as was for a long while thrown about the Dorian influx into that older Greece in the myth of the return of the Herakleidai. Chief of these littoral Teutons, however, judging from the extent of his homeland upon the main shore and by his after-predominance over the others in the new homeland in Britain, was the Engle. Yet the bloods were essentially the same. They seem to have been one in race just as was that older Greek, who within himself was not yet Greek, not Hellene, not Achaian even, but still Achaian, Ionian, Dorian, Aiolian, while in blood, speech, manners, customs, type of government, he was one, and, whatever might be his minor tribal differences, one as against all others, who to him were only οἱ βαρβαροι. Another parallel is to be found in the Germans. Out of that swarming hive of Mid-Europe, Istavones, Ingavones, Herminones, as Tacitus generalizes them, with all their confused and confusing tribal subdivisions and dialectic differences which left their pestilent legacy in the numerous petty German states of even a generation ago, and in the yet chaotic German speech - out of all this was slowly evolved a common race life for the German peoples.

So, out of the mixed kin bloods of Engle, Saxon, and Jute came a common race, and a common race name, for the peoples we now know as English; but it came through the predominance of the Engle over the others. The undue historical prominence of the Saxon in the early written history of that England which grew up in Britain has arisen probably from the fact that he settled in South Britain and so was first to feel the influence of Latin civilization, and first learned to keep written record of his deeds. The Saxon Chronicles magnify in the eyes of the historian the relative importance of the place and work of the Saxon in Britain; while the absence of similar chronicles among the more backward, or less known, Engles of the farther north unduly obscures their really far greater work. We must read the history of early English Britain in the light of after-events for the corrective of this error. When Saxon and Jute disappear from the after English history, and only Engle remains, it is that the greater absorbs the less. And the correction goes back of the Engle-land which grew up in Britain, to that older Engle-land which lay between the shores of the Baltic and the North Sea. The lowland Teuton was from the time we can first trace him already more homogeneous than his kinsmen of the interior; and so he anticipated the German by a number of centuries in the development of a national unity, a national literature, and in the working out of a common race life.

Not so very much is known of that older English, or Engle, land, and of the older Engle-man, for, as has been said, not only was the earlier life of the race lost sight of for centuries in the glare of the greater folk-life which grew up afterward across the water, but also it was lived before the Engle-man had yet learned to put pen to parchment in written speech. What knowledge we have partly comes to us through folk tradition, partly through the reflected light from an after-age as seen in the old Saxon Chronicles, partly has been dug out of the upbuilding of human speech. In the Song of Beowulf, possibly the earliest of the Teutonic epics, we have a picture of the lowland Teuton before he crossed the Channel. Crude, defective, lacking in detail, it yet throws much light upon the early life of the Engle-man. The true value of these race epics is often overlooked. They are pictures rather than history; pictures of man, rather than records of men. Their value does not lie in any accurate chronicling of events, for in this they are generally worthless; it lies in that other fact that they are mirrors; that they reveal to us the man of the long-buried past, his mental and social life, his race characteristics. For this they are invaluable. They show to us after all the centuries the things which were long neglected as history, but which we now value more than all else - the daily life; what those old-time men ate; what they drank; the clothing they wore; how they were housed; after what fashion they made war; what weapons they had; the type of their government; what gods they revered, and their manner of worship; how they cultivated the soil; what grains they raised; how they kept house; and how they prepared their food; how they buried their dead; and what they knew, or thought they knew, of the life to come. Herein, and not in the mere chronicle of battling about the walls of Troy or the sea wanderings of Ulysses, lies the undying charm of the "Iliad" and the "Odyssey." We know the men and their manner of life as we know our neighbors. It is the charm of Herodotos; for Herodotos, also, wrote an epic. The Greek audience at Olympia recognized this when they named his books after the nine Muses. One booklet of Herodotos is worth more to us now than all that Thucydides wrote. And yet the world long classed him only as a teller of tales. We have learned the value of such tales; for we have learned that true history is not simply a chronicle of kings and of arms, but is the story of the evolution of man.

Of the life of the Engle-man before the days of the coming to the new home in Britain this much at least is known, that in the lowlands of West Europe the race differentiation from the other branches of the Teutonic peoples was already well advanced, and the Engle-man stood as a folk by himself, with his own folk manners, customs, traditions, and the beginning of his own separate folk literature. The germ of the free institutions of all after Engle-lands is to be found there in the free village life of that older folk home in the Netherlands of the West European shore. In the *ceorl,* the free man of the people, with voice heard by right in public assembly, was the free man, the voter of the Engle-man of to-day wherever found. In the village-moot was the prototype of the town-meeting of New England. In the hundred-moot was the first form of state government as found now in America; while in the greater folk-moot, the gathering of all the free men of the tribe for deliberation and counsel, was that which has now, for convenience because of numbers and distance, become the delegated gathering of Parliament or Congress. It was as essentially "government of the people, by the people, for the people," as that concerning which Lincoln gave voice.

The broader national life of the Engle-man was not, however, to be worked out in the older lowland home. The newer and greater Engle-land that was to be lay across the waters of the British Channel, and as yet was possessed by other bloods. The Celt was there as dweller in the land before him; and that other, and still older, of the Celtic speech, but not of the Celtic blood. In the fifth century the historic overflow began. Whatever may have been the apparent political factors inviting the migration - whether the old historic wrangle of Briton and Pict after the Roman withdrawal, and the traditional cry for help sent over the water to the lowland Teuton, or what else, the true motive force was more probably the need of a broader homeland for a rapidly multiplying people, together with the pressure of the German from behind; and added to these possibly a race unrest which has made of the Engle-man and his descendants to this day the pioneers and frontiersmen of the world. Already in the third century, before the Roman had left the land, his fleets were busy repelling the constantly recurring incursions from oversea. History points to Ebbsfleet on the Isle of Thanet, and the year 449, as the place and time of the onset of Saxon and Jute, and to Hengest and Horsa as leaders of the bands which made up the southern line of assault of the lowland Teutons upon the insular Celt. These answer for historic milestones for a portion of the Teutonic onslaught, but the greater movement was, as before stated, one of which early history has taken less note, possibly because of possessing less of the dramatic element in it; this was the steady migration of the Engle-man across the waters to the long Northumbrian -coast line of Eastern Britain, reaching from the Cheviot Hills southward almost to the north bank of the Thames. This migration had probably been going on long before. It was just such an onset as that which, a thousand years later, set in across the wilder waters of the Atlantic to dispossess the Red-man of the broad lands of America; or as that which, still later, swept over the crest of the Alleghenies and down the valleys of the Ohio, the Tennessee, and the Cumberland, to drive out Frenchman and Spaniard from the heart of the continent.

Engle, Saxon, and Jute crossed the waters of the British Channel to the new land. But it was the Engle who stamped his name upon the resulting common race; whether through mere weight of greater numbers, or whether through a more forceful tribal character, does not now appear; possibly because of both. This much is clear, that while the Jute has fixed his name upon Jutland (Jute-land) between the waters of the Baltic and the North Sea; and while a Saxon name (we may hardly say the) lingers in Mid-Europe by the waters of the Elbe; it was the Engle who gave name to the new race-home oversea, while his name disappeared from the mainland. Here the Engle-man became through word-change the English-man. Yet not all at once. Nearly four centuries passed by in the new home before the old tribal distinctions had entirely faded out; but fade they did until no trace remained. The stronger blood prevailed. And from the Roman wall to the Solent the land knew one master, one kin, one name - the Englishman.

Chapter Sixteen - The English Man of Britain

Whatever, in the ages to come, the English-speaking man may forget, one thing he can not forget that for a thousand years there was only one English land. For a thousand years Britain to him was home. Could he forget it, he would be unworthy of his name. In the great race upheavals which came to Continental Europe during and after the decline and fall of the Roman Empire, the name of the Engle soon disappeared from the mainland. Fragments of the Saxon and the Jute folk still lingered, but feeble and helpless; for their smaller numbers were scarcely felt in the presence of the mighty masses of Goth, and Vandal, and Hun as they swayed to and fro over the lands of Mid-Europe in a titanic grapple for empire. The branch which crossed the Channel, however, found behind the watery barrier of that narrow sea a home where, secure from the storms which for centuries kept its Teutonic kin of the mainland rent and torn, it might work out a race destiny. That twenty miles of water, in the crude maritime skill of the would-be invader, was to the Teuton in his new home what the two thousand miles of ocean was to the early American in the face of the better seamanship of after-ages a wall of safety behind which, with little molestation, he might go on to develop his own race individuality and consolidate his race power. That twenty miles of water made possible the greater Engleor English-land of the British Isles, and the whole after-history of the English-speaking peoples. It saved that early Englishman from the chaos which for ages swallowed up all possibility of a united national life for his Teutonic kinsman the German; and from which only within the recollection of the present generation is the wrangling brood of petty German states beginning to emerge.

Here, behind the barrier of the sea, the race character of the Englishman, as he afterward came to be known, began to take permanent shape. The germs of the older and narrower homeland here found a broader soil, a freer air, a more genial sun, and took on a new and richer life. Here the new Briton grew up; not the Briton of Caesar, who was Celt and that Pre-Celt whom he had absorbed, but the Briton of Teutonic blood who absorbed alike Celt and his predecessor. Here the primitive germs of civic life, as seen in the various folk-moots of the Continental Lowland Teuton, developed into the fixed order of a settled government. Here the rude cadences and the crude imagery of the Lowland Song of Beowulf rounded out to the measured speech and the richer mental life of the Elizabethan age. Here, putting aside the later Teutonic belief in Woden and Freya and Thor and all the woodland theogony which had covered over as with an after-growth the primitive Proto-Aryan faith, he went back in spirit to that older Teutonic trust in All-Fader, him of whom the Aryan man of the early Vedas sang ages before in the highlands of Mid-Asia, "His shadow is immortality: He alone is God above all gods"; and who to him in the newer light broadened out into the All-Father of all men. The Lowland Teuton who came to the British Isles might possibly, with different .surroundings, have developed into a different type of man. The Englishman who, after a thousand years, has gone out from the British Isles could not possibly be other than he is. A thousand years in the one mold has set the cast; and now wherever he may go he carries with him the stamp.

The conquest of Britain by the Lowland Teuton was the conquest by a people who had never yielded to the power of Rome over a people among whom Rome was dying out. The result was, a Teutonic folk who never knew Rome as the German has known it. Then, too, isolation saved them from any undue after-influence of Roman civilization; for what of Rome had been in Celtic Britain the incoming Teuton destroyed; while Continental Germany after it ceased to be a battle-ground for Roman arms remained a battle-ground for Roman ideas and Roman influence. The Englishman, like the Norseman, escaped this, and so he and not the German most nearly represents the primitive Teuton. Then, too, the immediate after-waves of incoming population were of pure non-Romanized Teutonic blood, so that the race type became fixed and set in the new home unwarped by alien forces. That the Teuton did not find the conquest of Celtic Britain so very easy is shown by the slowness of his spread over the land. Of the Engle spread in Middle and Northern Britain we have less accurate account; but south of the Thames it took the Saxon thirty years to win Kent alone. It was sixty before he had overrun South Britain. While two hundred years had elapsed before the combined Teutonic forces had become possessed of what, is now known as England in contradistinction to Scotland and Wales; and Cornwall and Devon were still West Wales. The slowness of the Teutonic progress may be explained by the fact that, like the spread of the Englishman among the Red-men of America a thousand years later, it was not so much a subjugation as it was an expulsion. When the contest ceased it was the Teuton and not the Celt who dwelt in the land. It had to be expulsion or annihilation; for, like the Redman, the Celt fought long and hard for his home. The Celt has always been a hard, tho not often a successful, fighter; some race lack of unity apparently lying back of it all. But he strikes out fiercely. Indeed, so determined, so persistent, so vigorous was the Celtic resistance to the Teutonic aggression that it casts some shadow of doubt over the historic tale that the Teuton first came to Britain in response to an appeal for help against the Pict which the Celtic Briton was fabled to have sent across the water. If the Celtic Briton did invite that older Lowland Teuton to cross the sea to his help, he soon found out his mistake, for the Teuton, then as now, has staying qualities. If he really did come to assist, he remained to hold. The Pict had indeed to go; but so also did the Celt. It was the Teuton who remained; for the land was much to his liking.

Upon the more generous soil of the new land, under a more genial sky, the Engle-man and his kin began to take on a broader growth. Now for the first time the prophecy of the race future began to show more than a mere tribal life. Yet much of the old life remained unchanged. With him he brought to the new land his older institutions and forms of civic life. The *wick* and *ham* and *tun* of the older home became the wick and ham and ton of the new. The various moots of the older kin life became the moots, or meets, of the newer English life. Even the theogony of the beechwoods of the older Teuton land quickly supplanted the weak Romanized Christianity of the Romanized Briton; as it in turn had supplanted the Druidical rites of the Celt. The coming of the Lowland Teuton to Britain was not simply a conquest; it was the migration of a people. In this, Ebbsfleet, and Southampton Water, and the Northumbrian Coast, were only the foreshadowing of that other migration of a thousand years later at Jamestown, and Massachusetts Bay, and up and down the long Atlantic shore. Yet even with the conquest of Mid-Britain completed, even with the Celto-Briton driven back to the rocky fastnesses of Wales and to the Devon-Cornwall peninsula, and with the Pict forced northward beyond the Roman wall of Hadrian, the Teutonic kin were not as yet one in national life. The conquest had been, as has been told, by separate bands each with its own independent tribal leader. The result was the petty English kingdoms of the Heptarchy; and while a common national life was slowly evolving in the new land, it required defeat rather than victory, disaster rather than success, to bring it about by forcing together for better mutual defense the separate units. It was so that the pressure of a common peril forced the English colonies in America together a thousand years later. A few centuries of this separate tribal life passed by, centuries of quarrels and battling between the various and ever-changing minor kingdoms of the land, and then again came another wave of population from oversea; and now in turn this Englo-Teuton of Britain had to fight to hold the land of which he had dispossessed the Celt. But this second wave of population, tho coming as invader and hostile, was not of alien blood as Teuton had been to Celt. It was of like kin, the Lowland Teuton of the Dane-mark. In this onrush of invasion the minor kingdoms of Britain disappeared, first forced together by a common danger, then overwhelmed in a common fate. Early in the eighth century the Norse peoples of the Danish and Scandinavian peninsulas, driven out by the scanty food supply of a too narrow homeland and led on by tales of rich, defenseless lands beyond, began to make their way southward along the West-European coast. It was the working of the same motive forces that had impelled their old Aryan kinsmen as they broke southward over the rocky defiles of the Hindu Kush into the fertile lands of the great Indian plain; the same that led the overcrowded peoples of Western Europe across the Atlantic to the shores of the New World. It is the underlying cause of all great race migrations - the hope of a homeland where life shall be less arduous, the returns of toil more generous. In the thought of these, men willingly endure the hardships, the perils of the change. Thus forced out, and thus led on, two well-marked lines of Norse overflow began to show themselves early in the eighth century - one directly across from Norway to the Shetland Islands, and thence southward to the shores of what are now known as Scotland and Ireland - the other from the Danish peninsula directly southward along the coast to the shores of what is now France. Here the latter stream divided. One branch, seizing from the weak grasp of Charles the Simple the rich lands of Northern France to which they gave their name, Normandy (North-man-dig), spread thence still further southward, and even to the Sicilian shores of the Mediterranean. The other branch, crossing the narrow waters of the Channel, began to battle for the fertile lands of the east coast of Britain. They met here a fiercer resistance than their kin found upon the other side of the Channel, and for two centuries the contest raged with varying fortunes before the end came, and Danish Knut sat upon the throne of all England.

The first effect, however, of the common danger had been to force the various minor kingdoms of the English peoples together. The despairing cry of that old litany, "Lord, save us from the fury of the Northmen," heralded the coming together of all the English kin. Two centuries before Danish Knut finally sat upon the English throne the fury of the Dane upon the long Northumbrian coast and of his marauding kinsmen further south had broken down all minor differences, and in the pressure of a common peril had brought English Egbert (year 827) to the throne of all England. From that day all the old tribal distinctions disappear in the one common name. There was no longer Saxon, or Jute, or Engle-man - only English men. And from that day all Britain became, and for eight centuries remained, all England. From the day when Egbert, first king of all the English peoples, sat upon the throne of Britain, England as a political entity, England as one of the powers with which the world has had to deal, became a fixed and sturdy fact.

Yet the perils of infancy were upon the new-born kingdom. Scarcely was Egbert seated upon the throne when the storm which had so long been threatening burst in full fury. After a troubled reign of battling with the foe, Egbert died in his bed in peace; but no peace came to the land. Nearly two centuries more of a war that had truces and temporary cessations, but no abiding peace, and then at last Danish Knut became king of the English folk;

but not before the long contest had given to all English peoples the memory of one character so purely unselfish, so entirely lovable, that he stands side by side with Washington as a common race heritage. It is as a gleam of sunlight in the dark woods, this story of English Alfred. Coming to the throne in the year 871, reigning thence until 901, his thirty years cover one of the most trying periods of that older English history. Northumbria, the land of the Engle especially, had passed under the domination of the Dane, and as Danelagh was a constant menace to the established order. And back of Danelagh was the power of the whole northland of the peninsulas. For thirty years Alfred headed the defensive fight. Sometimes a truce patched up for a few years, only to be broken; sometimes the storm of battle; and all the while the land growing poorer as the hunger of war ate up its substance. And Alfred? - sometimes as king upon the throne; sometimes at bay in a swamp stronghold; sometimes a fugitive among the swineherds of the beechwood; but always Alfred, king of the English folk, never despairing, hiding the gloom in his own heart that to his people he might present a face of hope. The warm, loving, helpful, hopeful, unselfish cheer of the man, strong to do and to bear, has made him to all after English men the typical English man of the days of the beginning, as Washington has become to all English men for the days that were yet to be. Of all English men of history British Alfred and American Washington seem most alike. There is in each the same calm equipoise, the same strength back of gentleness, the same strong hopeful looking beyond adversity to the promise of the better things before, the same broad forecasting of the future, the same unshakable trust in God both born leaders of men; and to both, each in his own land, the hearts of the after-generations have turned as Father of his Country; for while Egbert sat as first king of all the English folk, it was Alfred's patient cheer that first welded together the hearts of the English peoples into one. Thenceforward there might be English peoples many, but only one English man.

There are, indeed, some striking similarities in the details of the public life of these two men. Alfred at Reading and Ashdown at the age of twenty-two is as Washington at Great Meadows and DuQuesne at twenty-three. Alfred with his tattered forces in winter camp in the marshes at Athelney is as Washington with his tattered forces in winter camp at Valley Forge. Alfred with his untrained men of the fyrd to do battle against the trained soldiers of the Dane was as Washington with his raw levies of colonial militia against the regulars of King George; each had to make out of such crude material the army with which to do successful battle; and each did it. When in the after-years all English peoples shall have learned to know divisions no more as between themselves, and shall gather once more, as at the beginning, in folkmoot of all the kin, these two names are meetest to stand in the presence of them all as the two foremost builders of English nations; the one for the Greater England which grew up across the Channel; the other, for the yet Greater England which has grown up in the broader lands across the sea.

Might not Beowulf, kingliest of kings of the old-time English of the Lowlands, stand with them?

Like Egbert, Alfred died at the last in his bed in peace (901); but the struggle went on with varying fortunes until, as said, Danish Knut sat on the throne of all England, and went back no more to Dane-land to abide; for in the broader English kin Danish Knut soon called himself only English Knut, and reigned as an English king leaving the old English ways unchanged. England had simply gained one more English man; for, after all, the blood was the same.

But the end was not yet as between the English land and the Northman. Knut again brought all the English land under one king, and died as an English king in 1035, and the Dane came no more to the land as conqueror; but instead came Northman William from over the Channel, claiming the throne through right of succession. The battle of Hastings (1071) placed him upon the throne of all England. Yet again, as with the Dane, it was not an alien but a kindred blood, the Norse blood of Rolf the Ganger, that came in with William to possess the land as conquerors and overlords. And as with Knut, so with William; Knut came Dane, he remained to rule as Englishman; William came as Norman, he, too, remained to rule as Englishman. But after William no other ruler from oversea ever sat on an English throne by right of conquest. Knut and William in themselves as rulers would have left scant impress upon the English race life. It was the influx of Norse blood of which they were only the figure-heads with which we have to deal. That a change did come to that older English blood through this influx of a newer kin blood the whole after-history of the English folk makes clear. The England of the days before Knut and William was not in all respects the same as the England that was after them. Engle, and Saxon, and Jute seem to have grown into rather a patient, plodding folk in the new land, tilling the soil and avoiding the sea after the first crossing of the Channel. But now began to grow up a wilder, freer, more adventurous spirit in that after England because of the infusion of this wilder Northland blood. The instinct of the sea was strong in that older Dane who came to the English land. The "long ships" of the invaders made possible the greyhounds of the sea that now fly the Cross of St. George and the Stars and Stripes. And the Norman - he ever loved the twang of the bowstring, as his far-off descendant by the banks of the Ohio and the Cumberland loved the crack of the rifle. Norman William made possible the Old French War and the wresting of all the broad empire of the Mississippi from the hands of the Celto-Latin.

Yet that older, staider English blood of the land of Alfred and Harold had its share also in the after-results; for the Norse blood was a restless, lawless blood, a blood of battle and storm and stress, and lacking in some of the elements which are needful to permanent dominion. If the Norse blood toned up the slower-going old English blood, the more persistent English blood toned down the wilder mood of the Norse, and taught it to abide. The Norse blood made possible the Sea Dogs of Elizabeth; the staider English blood made possible Jamestown and Plymouth Rock. The Norse blood made possible Crecy and Trafalgar; the sturdier English blood made possible the England of Britain and America. The English blood has held what the Norse blood has won. And that older England of Eadwine, when "A woman with her babe might fare scathless from sea to sea," the England of Alfred with justice and right and law, has always been the great solid foundation upon which the superstructure of all after English greatness has been reared. Either of these bloods alone might have meant failure. Together, they have won and held empire. Knut and William both instinctively recognized this fact when, after the conquest, they each turned to the older English moot to confirm their right to the throne, and by its voice reigned as English kings.

Yet in Britain the line between conqueror and conquered has never been entirely obliterated. The fusion of bloods which in the Greater England across the sea has been long since an accomplished fact, in the older England of the British Isles is still incomplete. Gurth the Saxon still dwells in the land; and still he is thrall. Still he feeds the swine, digs the ditch, toils in the mill. And still his Norman master rules in army and church and state, and dwells in the castle on the hill, or walks the quarter-deck looking down upon Gurth before the mast. The years have changed names and forms, not facts. Only, at last Gurth is awaking, and begins to feel the stir of the blood of Saxon Harold in his veins. It is only in the newer and greater England beyond the seas that the old lines have disappeared, that the bloods have finally mingled; and there is no longer a bar between Saxon Gurth and his Norman lord, for they have met about the fireside, and are one. It is in view of this fact that the newer England of the west shore of the Atlantic may be spoken of as the truest England of all.

Chapter Seventeen - The Making of England

The period which reaches from the closing fourth to the mid-seventeenth centuries, that is, from the first incursions of the Lowland Teutons upon the shores of Britain until what is known as the English Revolution, may be spoken of as the period of the making of England - England as the world knows it to-day. These centuries brought many changes to the Engle people; some as belonging to the normal evolution of race type; some, as incident to the times and the varying exigencies of national life. Among these changes may be enumerated:

1. The formal and complete transfer of the home of the English folk from the lowlands of West Europe across the Channel to the British Isles, with the more complete evolution and fixing of the English race type.

2. The development of the hereditary kingship, and high tide of the principle of kingly authority; a consequent restriction of the older English idea of government by the people; the long contest between the two conflicting prin-

ciples of government, ending in the final victory of the people, and the practical reassertion of the primitive English idea of government by the people.

3. The change from the older Teutonic faith to Christianity; the growth of the church as an ecclesiasticism; and then the long contest of the church for civil power, ending in its final defeat. In it all, the adjustment of the spiritual nature of the English folk to a new faith.

4. The beginning of the segregation and differentiation of the Greater England across the Atlantic from the older England of the British Isles.

5. In this period also was shaped the permanent type of English speech, the old inflected forms which the Teutonic in common with the Graeco-Latin and other families of Aryan folk-speech had inherited from the Proto-Aryan mother tongue being finally sloughed off, and the resulting simpler and more direct type of speech becoming fixed and made permanent by the rich literary flowering of the Elizabethan age, and notably through the translation and popularizing of the Bible in this speech of the common people.

6. The growth of a race literature before any separation of the kin had come about through further race migration, and while the English folk yet remained one in the common home, and which consequently became and continues to be a literary heritage belonging in common to all the after-divisions of the English-speaking peoples.

I - The New Home, and the Changes which it Brought about in the Physical Constitution of the English Folk

The migration of the English man from the mainland of the Continent was a change to sunnier skies, a better drained land, and a more fertile soil. It brought to him a consequent betterment of the means and ways of living - a more certain and nutritious food supply, less fish, more meat; better shelter in his home; warmer clothing; less arduous toil. The result would naturally be, the development of a more vigorous bodily constitution. That this result did actually follow, a comparison of the English man of the British Isles with the man of the Continent, and especially before the days of factory life and overcrowded cities, clearly shows. Yet another and no less potent cause may be noted which soon began to differentiate him from even his kin over sea. The crossing of the water to the new race home removed him from involvement in the ever-recurring and harassing warfares of the unsettled bloods of the Continent, and through the very isolation left him free to work out a race destiny of his own. The twenty miles of water of the English Channel made possible the whole after-history of the English folk. Without it they would have been only as the Hollander or the Dane - a people existing by sufferance of the more numerous, and hence more powerful, races of the great Mid-European kingdoms. It was this narrow strip of water which saved them from Charlemagne, and absorption into the empire of the Franks. It saved them from the anarchy which followed the breaking up of that power. It saved them also from the anarchy of the Middle Ages. It shielded them from the armies of Philip of Spain in the sixteenth century. It was the impassable wall to the European coalitions of Napoleon.

And now the result of all this. The strength, the vitality, which Continental Europe was forced to consume in its great wars of offense and defense, the English folk, thus sheltered behind the barrier of the sea, were enabled to expend in the building up of race vigor at home until through the surplus of power thus stored up, as one stores up a bank account, became possible the wonderful race expansion of the seventeenth, eighteenth, and nineteenth centuries. It is an interesting question, How much of that robust physique, that enduring vitality under continued strain, which made the English sailor master of the seas, the English colonist master of the new lands of the world, may be due to the fact that thus secure behind the barrier of the sea the race has not during all these centuries been forced to consume its vitality year by year in drafting into its armies the young able-bodied men, those best fitted physically to beget a strong, vigorous race, leaving the old, the feeble, the undersized, at home to beget children and renew population? Every stock-breeder knows the effect upon his herd of such a policy; and the same laws hold good among men. It means inevitable deterioration of race, in size, in vigor, in endurance, in vitality. This the English man in large measure escaped because of the protection given to his land, his home, by that twenty miles of water. And this the man of the Continent did not escape, but went on age after age consuming race vitality in army and camp and field. But this curse of militarism, even tho enforced, brought to the man of the mainland yet another factor of race bane and race deterioration. Vice has ever been an accompaniment of camp life; vice that leaves the blood contaminated, and the physical constitution poisoned. The less general military service of the English peoples has kept a cleaner blood, a purer home, while Continental Europe as a vast military camp for ages has meant the very life blood of the race poisoned. The wars of the Caesars and their accompanying vices consumed the wonderful vitality of the older Roman farmer folk, the men of pure blood who had made Rome. The Spanish wars from Ferdinand to Philip consumed the splendid vitality of that mixed Latin, Iberian, Gothic blood which had found home and built up empire south of the Pyrenees. The wars of France, from Louis XIV. to Napoleon, consumed the vitality of the mixed Teuto-Celtic blood which had given to her her power. This is possibly of all the most insidious and far-reaching of the curses of war; for it is carried back to the home and helps to poison the life blood of a nation at its very source.

It is also a question of no little interest, How much of what we call nerve in certain races, the calm, cool equipoise which gives the staying quality in times of continued stress, and which is in marked contrast to the impulsive but short-lived enthusiasm of others, may be due to the heredity of long exemption from constantly recurring harassment of siege and battle? This nerve tension has been upon the races of Mid- and Southern Europe for ages. It has been as the sword of Damokles at every feast; the shadow of a cloud over every household; the unbidden guest at every wedding dance. It has worn upon the mother carrying her unborn babe, giving a prenatal cast of nerve strain to the yet dormant life. It has followed that life through the youthful school-days with the thought of the conscription, and the exile from home of enforced army life. And all this has not conduced to a reserve of nerve power. It has worn insensibly upon the race. Every physician knows the greater tendency to convulsions, to epilepsy, and to the whole train of nervous diseases which have their primal origin in lack of nerve power, as shown in children begotten and reared in times of civil strife or of home peril from foreign wars. These race harms the English man in the unassailable security of his home lands has for ages escaped. Yet he has not entirely escaped; for the English man both in the old home and the new across the ocean has had his civil wars. And then when he was still young he knew the harrying of the Northman upon his shores. The cloud recurred for a space when the bale fires were lighted for the coming of the Armada. And then it cast its shadow once more over English homes when Napoleon's flotilla was gathered in the French ports just over the narrow strait, and the Channel fleet kept watch for English firesides. Yet, as contrasted with the unrestful lives of the Continental peoples, scarcely out of one war of invasion before the threat of another has been upon them, the home life of the Englishman has for generations been one of security and repose. And the result shows in the steadier nerve, the greater reserve of endurance under long strain which is the English man's heritage.

It is a well-recognized fact that the men who best endure the strain of modern city life, who make up the greater number of the successful "Captains of Industry," and the leaders of commerce and finance, are not the men whose boyhood was spent in the incessant strain and stimulus of city life, but those who were born and bred in the quiet of the country. They come from their quieter homes to the burden and the strain with a reserve of nerve strength and endurance which the men of city birth and rearing do not possess. Why should not the law which holds good in the case of the individual hold good in the case of the race? for the race is only an aggregation of the individual men. History shows that it does hold good; and that the harassed, unresting races of Mid-Europe have ever been at a disadvantage when pitted in race rivalry against the insular and the continental peoples with a heredity of less turbulent national life. In the long contest for world dominion their endurance failed. In other words, nerve gave out. Rome's long-continued dominance and endurance under the strain of almost incessant warfare is explained by the fact that her armies were recruited, not from the Roman people, but from the fresher unworn life of the provinces, and from the ranks of the Goth. Indeed, militant Rome of the later centuries was no longer Rome; for the Goth seized upon and exploited that old blasé, worn-out land of the Latin. It was a new man - upon the throne - in court - in the army. Of the old, little more than a name remained.

The English man, as just said, in a measure escaped all this; and while other races went on consuming vitality, he went on storing it up. This is one of the secrets of the physical endurance of the English peoples; for America, Australia, New Zealand, in their oceanic isolation are repeating upon a vaster scale this phase of the history of their fathers in the British Isles.

And then the English man alone, of all the West-European races, retained in his type of Christianity the restfulness of that old Hebrew Sabbath - one day of every seven when the worry and overstrain of the struggle of life were put away, and the wearied nervous system had a chance to recuperate and thus escape premature exhaustion in both the individual and the race. The adoption of the Hebrew Sabbath is a factor of no small weight in accounting for the superior wearing capacity of the English man in his contest for race supremacy with his fellow Aryans. There was the working of a far-reaching physiological law back of the words of the old prophet when, as the mouth-piece of the Lord, he said that day to Israel, "If thou turn away thy foot from the Sabbath, from doing thy pleasure on my holy day; and call the Sabbath a delight, and the holy of the Lord honorable; and shalt honor it not doing thine own ways, nor finding thine own pleasure, nor speaking thine own words: then shalt thou delight thyself in the Lord; and I will make thee to ride upon the high places of the earth; and I will feed thee with the heritage of Jacob thy father; for the mouth of the Lord hath spoken it."

Grant said, "There comes a time in every battle when, if the one side does not run, the other will." It was merely another way of saying that every battle is only a test of nerve; and nerve means the vitality which endures. The capacity to fight harder and longer, other things being equal, is what decides victory. It was this quality of endurance which finally decided the two centuries' duel between French and English blood for the possession of the broad lands of North America. The French man had every advantage. His colonies were first established. He seized and held the one great direct waterway from the Atlantic to the interior; while before the English man were the mountains and the trackless forests. The French man had tact to make friends arid allies of the Indian; the English man could not. The French man flanked and hedged in the English with a chain of forts stretching from the Great Lakes to the Mississippi. He had a reserve home population in the mother land, and a home wealth double that which lay back of the English man. Yet when the duel of the two hundred years was ended, it was the Cross of St. George and not the Lilies of France that waved over the land from the St. Lawrence to the Ohio. It was not superior generalship that did it. Braddock's defeat was only one of the countless military blunders of the English campaigns. It was race vitality, the capacity to go on stubbornly fighting after defeat; which was ready to take up the fight again the next day, the next month, the next year, and on indefinitely - it was this which won in the end. The English man simply worried the French man out.

2 - The Kingship Versus the People

The long battling, first of the Engle-Saxon wave of invasion with the Celtic Briton for possession of the land, then of Engle and Saxon and Jute between themselves for supremacy, then of all three united against the Danish invader, then of English and Dane against the Norman onset, covering in all a period of somewhat more than six centuries, brought, through the necessities and the exigencies of war, a new political factor into the English race life, The King. In the older English of the Continent the fully developed kingship had as yet no place. In its stead was as yet only the leadership of an elective and ever-changing military chieftainship. The word King did not as yet carry with it among the Engle folk the significance it afterward acquired among them in the new land. It was this kingly chieftainship that came to Britain with Hengest and Horsa, and inferentially with the Engle men. But as the long wars with the Celtic Briton in the new home dragged on, the military leader who proved to be competent and masterful would naturally have the period of his leadership renewed or prolonged, until finally the formality of a popular expression fell into abeyance, the office became virtually one of life tenure, and then, through association in office and through family ties and family influence, was passed on from father to son, and the elective military chief had become the hereditary cyng, or king. It was thus that the temporary and elective war-lordship of Engle and Saxon and Jute had insensibly merged into a political rule which passed on from father to son until the hereditary principle became fixed upon the civic life of the various tribes; and then in the warring between themselves for supremacy as the one tribe or the other gained the victory the warlord of the victor naturally and logically became the overlord or cyng of the vanquished, until Egbert, War-lord and Cyng of the West Saxons, sat upon the throne as Over-lord and King of all the English. From that day, whether under Egbert, Alfred, Danish Knut, English Harold, or Norman William, down to Edward VII., the kingly idea has never been set aside by that branch of the English folk inhabiting the British Isles. Yet even with them the king has never been *the king* as the Latin bloods have known him, or as yet other branches of the widely scattered Aryan kin have known him. Even in the days of the highest claims of the kingship the historic fact that it was a power held as from the will of the people was in some shape always recognized. This is shown by that other pregnant fact that the confirmatory voice of the people, whether in folk-moot or by representative assembly, was never permanently set aside, but was constantly invoked to establish and make sure the kingly title. English Harold, when the succession was changed, held his crown at the vote of the kingdom. Even Danish Knut, and Norman William, coming to the throne by the elsewhere recognized medieval right of conquest, yet felt impelled to seek confirmation of that right at the voice of the folk-moot. This fact of the people as the rightful source of power is also implied in the fact of an oath of office upon the part of the king, and further in the very wording of the oath itself, "To govern well; and to abide by the ancient ways." And that the people upon their part thus looked upon themselves as the source whence the king derived his right to reign, was shown when in 1135, putting aside barons and prelates, the city of London gathered together the folk-moot and elected Stephen to be king, and as the delegating power received from him his oath of office. And that this delegated right might, if need were, be recalled by the people, is shown in that memorable scene in 1327 when Parliament, exercising upon behalf of the people the older folk-right, deposed Edward II. as a king unworthy to rule. When Sir William Trussel stood before Edward and as spokesman and representative of the "Earls, Barons, and others" took back the pledge of fealty, declaring, "We will hereafter account you as a private person, without royal authority," it was only the English folk resuming their primitive right of the initiative in the government. The same right was reasserted in 1399, when by vote of both houses upon behalf of the people Richard II. was deposed and the line of succession changed.

Yet the reserved and underlying final authority of the people was shown in a sharper lesson than that of Edward and Richard. Whenever an English king has felt tempted to say with Bourbon Louis, "L'État c'est moi," the specter of 1649 and the headsman's ax have come up before him as a warning. The Long Parliament finally, by the execution of Charles I., settled, and once for all, the relative positions of people and king; for tho it seemed for a little while, with the coming back of Charles II., that the lesson had been lost, yet time quickly showed that the days of Charles I. even were no longer possible in English land, and with the expulsion of the House of Stuart thirty years later the throne quietly accepted the decision, and with what grace it could abided by it. The king remains; the kingship is gone.

Yet the introduction of the kingship at all, even in a modified form, into the civic life of the English folk, was the bringing in of a factor so new, so entirely alien to the whole spirit of their primitive institutions, that it must needs follow that much clashing would be the first result, and that a long time must elapse before the genius of their political life would take in, and readjust itself to, the new order of things. That it never did quite thus readjust itself, the long-drawn-out contest between people and crown of the Older England in Britain, and the entire repudiation of the kingly idea by the Greater England in America, well show. That the divine right of kings to govern never found unquestioned lodgment in the English mind is shown also by the battle which never ceased until the head of Charles dropped into the executioner's basket. For this tragedy was only the culmination of the conflict which in one form or another had torn and tent the English folk for nearly twelve centuries.

In the unceasing contest of king against people and people against king that preceded the Long Parliament, the year 1215, which saw the memorable locking of horns between people and king on the green sward of Runnymede and the recognition of the people's rights in the Magna Charta, is looked to as the great landmark. And so it is. Yet it does not mark the beginning. It is only a roadmark, a milestone midway upon the journey. This was *Magna* Charta, the *Great* Charter. Back of it lay a Lesser Charter upon which it was based, and of which it was only an amplification and a reassertion, the charter of Norman Henry in the year 1100; and this again carried in it the pledge to re-store "the old law of Edward" - English Edward, last of his house, son of Al-fred of blessed memory. And back of Alfred, and the closing half of the ninth century, is only a step to Egbert, first king of the English, in the first half of the same century; and then the Heptarchy, and the kingship nominally he-reditary but really elective, with no right to make or enforce law without the assent of the people through the Witan, or Wise-men, in Moot gathered. The very oath of coronation, "to govern in accordance with the old ways" reaches back to, and brings up, the whole of that common law of the primitive Eng-lish folk which was before its kings, and which has always remained more potent than its kings. There is a common law to every community however humble, to the hamlet by the mill, to the fisher folk by the sea, to the moun-tain settlement of Kentucky, to the mining camp of the Sierra, to the mir of Russia, to the village of China: it is the custom of the people; not written; not formulated maybe; yet living and lived. It is The Way of the Land. "Our fa-thers so did," is the authority. This common law has always been the barrier between the liberties of the people and the exercise of kingly power which no king has ever been able permanently to break down. It was this that the English kings swore to observe and rule by. So far as the English man of Brit-ain may be said to have a political constitution, the ancient ways, the customs of the fathers, may be said to be that constitution. For these the English man of Britain battles as the English man of America battles for his written consti-tution; and for the same reason. Each instinctively recognizes the fact that therein lies the safeguard of his liberties.

The question is sometimes raised, When did Parliament, that public voice of the English man of Britain, have its beginning? The question might better be asked, When was there not an English Parliament? Not necessarily the two formal Houses with all the fixed rules of procedure, the presiding officer, the mace, the insignia; these are only the non-essentials, the rubbish gath-ered of the centuries. But when was there not the voice of the people, in body assembled, heard officially in their own government? The primitive ground-work of Parliament is to be found in the system of Moots of the older English folk in the Lowlands of the west shores of Europe, before the transfer of the race home to the British Isles. The initial germ lay in the Village-moot. It had its expansion in the delegated Hundred-moot of adjacent villages, as common needs and common dangers began to force the separate communities into closer union. It had its broadest foretype in the great Folk-moot, when all the kin met in times of stress or danger to consider matters pertaining to peace or war or to grave concerns of public weal. There is no clear consecutive his-tory, for the earlier records are few and faulty, but out of the maze of tradi-tion, of word unbuilding, of old chronicles, defective tho they be, one fact stands forth plain and unquestionable, that the voice of the people in their own government, and which at the first was supreme, came to the shores of Britain as a part of the folk civic life; and while in the after-growth of the race it was sometimes obscured, sometimes for a season overridden, it was yet never lost, but always reasserted itself, and was always the final and decisive authority.

This much of the history of the folk power in the government is upon record - scarcely was the first battling over and the race settled in the new land, when we find mention of the Witenagemote, the gathering of the wise men who are both the counselors and the restrainers of the king. His very office was dependent upon them, for while the succession was ordinarily in the same family line, their voice must confirm, and they could pass over, or set aside, one unworthy or unfitted to rule. Their voice must assent to the making of war, to the enactment of laws, to the division of public lands, to the levying of taxes, to the appointment of public officers. The administration of justice as between man and man, or as between a man and his community, was not in the king's hand, but was the reserved right of the people in Moot assembled. The manner of the selection or appointment of the Witenagemote from the body of the people is not quite clear; yet this fact is clear, that it was the people as against the king. The king was, in fact, but little more than a hereditary war-lord without a standing army.

To all this much change came, however, as the years passed by. About the war-lord grew up a personal following of those who owed to his power their advancement in war, and who owed to the same influence the rewards of land for public service. The king's thegns in time became the king's nobles; their interests tied up in his as against the interests of the people from whose ranks they had come. As the kings' men they claimed and gained exemption from the law of amenability to the local Moot, being amenable only to their lord for their conduct, and having support from their holdings of land for which they were to render service to him. A new order had come to the body politic. The king had gained a following whose interests were no longer the same as those of the people from whom they were thus separated, and the battle of king and people was on, a battle which never ceased until the headsman's ax a thousand years after reasserted, and once for all, the old right of the people as the supreme authority. The Long Parliament, the Parliament of Vane, and Hampden, and Pym, was the old English Folkmoot resuming again the power which ten centuries before it had in part delegated to the warlords whom it had created. "Resolved, that the liberties, franchises, privileges, and jurisdiction of Parliament are the ancient and undoubted birthright and inheritance of the subjects of England," was the wording in which the people, in delegated Moot assembled, reasserted the authority of this their representative body. The great uprising of 1642 told to all men that the Parliament, and not the king, was corporate England.

Yet while thus Parliament, and not king, is corporate England of the British Isles, even it is not England in the ultimate sense. Back of the Parliament, as back of the Moot - Witan, Hundred, Folk even - has always been, and is now, something still greater, the right and the personality of the individual, and the old ways of the folk. The English blood at least, of all the Aryan kin, has never at heart forgotten the old days when each Aryan man was still a law unto himself, his own right arm his defense, his home his castle, wherein was acknowledged no other as over-lord. It shows itself in the sturdy assertion of personal rights in the English man of the banks of the Thames. It shows itself equally in the significant pat on the rifle stock as a last court of appeals, in the English man of the mountains of Kentucky and Tennessee.

The Parliament of Britain has power to make or unmake kings. It may even abolish the kingship. But it may not abolish the right of way to mill and market of the humblest farmer. It may add to or cut off empire. It may not close the footpath under the hedge which ancient custom has made a public way. Authority to legislate upon and change the "Ways of the Fathers" has never been delegated even to Parliament. This reserved right of the individual, with the spirit of personal independence which is its concomitant, is the basic safeguard of the corporate rights of the English peoples. It has to be dealt with as an ultimate fact in any consideration of the civic life of all Aryan peoples; but most of all among English peoples. The failure to appreciate this fact is where Charles I. made his fatal mistake. And it was where the Parliaments which immediately preceded the revolution of 1776 made their fateful mistake. They had forgotten the lesson of 1642. In its exaggerated form this reserved right of the individual to act of and for himself lies back of the chronic feuds of the mountains of Kentucky and Tennessee. It is the underlying thought, tho often abused, in Lynch law. In contradistinction to the surrender of individual rights in our complex civilization, it is primitive savagery; yet it is that essential touch of primitive savagery which civilization needs to keep it from crushing out the individuality of its basic unit, man. It is the salt which keeps civilization from premature decay through over-organization. "But if the salt have lost its savor" - what then? Better even the excess, tho it may sometimes mean lawlessness, than a civilization tainted with the dry rot which quickly follows when the individuality of the man is lost in the machine. There may be something in the race-life of a people more baleful even than Lynch law.

Chapter Eighteen - The New Faith

The English man who came from the Lowlands of West Europe to the shores of Britain in the fifth century was not yet Christian. He still held stoutly to the gods of his fathers. And for gods of man's making they were no mean gods. The abominations of the Semitic theogony had never touched them. The lewdness of the Graeco-Latin Olympos was to them unknown. He could make no gods higher than himself, but they were the best of the self that was in him. Gods of the woodland, the winter skies, and the sea, they were like himself, only great, strong, simple-hearted men, true to the faith that was in them, true to their wives, true to a rude yet healthy and healthful code of high manly honor; not overly peaceable; rather given to brawl and battle, yet in an open, manly way; and, like the men who had made them, not pretending to have pierced the mystery of the far future, but looking forward to fate, and Ragnarök, and the end of all things when they, too, should go down in final and hopeless battle.

It is well to pause a moment and consider that old-time faith of our forefathers somewhat carefully, for it furnishes the key to much of the after religious life of the race. And especially does it furnish a key to the differences between the Teutonic and the Graeco-Latin types of the Christianity which grew up upon the wreckage of the older faiths. Indeed, it may be questioned whether any religion ever wholly escapes, or succeeds in emancipating itself from, the modifying influence for good or for ill of the religions which preceded it. The rule is that it does not. Assuredly Christianity in its many variant forms is no exception to the rule. In this sense all religions are to a certain extent composite. And in this more careful examination of the faith of our fathers we have to depend not so much upon any written records of our forebears, for we have not much that is direct and to the point. They were too busy fighting to do much else; and then their fingers were not yet skilled to the stylus or to the pen. It is from the Norse, more especially from the Icelandic man, that we gain largely what light we have; for he, in the isolation of his ice home, carried the old heathenism of the Teuton with its myths and legends down to the time when pen and ink-horn became comrades to the sword. The great underlying difference of that old Teutonic religion of our forefathers as contrasted with the Graeco-Latin religions of Southern Europe is its manliness. It has left a mythology marked by strength, earnestness, honesty. Its gods might be rude, but they were true. Valhalla might lack the polish, the courtliness of Olympos, but it had the merit of sincerity. It was only a larger and somewhat idealized Teuton-land, home of the gods and of stout-hearted Teutons. Woden (or Odin) himself, the All-father, is a great, strong, homely, simple-hearted man of the woods, rough but leal and true. Jove upon Olympos was more as the courtly man of the world, somewhat cynical, insincere, ready for his own gratification to betray innocence and purity. And when we speak of Woden and Jove it is to be borne in mind that we are virtually speaking of the men back of them; for Woden and Jove as gods of man's own making were only to him his embodiment of the ideal man, each for his own race, possessing in typical degree the traits which to him were race characteristics. All through the old Graeco-Latin religions run the same elements, only growing more base as you descend in the scale intriguers, jealous, untruthful, impure, betrayers of women, temples that were only houses of debauchery. Ovid's "Metamorphoses" in English would be banished from the shelves of any family library. Men, to their credit be it said, at last even grew ashamed of their gods, and the whole fabric was falling to pieces through its own rottenness when Christianity came to give it the final blow. Yet it left its baneful seed in the type of Christianity which grew up in the Graeco-Latin lands as its successor.

But in the Teutonic religions, with all their battling and bloodshed, their exaltation of brute force, we yet find truth and purity, and reverence for woman, and loyalty to the home and the fireside, with sacred regard for the marriage tie. When we look back beyond Christianity to that older religion of our forefathers, we find nothing to be ashamed of. It brings the blush to no cheek. Its myths may be read by simple-hearted children at the fireside. It was a religion that grew up in the pure air of the open sky; under the solemn shadows of the great forests where the lone winds sang anthems amid the swaying pines; out upon the stormy Northern seas where the wild waves dashed and leaped to the lashing of the wilder tempest above. What wonder that it was a religion with a certain sternness of purity about it? With such a birth-land it could not be otherwise. And this stern Northland religion also left its impress, and it was no light impress, upon the type of Christianity which followed it; for the law of heredity holds good in spiritual as well as in mental and material things. It is deeply interesting to note that older English man in the simplicity of his primitive faith groping, after his earnest, homely fashion, his way heavenward. True, neither he nor his gods saw very far into the depths of spiritual mysteries. Neither professed to. The gods themselves were too busy, battling with the giants and the dwarfs for possession of the land in which men were to make home and fireside, to trouble much about the unknowable which might lie beyond. And then with Ragnarök, and the end of all ever before them, why should it matter much? And so they battled, and toiled, and subdued the evil forces that the land might be less forbidding and men might bide in peace. It sounds all very simple, at times almost child-like, this story of Odin, the All-father, and Thor with his mighty hammer, and the battling with giants and dwarfs; and it is childlike; but it is to be remembered that this man of forest and field was as yet only a child; and this was still the infancy of the race.

Such were the gods of our fathers - only great, bighearted men, co-dwellers with themselves in the land; journeying across the craggy mountains to visit each other; trudging through the snow-drifts to Jötunheim; trying their might in games of strength with the giants; eating, drinking, making merry in the ruddy firelight, as the darkness of the Northern night-winter settled down upon the earth when the sun had fled southward from the presence of the ice-wind and the hoar-frost.

And then came that sudden burst of a softened tenderness in the soul of that stern old Teuton such as we sometimes, to our surprise, find in the rugged, weather-beaten man of the woods, or in him who is tanned and seamed by the salt spray of the sea. Baldur, the Beautiful, the Northland Apollo! How the hearts of those grim Northern races clung to him! His worship came to them as the caressing touch of a babe's hand to the wrinkled cheek of some unloved and sorrowful man. Baldur, the Beautiful! He stood among the strong, battling deities of the Teutonic mythology like the one fair, tender child that is sometimes born to a house filled only with rough unsmiling folk. Baldur, the god of sunlight, of springtime, of green grass and running waters, and the singing of birds, and whose coming brought a smile of gladness to the frozen earth; the god into whose dwelling-place nothing impure could enter, and at whose death "There was long silence in heaven; and then with one accord there broke out a loud voice of weeping." But the heart of that stern, rugged folk could not give him up; for to them he represented all that was brightest and gladdest in life. To the new earth that was to be after Ragnarök Baldur would return again, risen from the dead. For in one thing the men of that older Teutonic blood were greater, more prescient than the gods they had made; after the gods, after Valhalla, after the Norns and Ragnarök, these old men of the beech-woods felt somehow in their inmost souls that there *was* more. They, too, had a dim Northland vision from afar of what John saw upon the island of Patmos - A new heaven, a new earth, and the coming of one who was above the gods, unnamable yet sure, and he should right all wrongs, sever ill from good; and Ragnarök should return again no more forever. And in this simple old-time woodland faith men lived, served God in their homely fashion, and died without fear. "Fifty winters have I this folk ruled," says Beowulf as the death damp gathers upon his brow, slain battling for his people. "I kept mine own well; sought not treacherous war; swore not falsely; waited the appointed time. For all this, tho sick with deadly wounds, I gladness now may have. The Ruler of men may not me charge with murder of kinsmen when my life shall depart from this body." It was of such Paul wrote, "For when the Gentiles, which have not the Law, do by nature the things contained in the Law, these, having not the Law, are a Law unto themselves; which show the work of the Law written in their hearts, their conscience also bearing witness ___ " Beowulf's conscience bare him witness; and in death it was peace."

There is an especial interest attaching to the topic of the religion of our far-off forefathers in this, that as the older heathenism of the Graeco-Latin lent its molding influence to the making of the type of Christianity which Southern Europe developed, so that older heathenism of our forebears had no small share in settling the type of all our after-religion. It is an open question, How far the rude yet pure heathenism of the Teutonic races was father to the sturdy Protestantism of the Reformation? Maybe after all it was pagan England which was largely instrumental in making Protestant England. We may after all owe a greater spiritual debt to Woden and Thor and Baldur than we have been wont to acknowledge; for these were only the embodiment of the nature-faith of these "Gentiles which had not the Law."

Not without a struggle was the older faith given up. And it only was given up when the soul life of our forefathers had outgrown it; and with hungry hearts they began to grope in the twilight for something more.

One day a wandering monk came to the court of Edwin of Northumbria, that Edwin, or Eadwine, who built a city upon the hills by the banks of the Forth and called it Edwin's-Burg. The monk had a rede, or tale, to tell. It was of a faith which claimed to give to men this something more for which the hearts of those old forefathers of ours were thus beginning to hunger, and for which in the dimness they were reaching out. When the tale was told one of the ealdermen arose and said,

"It may be, O King, thou dost remember that which sometimes happeneth in the chill winter when thou art at table with thine earls and thegns. The fire is lighted, and the hall warmed, and without is the rain and the snow and storm. Then cometh a swallow flitting across the hall; by the one door it cometh in; by the other it goeth out. Pleasant to it is the brief moment the while it is within; it feeleth not rain nor the cheerless winter; but it is only for a moment, as the twinkling of an eye; and the bird is gone again out into the darkness and chill whence it came. So, it seemeth unto me, is the life of man upon earth by the side of the unknown beyond. It dureth for a little space but what is that which cometh after? that which was before? We know not. If then this new teaching mayhap shall be able to tell us somewhat of greater surety, it were well that we should heed."

And so Woden, and Thor, and Baldur, who could give no sure rede of the hereafter, were put aside; and Christ, the Christ who at the mouth of the tomb had said, "I am the resurrection and the life; he that believeth on me shall never die," the Christ from the land oversea came in in their stead; not at the point of the sword, as to Charlemagne's Franks; not because they must, as with King Olaf's bonders; but because the hungry heart of a free folk opened out to him. In that free-willed, self-respecting choice of Christianity possibly lies the key to the steadfastness with which the English folk have always clung to their faith.

Chapter Nineteen - The People versus Ecclesiasticism

Yet scarcely was the new faith seated in the land when the battle was on to keep it in its purity, and as a matter of free will. It is to be remembered that Augustine brought two things to Britain Christianity and Rome. The political power of the Roman Empire had, in the ages after the Goth, been gradually merged into an ecclesiastical power which sat in the old seat of the Caesars upon the Seven Hills. The Tiber had simply changed masters. And the spirit of the older regime passed on to the new. The Rome of the Caesars, which could brook no rival, no dissent, passed on in spirit to the Rome of Hildebrand, which likewise would brook no rival, no dissent. It was the old Roman Imperium reasserting itself within the kingdom of Christ. The nations which before must bow to the Eagles, now must bow to the Tiara. The form of submission was changed; the fact remained. The Latin races accepted Rome with Christ; the Teutonic races at heart never did; and from the very beginning the battle was on to sever the two. The battle began with the English man; it came later to the other branches of the Teutonic folk.

There is a curious parallel between the development of the kingship and that of the Roman ecclesiasticism in Britain. They rose together; they flourished side by side; they fell together; for Charles, not Henry, marks the final struggle. It is true that both had apparently a new lease of life for thirty years under the second Charles and then James, after the Restoration, but men quickly found that it was only an attempt to galvanize a couple of corpses - a few contortions, a few spasms as of life returning, and James and the Stuart dynasty and Romanism quietly slipped out of the land in 1688, unresisting, unmourned, as William of Orange came in; and no Romish king ever again ruled over an English people. The men of York, with the quick instinct of the people, recognized what the crisis meant as they rallied to the shout, "A free Parliament, and the Protestant religion." The first James had made the second James with his Romanism an anachronism and an impossibility to English peoples when, seventy years before, he had officially placed the open Bible in the hands of all English men.

Yet the change was not really a sudden one. It had taken a thousand years for it all. Rome came to a simple folk that did not foresee the end. And then Rome herself was no longer the same. The Rome of James in the seventeenth century, the Rome of the Gregory of the eleventh century even, was not the Rome of the Gregory of the sixth century; much less was it the purer Rome of the ages before. Neither was the Rome which came to Britain with Augustine the Rome which went out from Britain with the Stuarts any more than the kingship which came to Britain with Hengest and Horsa was the kingship which went out from Britain with James. Both had changed; for Rome also is an evolution. In the ten centuries the English man had traveled a long way; and Rome had traveled a long way; only, the ways had been by ever diverging lines. The Rome of the early, simple faith, humble, devout, had become the Rome of Mariolatry, of the confessional, the indulgence, of saints' worship, the wonder-working shrine, the closed Bible, the Inquisition, the grasping after worldly power. It was getting ready to become the Rome of the infallible Pope. That old cry of the Apocalypse which ceased not day and night before the throne, "Sanctus, Sanctus, Sanctus Dominus Deus Omnipotens!" was become to Rome, "Sancti Patres et Virgines Ecclesiae, et Sanctissimus Pontifex Maximus."

And the English man - he was more and more becoming a man of the open Bible, of the primitive Christ faith, of looking to God alone. To him there was but one Sanctissimus, and that was not at Rome. It was the purer, simpler faith of the old beech-woods, the childlike, reverential belief in a kindly Allfather, reasserting itself. It was Teuton versus Latin; Woden versus Olympus;

or, truer still, it was Christ versus Peter. Not the Peter of the coarse fisher-man's cloak, and the home, and the "wife's mother that lay sick of a fever," but the Peter of the Pontifical Palace, and the scarlet robes, and celibate vow, the pseudo-Peter who was not of the Twelve.

We sometimes make the historical mistake of classifying the religion of a people by the religion of its court. Thus we ordinarily say that Britain was Roman in faith from Edwin to Henry VIII.; then Protestant until Charles II.; then Roman again under Charles and James; and finally Protestant under William and Mary. We might as well accept as a gage of the current of a great river the boats that ply up and down and across its eddying surface. The reli-gious history of a people is not to be found in the life of its courts. It would be more correct to say that England never was Roman in the sense that South-ern Europe became Roman. When Bede, the Venerable, that long dying day with failing breath added line by line to his English rendering of St. John's Gospel, until, the last line written, the "*Gloria in excelsis*" floated out on the evening air as he "Fell on sleep," he had done that which time and change and Romanism never could undo - he had planted in English hearts the thought that the Bible was to be an open, and not a closed book. From that hour the open Bible became to the English-speaking man, whether Master Ridley at the stake on Oxford Common, or the Scotch cotter by his peat fire, or in the log cabin of the pioneer on the banks of the Ohio, a part of the daily life. And the English folk never from that day lost its Bible in the speech of the people, whether in the partial versions of Bede, or the Rush worth Gloss, or Alfred's Vulgate Interlinear, or the work of Alfric, or the Ormulum, or the completer works of Wycliffe, and Coverdale, and Rogers, and others, on to the author-ized version of King James in 1611. They have been trained and bred in the Scriptures by the fireside and at the mother's knee until the whole mental and spiritual life of the race has been tinctured and shaped by it. This, with a purer antecedent atmosphere of the old heathen faith, saved them from the degenerate Romanism of the later centuries. Altho Christianity came to Brit-ain, as it did to the whole West, via Rome because Rome was then the center of Western civilization, just as it spread out from the city of Constantine to the east and north from that center of Oriental civilization, and as from Alex-andria along the south Mediterranean littoral, yet the extreme West went back of Romanism to Christ for its faith. We should not confuse the messen-ger with the message.

Many things pertaining to and originating with Romanism, came to Britain with Rome, the monk, the monastery, the abbey, the nun, celibacy of the priesthood, saints' worship, the papal legate; and for a while these bade fair to become, as in Southern Europe, a part of the race life. But they were only the excrescences which time and the older heathenism had foisted upon Rome, and which the healthier, sturdier race life of the English man only for a while, and impatiently, tolerated, then ridiculed and repudiated. Yet the Eng-lish folk was not saved from these without penalty. Saved as by blood and

fire is written in the race history by the headsman's ax and the stake and fagot; for the Inquisition has left its baleful traces on English soil also. Bloody
Mary, and Smithfield, and Laud's troopers, are a part of the price the fathers
paid for the boon of a purer faith; just as France paid St. Bartholomew's - and
then lost the prize.

What Romanism had become in the eyes of the English people is well told
in the "Canterbury Tales," for Chaucer as poet of the people only voices the
popular judgment. The picture is of the "wanton friar," full of the tricks of his
trade; the nun with the dubious motto, "Amor vincit omnia," engraven upon
her golden brooch; the "pardoner," a fourteenth-century Tetzel and upon the
same errand of sacrilegious gain, for -

"His wallet lay before him in his lap,
 Brim full of pardons come from Rome all hot."

And then his unfailing supply of fictitious saints' bones to sell to the credu-
lous at exorbitant prices. The tale has the scoffing sneer of Boccaccio in it;
but it had back of it what Boccaccio's sneer failed to find in easy-going Flor-
ence, a race conscience still healthy and true. Yet it was Rome, not Christ,
that the biting sneer is aimed at, for there was another to the little company
which set out together that April morning from the Tabard Inn; and the voice
of the scoffer drops to a tenderer tone as of him he speaks. Among the frauds,
with the quick instinct of a heart yet unspoiled he recognizes and pays tribute to the true priest of God:

"A good man was there of religion,
 And was a poore parson of a town;
But riche he was of holy thought and work.
He also was a lerned man, a clerk
That Christes gospel truly wolde preche."

"This noble ensample unto his sheep he gave,
 That first he wrought, and after that he taught."

"He was a shepherd, and no mercenarie." .

"But Christe's love, and his apostles twelve
 He taught, and first he followed it himselve."

There is no sneer in this. It is the honest, true heart of the old Woden wor-
shiper putting aside monk, and nun, and pardoner, and Rome, and going back
reverently to the man of Galilee. It was this spirit that was working everywhere in the English heart. It had never, even in the palmiest days of Rome
on British soil, quite died out. The Tower never could smother it; the fagot
could not consume it; the ax could not kill it. It, and the open Bible, saved the
English man from Rome. The Puritan was the outcome of it all; for the Puri-

tan of the sixteenth century was the joint product of Woden and the Bible and Rome. He was the protest of the aroused conscience of the English people against what they held to be an apostate faith. To the Puritan, Romanism with its images and its shrines and relics, and its Mariolatry, was only an Olympus redivivus. His very excess of austerity was only the recoil of an overbent spring. It was the reaction from Roman license. "Fanatical?" - Yes! The "wanton friar," and the "pardoner" with his indulgences for sale "all hot from Rome," and the Tower, and Smithfield, and Laud's troopers, and the studied insult of the "Book of Sports" read by royal order from the pulpit to a God-fearing people upon the Sabbath, had done their work. The fanatic upon the one side was the legitimate product of the fanatic upon the other. But the Jesuit zealot of the court was met, and in the end overmatched, by the Puritan zealot of the people, who was his normal product and antithesis. That the Jesuit did not produce the Puritan in Southern Europe, shows the difference between the peoples, a difference which is racial and radical. We go back of Christianity, back of Woden and Olympus, back of these to climatic environments probably for predisposing factors; and again still back of this, possibly, to some more subtle race variation for an ultimate cause. But whatever the cause, the fact is to be noted that the two types of Christianity, the Roman and the English, were essentially unlike, and produced essentially unlike men.

Chapter Twenty - The Puritan

The Puritan was the aroused conscience of the England of the seventeenth century. While Cavaliers jested and gambled and drank, and filled the public eye, and while king and court toyed and coquetted with Rome, the Bible had, unnoted, been doing its work among the people. The Puritanism of the seventh century was to its age what the Wesleyanism of the eighteenth century became to the English man of a later Britain, a quickening spirit. It became a flaming fire. Under its power the only half-way Romanized English man awoke to a higher soul life. Yet as extreme begets extreme, Puritanism was not a normal, spontaneous religious expression of the higher type of spiritual health, but the expression rather of a reaction which became even morbid in its intensity. So extreme was the reaction from the Mariolatry and the saints' worship which Rome had somehow foisted into the New-Testament teachings, that the Puritan in spirit virtually went back and ranged himself side by side with the Jew under the Old Law and the Prophets. While Rome developed a pagan Christianity, the Puritan developed a Jewish Christianity. To him the divine revelation came rather from the Jehovah of the fire and the thunderings of Sinai than from the pitying face upon the cross. When he prays, it is as Elijah at the cave of Horeb in the desert, alone; he only standing true, all others fallen away from God. When he speaks, it is as tho Jeremiah had arisen from the tomb to hurl forth his denunciations and pour out his lamentations. The Puritan, like the Scotch Covenanter, was rather a man of the Old Covenant than the New. Both were men of the Law, and of blood. Even their tenderness had in it somewhat of the fierceness of the men who came down out of the coverts of the rocks to do battle with Midian. It is "the sword of the Lord and of Gideon" that rings out as the battle-cry over Edge Hill and Marston Moor. There is not in him much of the "love that suffereth long and is kind"; there is much of the "eye for an eye, tooth for tooth, brand for brand, burning for burning." Adversity had made him hard; persecution had made him bitter; the frivolities and the profligacy of church and court had made him austere; a spirit of morbid introspection made him seem sour-faced and forbidding to the gay Cavaliers of the Stuarts; but weak no man ever called him; and when the clash came, the "Sword of the Lord and of Gideon" flashed in his hand upon the field of battle; and Cavalier and King and Church went down before him. It is no small debt we owe to him, the keeping for us of the faith of the fathers; for Puritanism saved England from Rome. More that Puritan revolution of 1646 possibly saved Britain from the wild upheaval of 1793 and the guillotine.

Foremost among Puritans, *primus inter pares,* stood out one figure, Oliver Cromwell, kingliest of uncrowned Britons. Stern, rugged, massive, filled with gloom, and yet rejoicing as an old berserker in the fierce joy of battle, he, possibly more nearly than any other one man, is representative of the spirit of Puritanism embodied. He was not Puritanism; it was born before him; it lived after him. He was not even, it may be, its most unselfish, self-obliterating exponent. By the pure light of Hampden's life the fires of Cromwell's passion burn with a lurid and smoky flame. Yet as the prime figure in a great drama which became the culmination of the Puritan reaction, no other man so stands forth in history as its living embodiment. Occasions are said to make men; yet some men fail under the stress of the occasion; others do not. This be it said of Cromwell, that when the occasion and the stress came, he did not fail.

In the battle King and Church went down. Then again followed the law of reaction, and the recoil from the overcompressed spring of Puritanism; and after the Puritan triumph and the Protectorate, came again to Britain Rome and a second Charles. But only for a little while. It was weariness, not exhaustion. England only gathered her breath. And then 1688 finished the work of the first revolution; and Puritanism returned to power again, a Puritanism shorn of its excrescences, a Puritanism broader, sweeter, more kindly-hearted, having no less of the firmness of the Old Law, but having with it more of that charity which is the loving αγαπη of which Paul spake; and Rome for the second time went out from Britain; went out to come back again no more to power in English land, unless the children forget the fathers, and the price the fathers paid for religious freedom.

It is not to be inferred, however, that Puritanism represents all of the religious life of the English peoples of that day. The Established Church which grew up upon the wrecked foundations of Romanism was narrow and intolerant at the first like the Rome which it supplanted; for to Henry VIII. and the Stuarts the Established Church was only a second Rome, and the ruler of England only a local pope. Yet it had in it a spiritual life which, altho sometimes cramped, and often for a time overgrown with the political fungi that sapped the soul of the Rome of the temporal power, still developed back of it all a sweetness and an ever broadening charity which have done much to make the home life of Britain wholesome and clean and true. Yet that Puritanism was the expression of the deeper national conscience of the race, and that it, and not the Established Church, has been the spur to keep the English man of Britain up to his spiritual best, probably no thoughtful student of the religious life of the English folk can well question.

For history repeats itself in ecclesiasticisms as in states; and the *Episcopus* of Rome, with all that this meant of conservative clinging to a form-bound and ritualistic past, remained with the Established Church; and as it was not these that had aroused the English people from the spiritual torpor of Rome, so could they not be a quickening fire to keep alert and active the spiritual sense among them, or to arouse them in the hour of religious peril. When the true hour of testing came, it was the Independents with their non-episcopal, congregational system in Scotland and Britain that kept the fires of religious zeal burning and saved England from falling back to the Papacy in the seventeenth century. It was Puritan and Covenanter, rather than the episcopal supporters of the King, who in that struggle saved the faith of the English man; as it was the revolt of Wesleyanism in the eighteenth century against the growing formalism of the Established Church which again fought the battle for a purer and a livelier faith. In Britain Wesleyanism remained prudently and safely non-episcopal in form. In America it has reverted; and is thus one step, and a long step, further back upon the ecclesiastical road which led out from the ways of Rome and all this means in church and state. And the Episcopus gives an ever growing bond of sympathy between all non-congregational types of ecclesiasticism.

It might be well to pause a moment longer before passing on from this question of the religious struggles of our forefathers. The world rarely sees at the time of their occurrence the full bearing of events. There was more involved, and more to result from that old struggle of the Papacy with English Puritanism than the mere question of religious beliefs. It was not merely Rome versus England. It was Latin versus Teuton. Religious fanaticism kindled the fire, but race rivalries kept it burning. The reply which Howard and his ships gave to the Great Armada in that long running fight up the British Channel was not the last word of the controversy. And it was more than the beard of the king of Spain that was singed by the freebooting Sea Dogs of Elizabeth. They harried the Spanish coasts; but they also swept the Spanish Main. That long-drawn sea-fight crossed the broader waters of the Atlantic, and was the first loosening of the hold of the Latin upon the New World and upon that broader sea which lay still beyond. It is a long way from Howard in the Channel and Drake at Corunna to Sampson at Santiago de Cuba and Dewey at Manila, three long centuries and more, but they are only the two extremes, the opposite ends, of the one struggle. Not foreplanned so to be by the governments involved; possibly not seen to be such by the peoples taking part; but the retrospection of history will so group them.

The defeat of the Armada was the first fatal wounding of the Papacy in its grasping after world dominion. And it betrayed the final emancipation of the English man's conscience from the political bondage of Rome; for Howard who was admiral-in-chief of the English fleets was a Catholic; and Catholic fought side by side with Protestant through those long anxious days against Catholic Philip and the Jesuit and the Inquisition and the Papal blessing and the commission to extirpate heresy in Britain. The defeat of the Armada was also the historical mile-post which marks the turning-point of Britain's political greatness. It settled her future as a world power. The "singeing of the beard of the King of Spain" by the sea-rovers, brilliant as it was, was still only a singeing. It still left the power of Spain and the Latin unbroken. But that long fight up the English Channel was a historic turning-point. As the gathering of the Armada had been the culmination of Spain's efforts upon the sea, so its defeat marked the beginning of the decline. From that day Spain ceased to be supreme upon the water; and from that day the loss of her vast colonial possessions was foredoomed. True, Philip defiantly said that he could easily build another Armada; and so, indeed, he might; but Philip never did; for he had learned anew that old, old truth which Xerxes learned ages before at Salamis, and which France learned at Trafalgar, and Spain had to relearn at Manila and Santiago de Cuba, that it is not so much the ships as it is the men who sail and fight the ships, that settles the question of the mastery of the seas.

Before passing on from the topic of the radical religious divergence which came between the two great Western divisions of the Aryan peoples, this might be said in common for all the Teutonic peoples, that they never at heart really accepted the spiritual domination of Rome. For a while, under the pressure of the political ascendency of the Latin peoples, a tacit submission was yielded; but with the throwing off of the Latin civil imperium it became only a question of time when the Latin ecclesiastical imperium should follow: for the whole spirit of the imperium, whether civil or ecclesiastical, was foreign to the free instincts of the Teutonic blood. Then, too, the direct-dealing Teuton, with an inborn scorn for indirect ways, never could in his soul be made to believe that God, the God of a universe of broad-based, far-reaching and eternal law, and yet a God of whom it was said that "Like as a father pitieth his children, so God pitieth them that fear him," would stoop from his high estate to trifle with the pleading cry of his children for spiritual guidance in the dark by giving as the seal of authority for his kingdom upon earth, and the way of salvation for man's soul, a supposititious pun upon a name, and a defective pun at that, for πετρος is not πετρα. A juster conception of the eternal fitness of things, and a nobler conception of God, was born

168

in the soul of that old Teuton, and he turned away in a lofty scorn, for he felt in the depths of his being that the pitying All-Father would not so trifle with his children. It was not so that God founded his church of the Old Covenant that day upon Sinai in the fire and the thunderings.

And Peter, poor impulsive, unstable Peter - this was not the *petra,* the solid mother ledge of rock upon which to found the Church of God. He was only, as his name, *petros,* the rolling-stone.

"Or what man is there of you who, if his son ask bread, will he give him a stone? If ye then, being evil, know how to give good gifts unto your children, how much more shall your Father which is in heaven give good things to them that ask him?"

The New England

Yet all this long battling of king, and people, and church, did not come to an end before Puritanism had done another work - Puritanism spurred on by the lingering spirit of Rome in the new ecclesiasticism of the England of the British Isles. And this thing which Puritanism did was the most fateful that ever came into the destinies of the English peoples in all their after-history. It was the transplanting of a scion of this intenser English conscience and English faith to new lands across the sea. It was the planting in a new and more fertile soil, under newer and broader skies, of the germ which in its growth was to become a shaping and dominating influence in the spiritual and mental life of the Greater England which was to be beyond the waters. It meant that this intenser English faith, this aroused English conscience, should no more be simply insular and local in its molding power upon the spiritual life of man, but should become continental, and then world-wide. It was the expansion of Puritanism.

When Pastor Robinson and his little band, grown weary, and hopeless of better days in the English land of the British Isles, recrossed the narrow waters to the shore of the old race home in Holland, and then after a few years of tarrying knelt down that day on the oozy banks of Delft-Haven while they commended themselves to God, and then, only a feeble band, set sail to find a new race home beyond the broader seas, they builded better than they knew. They were only the forerunners. They opened the way for that flood of Puritan migration which in the next twenty years sent two hundred ships freighted with twenty thousand souls of the best English blood, out from the old land into the new, self-exiled for conscience' sake. Twenty thousand! Not many as measured by the yearly statistics of Castle Garden in the year nineteen hundred, but enough to leave their impress upon the whole after-history of a continent.

Yet the Pilgrims, and the *Mayflower,* and the wintry seas, and Plymouth Rock, and 1620, were not the first of the English race life in the New World. Thirteen years before, Captain Smith and the London Company had laid the foundations of their town on the banks of the James. Neither did the New-

England folk of Massachusetts Bay supply the bulk of that after-stream of remigration which was to build up English empire beyond the mountains in the great interior valleys of the continent; rather did it long remain local and provincial in habitation and type. Its importance lay, not in its numbers, but in the intensity of the moral purpose which was behind it. It was the influence of a belief that really believed something, and believed it with all its might. The Puritan, and not the more easy-going blood of the Southern migration, struck the key-note for a new national life. It was the Puritan who gave to the new land, as to the old, its Jewish Sabbath, and its high moral purpose. In the new he gave also the revolt of the national conscience against slavery.

The continuation of this topic of the race life in the New World belongs later, and under a different heading. There remains still much of the life in the older home to be considered. Yet the historical fact is to be borne in mind, that the Puritan conscience had its awakening, not "On the wild New England shore," but across the sea, in the older folk-home of the Mid-English land.

Chapter Twenty-One - English Speech

The English speech was brought to the shores of Britain as an inflected speech. This form it had in common with all the other Teutonic tongues. Judging from the elaborate inflected forms of the Sanskrit, the member of the Aryan family which in point of antiquity seems to be most closely in touch as a written speech with the common origin; and judging also from the less elaborate, yet well-marked, inflectional framework of the whole group of Aryan tongues, an inflected structure which in each member of the family grows more elaborate as we trace them backward in their grammatical history; we may reasonably infer that the inflected type of speech has descended to them as a common inheritance from some highly inflected common Proto-Aryan mother tongue. Ten centuries after the landing in Britain, however, English speech stood shorn almost entirely of these grammatical forms, practically non-inflected, largely monosyllabic in type, while kindred German and the other Teutonic speeches have not so changed. On the contrary, the German in its word-joining seems to be entering again upon that agglutinative stage which precedes a more complicated structure. English speech has gone on yet further and rejected also some of the vocal sounds which seem to have been common to at least the Teutonic branches of the Aryan peoples. Some of its changes may be specified as follows:

The obscure ü and ö vowel sounds, and the ill-defined *ch* of the German, which the older English seems to have had with the other Teutonic tongues as a common heirloom, have disappeared.

The substantive, which in the Sanskrit had eight cases in its declension, and which in Latin retained six, in Greek five, in German four, and which in the older English had six, has in the changing dropped to two.

The varied forms of declension have narrowed down to one.

The dual number has been lost.

The verbal distinctions of an arbitrary gender, with the consequent perplexing declension of the article and the adjective, have been dropped. In contrast, German has sixteen case forms of the definite article *the* alone to be remembered and differentiated in speech. The adjectives and the adjective pronouns are similarly encumbered.

The verb in English has lost augment and reduplication; and the tenses have been brought to a simple and logical form.

Auxiliaries in the verb, and prepositions with the noun, have been made to do the work which was before, and in other Aryan tongues is still, largely done by grammatical changes in the structure of the words themselves.

In short, the English speech as developed in Britain by the fifteenth century had gone the round of the circle from the primitive monosyllabic, non-inflected form of some far-off ancestor of the common Proto-Aryan mother tongue, through the agglutinative stage of its help-words to that consolidation of root and helper which we call inflection, and is now again back nearly to the simplicity of the original starting-point in its use once more of the separate auxiliary, or time- and mode-helper to the verb, and in the use of the preposition with the noun to indicate the varied relationships of the substantive. The whole historic process of reconstruction has been one of simplification. And out of it all the speech has come broader, deeper, richer, more capable of expressing the varied and subtile thoughts of a race no longer in its childhood. Language and mind should keep even pace in race evolution. If they do not, if language in its development lags behind, it becomes a clog and a crippling force to mental growth. The Mongol tongues are cases to the point. They have become to the Mongol mind what the swathing bands have been to the Mongol foot.

That this law of returning simplification is one of natural evolution by the lines of a spiral which ever returns upon itself, only to a higher level, is shown by the same tendency to returning simplification in most of the modern tongues. The Neo-Hellenic tongue of the Athens of to-day is Greek in word; but it has sloughed off much of the older grammatical complexity of the days of the Greek dramatists, and is assimilating to the directness of modern speech. The daughters of the Latin have lost the grammatical intricacies of the involved Ciceronian sentence. Of all modern speech the German seems to have least felt the beneficent influence of this spirit of simplification. The verb has yielded; the noun, the pronoun, and the adjective remain cumbered with the older complicated inflections of case and gender little changed. It is a heavy weight the German has to carry in the competition for the position of a world speech. French, which even a century ago was still the recognized tongue of general intercourse between nations, has dropped out of the race entirely. German is falling behind. The simpler, almost grammarless English speech is distancing all rivals. Much of this no doubt may be ascribed to the rapid spread of the English peoples over the world, and to their position as its chief traders, yet the simple directness and force of the English tongue unquestionably have much to do with it. When the long delayed, but urgently needed reform shall be made in the spelling of the written English speech its spread will be even more rapid. This is its one drawback. For while of all languages English is one of the easiest to acquire as a spoken tongue, it is one of the most difficult as a written speech; and this solely because of its unphonetic and arbitrary orthography.

In tracing the evolution, through simplification, of language from the past we might easily fall into error, however, if we were to assume that all the complexities of the written speech of antiquity as it is passed down to us in the works of its scholars, were necessarily a part of the speech of daily life among the great mass of the people. The written speech of the scholar is preserved to us; the unwritten speech of the people, that which was heard upon the street and at the fireside, has little record. Yet this much we know, that side by side with the formal, elaborate language of the writer was another, simpler, more direct, Ἡ γλῶσσα κοινή of the Greek, the Lingua Rustica of the Latin; and this, and not its more scholarly associate, is in each case the true parent of modern speech. Possibly it might be more correct to say that out of the merging of the two has arisen the modern speech; and there are no longer two tongues, one for the scholar, another for the people. Yet the union has not been an equal one, for while the words are essentially the same for each, it is the elaborate grammatical forms of the written speech that have largely disappeared, the words as largely remaining. The speech of scholar and of peasant met; and it is the peasant that has triumphed. And. there is reason for this. It means that the great mass of the plain people has relatively grown in importance. It is only one of the indications of a mighty change in humanity. It shows that the current of modern life is reaching down past the surface drift of king and courtier, and schoolman to the great undercurrent of humanity. It is the evolution of Gurth, the swineherd. It means that man also, as well as his speech, is traveling back again upon the circling curve of the spiral to the line, but not necessarily to the level, of his starting-point. It means that as there was a day when king and courtier and schoolman rose above the level of the mass of humanity about them to a separate and distinct mental life in thought and in speech, so there comes again a day when humanity reasserts itself; and king and courtier and schoolman become the less and not the greater quantity in the problem of life. The change in speech is only the index of the more radical and far-reaching change back of it. A word in its grammatical transformations, as we trace it through the years, is often a truer key to the history of man than any of the pages of Buckle or Guizot. It is a palimpsest only waiting to be deciphered. As already stated, the German has shown less sign of yielding to the trend toward simplification than any other of the modern tongues. It might, not inaptly, be classed as a case of linguistic arrested development. The explanation to this is to be found in the race history of the German man; for of all modern peoples of Western Europe the

German remains the most unyieldingly medieval in his political ideas. Germany is still the land of the War-lord and of the divine right of Kings, while even the Latin, weighted as he is with the incubus of the Roman Church, is leaving these things behind.

In curious contrast with this general trend toward simplification in the evolution of modern speech is the unphilosophical attempt which has recently been made to frame a universal language. In Volapük not only were the obscure umlauted vowels and the deep guttural reinstated, sounds which to English throats are unpronounceable; but also the old, elaborately built-up verb of changing root vowels, and augment and reduplication, and substantive of many-cased terminations, were resurrected from the graveyard of buried tongues in the vain hope that the world would turn back in its pathway and strike hands again with the dead. It was a strangely blind attempt to arrest and turn back the whole current of evolution of modern speech. And curiously, but not strangely, this ignoring of the whole philological drift in the evolution of modern speech was by a German.

One feature of the English speech is not to be overlooked, a virility which has kept it essentially one and the same amid all the vicissitudes of race life down through the centuries. While it, in common with other tongues, has had to undergo the attrition which comes of contact and collision with other speeches, it has had inherent strength to withstand the contact and to overcome. It met the speech of the conquered Celt; absorbed and then assimilated somewhat; but remained English. It was held thrall by the Norman French for a season; but it absorbed and assimilated its ruler, and remained English. It was swayed for a season by the revival of the classics; developed the elaborate Latinized English of Milton, the pompous Johnsonese of Fleet Street; but kept them as one keeps upon a shelf the stiff collar and the elaborate but excessively uncomfortable dress-suit for ball or court; then went back to the simple, lucid, direct speech of Bunyan and the English Bible. The Romance languages under similar testing yielded to the strain, and drifted away from the Latin mother tongue until, while still Latin in name, they are only partly so in words and scarcely at all so in grammatical form. The virility of English speech which would not permit it to be conquered is in the end making it the world conqueror. And as of the speech, so of the man, for either is index to the other.

One other feature of the English language is to be noted. By the cessation of the use in common speech of the older grammatical forms of the second and third persons singular of the verb, and the second person singular and plural of the personal pronoun, and by a limited use of a few archaic words and forms, peculiarities so simple and yet so marked that the most unlearned recognize and comprehend them in a moment, a stately type of sacred speech is framed and set apart for the Scriptures and for devotion, making virtually a separate tongue. It is to the English-speaking peoples what the sonorous Latin is to the Roman Church service; yet it is not, as the Latin tongue, dead and devoid of meaning to the masses who hear. No other of the modern tongues has to the same degree set apart a portion of its linguistic forms as sacred to man's religious needs, and no other has reaped so inestimable a reward in the broadening and enriching of the whole spiritual life of the race. The great value of a sacred speech to the soul life of a people is little comprehended by those who would render the Scriptures into the hackneyed forms and words of every-day use. The attempt, in its degrading tendency upon the spiritual life of the people, may rank side by side with the secularization of the Sabbath and the banishment of the Scriptures from the schools. Rome so well understands the value of a religious speech which is separate and apart from the speech of every-day life, that she clings to a tongue dead for centuries, while certain short-sighted so-called reformers would cast away that priceless treasure to the English people, a sacred speech, vernacular, living, intense, and which has in the stress and battle of the centuries become interwoven with every fiber of the spiritual life of church and home and fireside, and which withal is so simple that it may be understood by the veriest child.

Chapter Twenty-Two - English Literature

Parallel with the development of English speech, accompanying it both as a causative force and also as a resultant, is to be considered the growth of English literature as distinct from the literatures of the other Aryan peoples. The literature of a race is simply the verbal expression of its mental life. As it comes down to us from our forefathers it is simply the family portrait gallery, showing what manner of men our ancestors were, what they thought, how they looked out upon the world about them, what glimpses they had of the unseen world beyond.

Of all the Teutonic kin the English man was first in the development of a literary life of his own. While the German was yet pouring over the monkish tales of the old Latin fathers, and while the Norse man was still the unlettered child of the fjord and the ice floe, the English-speaking man was already well advanced along the pathway of a literature that was native to the blood. The isolation of the English man in his new home, and his consequent exemption from the unceasing wars of the mainland, may probably account for this; just as the isolation and the quietude of the Icelandic shores were productive of the first and the richest literary life of the Norse peoples. But whatever the cause, the fact remains that by the early seventh century the "Song of Caedmon," with the yet earlier "Traveller's Song" and "Deor's Complaint," began to give to the English folk a historic literature; not to go back to the prehistoric "Song of Beowulf," which, like the Nibelungen of the whole Teutonic peoples, and the inherited cycle of the Arthurian legends from the Celt, takes hold upon a time to which, in the wording of the old common-law phrase, the memory of man runneth not back.

It is no part of the plan of this work to give a review of the literature of any of the Aryan peoples, but only to discuss and differentiate their respective lines of development and, so far as possible, to indicate briefly the causes, racial, climatic, or other, which may lie back of these differences. This much at least is an essential part of the comparative study of those race variations in type which we have found to exist. Consequently only such mention of individual works or authors is made as may help to bring out and throw light upon the principles involved.

Between the Teutonic and the Graeco-Latin literatures there is a well-marked dividing line. The easy life of the Mediterranean shore, and its sunny skies, have not been without their influence upon the mental type of the Aryan peoples who first settled there, as the inclement skies, the gloom, and the more strenuous life of the Northlands have been to the Aryan folk who made them their home. The "Iliad" could not have been first sung by the North Sea. The "Aeneid" belongs elsewhere in its very atmosphere than by the storm-tossed waters of the English Channel. Neither could the Song of the Nibelung or the grim chant of Beowulf have had birth by the sunlit waves of southern seas. In the one case the gleam and the cheer of the summer sun have illumined the whole spirit of song; in the other, inclement skies, the chill of winter, and the hard battle for existence are felt in every line. The only parallel to the fateful gloom of the Nibelungen to be found upon the Mediterranean shore is in the cycle of legends which centered about Boiotian Thebes, and which found utterance and undying fame in the somber dramas of Alschylos and Sophokles. The doom which hung over King Laios and his house, a doom unprovoked, unforeseen, unescapable, is as full of gloom as the closing scenes of the Nibelungen in the bloody feast-hall of King Atli; while Gunnar singing his death song in the adder pit, and Oldipous answering to the death-hail on the lone hill at Kolonos, are twin scenes of fateful darkness. But the Theban cycle is in spirit wholly exotic to the shores of the yEgean. In spirit it goes back past those days of the Greek by the Aegean as to some prehistoric legacy from the stress of the old Aryan struggle upon the rugged uplands before that ever the sea, and ease, and the laughter-loving southern sun, had worked their will in the mental cast of the Hellenic people. The Greek of the after-years forgot Jokasta, and Oldipous, and Kolonos, as he sang gleefully the Ionik wine songs of Anakreon. And the Roman - he drank, and hiccuped, and after his clumsy fashion echoed the tripping notes of the Greek lyre.

It is with the somber Teutonic mind, however, that we have now especially to deal. This takes in two great divisions, the German and the English; for the Norseland failed to keep up the fair beginning of the Icelandic Sagas. As contrasted, these two show marked differences in type. The German, dreamy, introspective, often morbid, tells of a race life hedged in and repressed. The centuries of tumult as the battle-ground of Europe, with the constant necessity of a crushing militarism which reaches down from the days of Caesar to the present, have left an indelible stamp upon the German mind. Forced inward upon itself, for ages cut off from the healthful stir of political life, depressed by the horror of sacked cities, of homes broken up, of families scattered, divided into little duchies, torn and rent by dissensions, without the spur and the aspirations of a common race life, it has missed the well-balanced virility of the English. From part of .this it is now emerging through the long-delayed but at last seemingly possible German unity. Prussia and the Hohenzollerns have done this much at least for the German peoples. Yet the very union brings with it a danger even more to be feared in its ultimate effect upon the German mind and its possibility of intellectual fruitage than were the old days of division. The life of the German peoples is to-day, as never before even in the darkest times of disaster, being absorbed into their armies. All Germany is only a vast military camp. The soldier is everywhere the dominant feature in the land. War, or the preparation for war, is the one all-absorbing idea of the race. The child plays with its toy soldiers. It hears the sound of drum and trumpet in the street. The youth looks forward to his years of enforced military service. The men think war, talk war, dream war. One people before in history did the same thing, trained, drilled, stood guard; and the mental life of the race became as dead, as unfruitful, as the desert. Sparta stands as a never-to-be-forgotten warning to the German. Historian, poet, dramatist, artist, while the Ionia of the Asiatic shore, Attika, the circling isles of Aegean, and even the Magna Graecia of barbarian vicinage beyond were their fruitful habitat, to them the arms-blighted plain of Hollow Lacedaimon was as fatal as the vale of the fabled upas-tree. No Spartan wrote a book, sang a song, chiseled a statue, drafted a play. Germany may remain the first military power of Europe (until the crash comes), but the price must be paid. It will be at the expense of her intellectual life which will become as barren as that of Sparta of old, unless the law of cause and effect shall change.

From all this the English man was saved. The twenty miles of sea-water which made possible the unhampered political life of the English people, made possible also a mental life as unlike that of the German as dissimilar surroundings could make of kindred bloods. No contending armies age after age ravaged and harried the English man's lands. Wars there were, as to all lands, but only for a little while; and then when the battling was over, peace returned; and no great standing troop absorbed the mental life of the people. No conscription thinned the ranks of the thinkers and the intellectual up-builders. No years of unquestioning military subordination throttled the freedom of thought. Every English man's house was, as the common law phrased it, his castle; and within its doors he dwelt and thought by his own fireside in freedom and peace. Instead of the repressing weight of a war-lordship over his land, even the mild kingships of the old Heptarchy soon became the powerless kingship of the England of the unwritten yet all-powerful English Constitution. Folkmoot passed on into Parliament. The assenting clash of spear and shield, and the mighty shouting of the armed host in council gathered, merged into the silent yet no less potent ballot. The right to bear arms, which the British English man held ever of unwritten right, and which the American English man has further guarded by written law, never was lost. Back of the literature of the English-speaking man lies as its very foundation-stone English freedom. Under the spur of freedom the English mental life became active, realistic, aggressive, because the race life was active and free to expand. The difference between the German and the English-speaking man is the difference between the student of the cloister, shut within monastery walls, and the man who goes afield, gun in hand, in the early morning, and so is in touch with all nature. The one is the recluse, possibly the more learned; the other, the man of the world about him, less scholastic it may be, but wiser. Of the two, the English mind would seem to be the saner, the more wholesome. And while the English mind is free from the mysticism of the German, it is equally free from the superstition of the Celt. It is a matter-of-fact mind of a type distinctively its own.

Not least among the molding influences at work in shaping the literature of the English peoples has been the Bible. It, more than any other one thing, has helped to fix and keep pure the English speech; and it more than any other influence has served to elevate and keep sweet and pure the whole mental life of the race. From the day in the first half of the eighth century (circa 735) when the Venerable Bede rendered the Gospel by St. John into the speech of the common people, on down through the various versions and imprints, the Scriptures have been a part of the daily life of the whole English folk. But especially in the older forms of the Prayer-Book, and in the somewhat later version of King James in 1611, have they been filtered into the whole thought and mental life of the race. Of all men of modern speech the English man is most in touch with the Hebrew; and of all modern tongues the English in the simplicity of its strength most readily lends itself to the work of rendering the Hebrew idiom. So idiomatically English have been the various versions of the Scriptures, that one loses sight of the fact that they are translations. It may seem strange that the most intensely practical and realistic of all modern peoples should be of all the most closely in touch with the Hebrew, who of all ancient peoples was the most unpractical, the least materialistic. It shows in the English folk a deep undercurrent of spiritual life which is separate and apart from the qualities that are making them world-masters in manufacture and trade. So closely does the idiom of the one speech lend itself to the work of rendering the idiom of the other that the thought of translation is lost sight of. To the great mass of English-speaking people the Bible is their Bible; it is in their tongue God speaks; the Law and the Gospel are primarily their Law and Gospel; they are the Chosen People; the New Jerusalem is to have English spoken in its streets as the tongue of the redeemed. The mighty hold that old Hebrew Bible has taken upon the English-speaking peoples is shown in the fact that they, and not the Hebrew, not the Continental European, are its missionaries, its evangelists to the world. The hundreds of millions of printed copies of the Scriptures which have gone out to all lands of the earth have been from the presses of English peoples, paid for by their money, distributed by their hands. It is a remarkable and a pregnant fact. Such a hold of the Bible upon the whole mental and spiritual life of the race could not but leave a deep and abiding impress upon its literature. And it has. The imagery of the Bible is found everywhere in the idealistic life, its phraseology in the style, its uplifting and restraining influence in the whole trend of thought. Even the writer who disbelieves and scoffs has yet been so imbued with its spirit through the very atmosphere around him that he can not write as the man who never knew the Bible and its God.

We are wont to speak of Spenser and Shakespeare and Addison and Johnson as the masters of English style, and exponents of English literature; yet if we measure by the standard of influence upon the whole after mental life of the English peoples it is not these men, but Milton and Bunyan, and the unnumbered and often unknown writers of their sacred songs, and over and above all the family Bible, which have most profoundly stirred the heart of the English folk and given cast and shape to their whole literary history. The literature of the English peoples is essentially a God-fearing literature. It has its excrescences; but they are, and remain, only excrescences which have failed to taint the sound, healthy current of the literary life of the race. The so-called realistic school, but realistic only in the sense of fleshly and unclean and immoral, has found an uncongenial field in lands trained under the purer atmosphere of an open Bible.

Another factor entered into the shaping of the literature of the English man in its formative stage, and a factor which gave to it a character peculiarly its own as contrasted with the literary work of his brother Aryan of Continental Europe, and that factor was The Sea. To turn from the literatures of the peoples of the mainland to that of this insular people is as a coming out into the fresh, cool breezes of the salt waves. It has in it the freshness of all the broad Atlantic. The sea air everywhere permeates and flavors it. Its imagery is full of allusions to the sea, and the ways of the sea. For the English man of Britain, like the man of that Tyre which sat upon her rock amid the waves, was a man who not only dwelt by the sea but who was wont to go down to the sea in ships. The mystery of the sea was ever upon him. It came to him as a child in the roll of the surges upon the rocky shore; in the wild sweep of the November gales inland from the far Atlantic; and in the cry of the gulls as they screamed their hoarse sea-calls about his harbors. The impress which the sea made upon him is written in the names of his towns Tyne-Mouth, Yar-Mouth, Ports-Mouth, Wey-Mouth, Ex-Mouth, Dart-Mouth, Ply-Mouth; the towns that sat where the inland rivers opened wide their mouths to be lost in the broader expanse of the sea. We are ever reminded of it also in the names which the forefathers gave to the prominences which look out seaward from the land Flamborough-Head, Spurn-Head, South-Head, Beachy-Head, St. Alban's-Head, Lizard's-Head; they all spoke to him of a land lifting its rugged front to look out upon the deep. And that long point of Cornwall at Land's End bade him in its very name to remember that here the solid earth ceases, and that beyond the ancient sea reigns supreme. And the Havens, and the Ports, and the great Washes where the sea rushes in upon the shore, all told him of the unending struggle between sea and land, and of a homeland about whose coasts the war of the elements was ever on. But when he looked out from his rocky headlands it was not the conflict so much as the mystery of the sea that was upon him, and the unknown beyond. He looked out as that man of Tyre looked out from the walls of his island home; for he, too, watched his ships sail on beyond the dim horizon line into the unknown West. What a pity that Alexander and his Greeks did their work of fire and sword so thoroughly within the walls of that old Phoenician stronghold; for Tyrian also, no doubt, wrote of what the mystery of the sea was to him. But his thoughts, whatever they were, perished with him in the ruins of his falling city. We possibly have lost somewhat in losing this, for he, too,

> Knew of the sea wastes; and the ships;
> And the curling breakers; and lone winds
> That out of the night-time sang the pain
> And mystery of the sea.

Then there was the element of romance from a new world as the veil was partly lifted from the mystery of the sea, and all the broad new life opened out. The fear of the sea was gone; for now men knew there *was* something beyond. And unlike the Greek with his dread of the graveless deep, and the wandering ghosts of the unburied dead, Sir Humphrey Gilbert in hopeful cheer found heaven as near by sea as by land. Possibly the knightly romance of the sea breathed most daintily into the spirit of English letters in the cultured words of Sir Walter Raleigh; yet the romance of its deeds came in through the sturdier work of Drake, and Frobisher, and all that long list of adventurers who made of the Atlantic an ocean highway; and of the Spanish Main a tourney-field for knightly jousts with the captains of Philip.

All this the nations of the mainland of Europe seemed in a measure to miss. The romance and the freshness of the sea somehow escaped them. Their literatures betray the lack. They might be termed subcontinental in type; for neither have they that subtile spirit of the vast upland plains of the deep mid-continent which breathes in the earlier Vedas. They miss, too, the cosmopolitanism of that island life of the English man, which through its ships quickly broadened to a world life; for the sea made all lands neighbor to the English man. Their life touched his; and he became of all Europeans most a man of the world. It broadened and enriched his literature. And it was the sea that made it possible.

But there was a Greater England yet to be; and it was to be continental, not insular.

Up to the end of the seventeenth century as there was practically as yet only one England, and only one English man, so there was as yet only one

English literary life; and all its products remain the common possession of all after English peoples wherever found. It is only after the seventeenth century that the lines of separation set in. Chaucer, Spenser, Shakespeare, Milton, Bunyan, the English Bible, are the common heritage by descent of all the English peoples. Hume, Macaulay, Carlyle, Tennyson, Green, Emerson, Longfellow, Irving, Bryant, are not. Different climatic and physical surroundings are accentuating the lines of cleavage which sprang from diverging race pathways; and time will only increase the differences, for these are causes which go on working through the ages. The probable future operation of these broad and far-reaching causes belongs rather in the consideration of the broader race life which has fallen to that English man who has ceased to be insular, and has become continental in type. It is upon the other shore of the Atlantic that the study continues.

Chapter Twenty-Three - Work and the Burden of the Years

When Macaulay's New Zealander stands upon the ruins of London Bridge and indulges in that historic retrospect of a closed book of race life, what will be his summing up as the one most fateful and most individual work which the English man of the British Isles did in shaping the destiny of all English men, and through them, as a consequence, in shaping the destinies of all after-races of men? It will hardly be Protestantism, for this was the natural religious outcome of all the Teutonic peoples. It will hardly be free institutions and representative government, much as he has done for these, for the germ of both is likewise to be found in the race life of all Teutonic peoples, and would, sooner or later, have found civic expression. It will hardly be his literature, rich as it is, for it is only one division of the great Teutonic contribution to the mental wealth of the world. It will not be in industrial development, for leader as he was in this for generations, this, too, belongs to all the Teutonic peoples as a birthright. It will not be free speech, for the revolt against a muzzled tongue was widespread among all the Teutonic kin.

There is one thing, however, which Britain did for the English-speaking peoples which no one else could have done, and which, if it had not been done when it was, and as it was, would have changed the whole after-history not only of all the English-speaking peoples, but of the world as well. Probably in the retrospect of the ages the greatest of all Britain's works will be seen to have been the seizing of the vast uncivilized regions of the temperate zone while they were yet open to contest, and holding them to be settled by the English peoples. Whether with deliberate foresight, or by a race instinct which is sometimes wiser than race wisdom, or whether in obedience to some unseen planning back of, and higher than men, the Briton seized upon and with grim tenacity held these lands as against all others. North America, Australia, New Zealand, South Africa - they were the only remaining unoccupied possible homelands for Aryan peoples; lands in which the Aryan blood might breed Aryan men free from deterioration or decay. It was the remaining untaken Aryan climatic belt of the world that the English man of Britain seized and held. Other regions might be held as tributary lands by Aryan peoples, but here only, of the untaken lands of the world, could Aryan men build up permanent homes and multiply. It settled the fate of the world; and it gave to the English man alone, of all Aryan peoples, the leadership. Others might hold tributary lands and gain wealth from them; he alone could breed his own race in his new lands and increase. Herein, as much as in race capacity and energy, lies the secret of the English man's rapid rise to power in the world. And it came through command of the sea. Howard in the English Channel, and Russell at La Hogue, settled the question of a wider empire than men dreamed of. It was more than a Catholic succession, and the fate of the House of Stuart, that those sea-fights decided. It was the fate of America, Australia, New Zealand, South Africa, the islands of the oceans, the strategic points for the world's navies, the vantage-points of the world's commerce, which were in the scale that turned in favor of the English peoples; and with these the whole after-history of the world. It marked the beginning of the receding tide with the Latin. Louisbourg, Trafalgar, Santiago de Cuba, and Manila were only the far-off resultants. Whatever remains yet to be written of the English man of Britain and his world work, let this stand first, that when, with a land hunger which was all-consuming, and an instinct wiser maybe than his reason, he seized and held the as yet open lands of the great temperate climatic belt of the globe, he made the English peoples who were yet to be, heirs in fact to the supremacy of the world. It is the debt which English men of all lands owe to that older English man of Britain.

There comes a time in the life of man when he says, "I am weary. I have accomplished enough. Let me rest." It is weariness - but it is also age. And it comes to nations as well as to men. It comes when they pause and say, "We are big enough. Let us cease expanding." But with man and race alike, there is no tableland of life; only a crest; then the descent begins. It is the law of vegetable as well. When growth ceases death has begun. When Augustus Caesar said, "Rome is big enough; let us abide content," he unwittingly spoke Rome's death sentence. There is no rest save in death. That old Roman god Terminus was not a god of rest. He could not abide. If he was not advancing, he must retreat; and when Augustus placed the statue of Rome's god at the boundaries of the borderlands and said, "The Empire is broad enough; here we will stay," it was the beginning of the end; for Rome did not stay. From that day she began to draw back upon herself. Augustus did not know his god. And he did not know the restless, seething world of men about him; for these were quick to recognize this sign of the coming on of age to their ancient foe. The Goth knew; and began to make ready. And the farthest tribe of wild Picts, with the instinct of the wild upon them, felt the subtile change, and began to get ready. It was the narrowing circles of the vultures as they scented the incipient decay. The danger line in the individual life is reached when one ceases to look forward and begins to look back. And it is so with races. It is the anticipation of something more in advance which alike in men and nations leads on and on, and postpones the approach of age and death. The secret of youth lies in looking forward.

Is Britain growing old? There is a cry of weariness going up; not loud, only a kind of an undertone, as when one speaks under his breath, but it is there. It is heard in the protest against any new movement in advance. It is the old plea of Augustus, "We are big enough. We have accomplished enough. Let us abide." I do not mean the querulous plaint of the chronic objector. All peoples, all ages have him. He is not an effect; he is born that way. If his country says, "Right," he says, "Wrong." If his country says, "Wrong," he is just as ready to say, "Right." And he generally poses as a moralist of a higher plane. This is one of the vagaries of the human mind to which ordinary rules do not apply. It is to be classed among the infirmities. Such minds are not amenable to reason. They are the inflictions which reason has to bear with and endure. They class themselves with Sokrates' gad-fly. They forget that all gad-flies are not Sokrates. Britain has her share of the gad-flies; but they are only gad-flies. And there are always men, honest, well-intentioned men, to whom all change is wrong - wrong because it is change; and who, failing to grasp the broader life of the nation, stand as obstructionists in the way of all movements in advance, and pronounce progress and growth as all wrong. To them the summing up of true wisdom is to be found in Pope's dictum, "Whatever is, is right." But there are also others, men who are not wrong-headed so much as wrong-hearted. Men to whom self, and party, and personal ambitions are more than country. These are the unbranded Benedict Arnolds of peace. Men who are not worthy of country or home. Ingrates with the spirit of the matricide in them. Every land has a few of such. It is to the credit of humanity that they are not many.

The symptoms of age in Britain show themselves also in the pessimism which crops out at times in her literature and in the public print. It is to be found rather in the reading between the lines; to be heard as the undertone to the chorus. It gives the strain of plaintive sadness to the prologue in Morris's "Earthly Paradise." There is no such note to be found in the song of Chaucer, as the little band of wayfarers sets out that April morning from the Tabard Inn. There every leaf of the hedgerows is aquiver with the gladness and the cheer of the springtime. It is still early youth, glad, sweet youth; and age is as yet afar. The chill of age is to be found rather in the covert sting of the cynic's sneer. The cynic is a product of decadence. Diogenes was born, not of the youth, but of the age of the Greek peoples. The cynical weariness of Thackeray's "Vanitas Vanitatum," echoing the cry of that blasé cynic of nearly thirty centuries before, has in it a more despairing tinge of melancholy than all of Carlyle's misanthropic howlings. Despairing, because it means the dying out of desire as well as of hope. It is age with the glad looking forward of youth gone; the play played out; the curtains rung down; the lights extinguished. Thenceforth remain only the gloom and the chill of old age and quick coming death which men and nations alike must know. Age betrays itself also in the growing mistrust of self, and of the national possibilities, as found in the daily press; and in an increasing minority which in every public movement of aggression hangs as a clog upon the wheels, and holds back. It betrays itself also in the dying out of enthusiasm; in the diminishing faith in an ability to bring things to pass; in the magnifying of obstacles, and the minifying of resources. It is somewhat of the querulous, complaining "Non possumus" of the later Papacy over again. It is Pius IX. - not Hildebrand of forceful and resourceful soul.

There seems to be a normal limit to the life of nations as to the life of man. Sometimes this is cut short by violence, as in case of the Aztecs and the Peruvians. Sometimes it is prolonged by isolation, as in case of China. But exposed to the ordinary attrition and battling of peoples a nation seems to conform to a like law as man, of whom it is said, "The days of our years are threescore years and ten; and if by reason of strength they be fourscore years, yet - it is soon cut off." The older Greek of the prehistoric times lived his life; but the tale of the centuries is unknown. His children by the Dorian invader lived out the Greek life to its end within some twelve centuries of time. The Latin of the older Rome lived his national life through the historic "*post urbem conditam*" to the Goth within about twelve centuries. His children by the free-born Teuton and the Celt, the Romance peoples, relived the Latin life from the Goth to their present decadence within some twelve or thirteen centuries. The grandchildren of the Latin in the newer lands across the sea are no longer of pure blood. They are the offspring of the bondwoman, born, as some tuberculous child, with the germs of premature decay already in their veins. From the landing of the English folk upon the shores of Britain until now more than fourteen centuries have already passed away. By the life measure of the Aryan peoples it is no longer to Britain the threescore years and ten, but the added years of the as yet unfulfilled fourscore; and they, too, have come "by reason of strength," for that old Teutonic blood is a virile blood, full of abounding life. The Latin has lingered on through his children to see the days of the degenerate grandchildren; degenerate largely because mongrel. The English man of Britain is living his life over again, and renewing his hold upon the world, in his children; and they are by the free-born Teuton. He has kept his blood pure. No mesalliance even has corrupted the current of his race life.

Yet it would not be strange if Britain were growing old; for she has lived much. She, more than any other modern nation, is the connecting link between past and present. And no other nation in the world's history has so widely touched the great currents of the world's progress. Even Rome had a narrower field. Rome was a Mediterranean power. Britain has been a world power. For a thousand years her flag has floated upon the seas. And now comes a new lease of life; for she, as no other nation, is renewing her life in the yet broader life of her children. Her own people are constantly going out and mixing with the younger blood of the Greater England beyond the seas, and coming back to bring to the old home the freshness and renewed vitality of the newer life which is there growing up. No others of the European peoples are thus revitalized. They, on the contrary, are largely self-centered; and the self-centered life, whether of man or nation, ages quickly. And the day will come in the race battlings of the future when the strength of the children will be the safety of the mother; and they will repay the debt which the English-speaking peoples owe to Britain for seizing and holding the great unoccupied lands of the temperate belt of the world, and so making possible that greater Engle-folk which so largely has the future of the world in its hands. There is a debt of gratitude for this due to that older England of the British Isles which the English-speaking peoples can never forget, and which it would ill beseem them to ignore. British imperialism of the sixteenth and seventeenth centuries made possible the Engle-land of the Thirteen Colonies, just as American imperialism in the acquisition of Florida, of the Louisiana Purchase, of Texas, of California, of the Gadsen Purchase, of Alaska, has made possible the Engle-land of the Western Continent, and as Britain's after-work in Australia, in New Zealand, in South Africa, in India, and America's work in the East and West Indies and at Panama, are making possible the yet broader Engle-land of the future.

But the germ, the possibility of it all, lay in that landed expansion of the England of the sixteenth and seventeenth centuries which came of British imperialism. The years have shown that those older Britons, in the far reaching out of their earth-hunger, builded more wisely than they knew.